The Frien

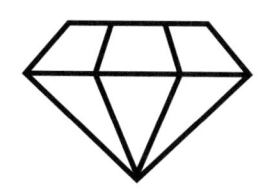

Facets of Jesus Christ
Volume One: January – June

*"Let [the one] who boasts boast about this:
that [they] understand and know Me..."*
Jeremiah 9:24 (NIV)

Jesus Christ is still the most accessible Being in the universe.
James W. Alexander

Compiled, updated, and edited
by
Bryan L. Herde

Bethel
Psalm 27:14

**Available on Amazon
in print and Kindle formats**

Published April 2022

Sovereign Grip Communications
www.sovereigngrip.com

Scripture taken from the HOLY BIBLE, NEW INTERNATIONAL VERSION Copyright© 1973, 1978, 1984 International Bible Society. Used by permission of Zondervan Bible Publishers.

Scripture taken from the Holy Bible, New Living Translation, copyright © 1996, 2004, 2007, 2013 by Tyndale House Foundation. Used by permission of Tyndale House Publishers, Inc., Carol Stream, Illinois 60188. All rights reserved. (NLTSE)

Scripture quotations taken from the AMPLIFIED BIBLE, Copyright ©1954, 1958, 1962, 1964, 1965, 1987 by the Lockman Foundation. Used by permission. (www.lockman.org)

Scripture quotations are from the ESV® Bible (The Holy Bible, English Standard Version®) copyright ©2001 by Crossway Bibles, a publishing ministry of Good News Publishers. Used by permission. All rights reserved.

Dedication

To George H. Morrison, whose many sermons from over one hundred years ago addressed a large number of Jesus Christ's facets, and inspired me to research and discover the 286 which are contained in these two volumes. I have come to know George pretty well over the years and very much look forward to an extensive chat with him when I join him in Heaven.

And especially to my Lord Jesus Christ. In one way, You are indescribable. But in another, You have made Yourself knowable, understandable, and relatable. May you, my Friend, be delighted to use this second year of daily devotionals to bring honor and glory to Yourself, and to help many others to know You, and our Heavenly Father, and our Holy Spirit, better and more intimately. Thank You for the honor of doing this through me.

Powerful Quotes from Inside

If we would be conformed to the image of Christ, then we must live closer and ever closer to Him. We must become better and better acquainted with His character and His ways; we must look at things through His eyes, and judge all things by His standards.
Hannah Whitall Smith

It is a wonderful measure of nearness that is thus made possible to us — we shall abide in Christ's love, even as He abides in His Father's love. It seems almost incredible that such intimacy, such closeness, as that which existed between Christ and His Father, should be possible for us. Yet it is nothing less than this that is promised.
J. R. Miller

Christ comes into me and becomes my very life. He comes into the very root of my heart and being. He comes into my willing and thinking and feeling and living, and lives in me in the power which the Omnipresent God alone can exercise. When I understand this, my soul bows down in adoration and confidence toward God. I live in the flesh, the life of flesh and blood, but Christ dwelling in me is the true Life of my life.
Andrew Murray

The secret of joy and love simply lie in nearness to Jesus, and His joy and love will spring within us from the Head. The most effortless and spontaneous life will ever be the best. Oftentimes He may wish us to be inactive. Let us be submissive in this, and when He rests in His love, let us rest with Him, and when He rejoices over us with singing, let us swell the chorus in glad response, our hearts keeping time to His.
A. B. Simpson

There is a cup that everybody must drink; there is darkness for everyone; there is a Gethsemane for every human creature with or without Christ;

there is a night, a period of sadness and sorrow. There is a time when the firmest hopes grow insecure, when the sweetest pleasures cease any longer to please. Have you made any provision for that hour? Is there between your souls and Christ a sacred union? Do you now call Him Savior and Lord? Have you laid your head upon His heart? Have you so given yourself to God that if He forgets you, He forgets Himself?
William L. Gaylord

Jesus insisted on living a simple true human life, dependent upon God and upon others. He struck the keynote of this at the start in the wilderness. Everything He taught He put through the test of use. He was what He taught.
S. D. Gordon

It is in His love that we are to find our happiness, not in anything apart from His love. What He gives is precious as the gift of love, and we may trust Him, trust Him even when He does not speak. Do not ask for texts for everything. There are those who cannot believe the Father of the spirits of all flesh unless He is bound down by black and white. But let us have faith in the heart of things. Trust Christ in His promises, trust Him in His silences. Golden is the speech of Christ, golden also is His silence.
William Robertson Nicoll

If I allow the living Christ to take possession of my will and desires, I can walk even as He walked. Let us come to the life of Christ, and try and find out what is that life that He lived on earth with His Father. That is exactly the Christ who lives in us. There are not two Christs, only one, the Christ that lived on earth is the Christ that lives in my heart.
Andrew Murray

Editor's Notes

All of the excerpts in these volumes are taken from books and pamphlets that are considered to be "public domain."

I continue to be extremely grateful to Internet Archive for the vast resources they are still building by converting ancient, printed materials (and more) into pdfs that are made available to the public free of charge. Thank you!

When I began the process of condensing the material I found into a small enough portion to fit inside two volumes covering 366 days of two-page, daily devotionals, I started with more than 5,500 pages of text. It took me quite some time to leave so much material on the "cutting room floor." Consequently, what you will encounter are daily readings taken from over 300 hundred sermons and book chapters.

Additionally, I have taken the liberty of editing some content in four ways:

1. Exchanged archaic or difficult words with more modern synonyms;
2. Updated "King James" English into more modern terms, such as "thee," "ye," to "you"; and most words ending in "eth" such as "abideth," "trusteth," into "abides" and "trusts," etc.;
3. Reworked some phrases or sentences that were just hard to understand into what keeps the intent of the original; and
4. Capitalize at all times the pronouns that are used to refer to God. I do this out of respect and to ensure that you, the reader, will not be confused as to when it is that God is the Person of note.

Given the timeframe in which all of these contributors lived, the generic use of the words "man" and "mankind" were common and referred to all of humanity. These terms have been retained pretty much throughout because to change all of those uses would have required some substantial rewriting of their texts in order to use contemporary language. To me, this did not seem necessary in order for you to grasp the overall content. Thank you for adapting to this.

You will also quickly notice that I did not go so far as to change any of the messages completely into 21st-century English. They are still, in both tone and voice, true to their age, though as you will quickly discover, most of the writings are actually quite timeless, and highly relevant to our own age.

Introduction

How does one describe the Infinite?

How much difference does one shovel of soil off Mount Everest make to the size of that mountain?

This is what I felt while compiling this book.

My friends, this book is that single shovel full of soil from Mount Everest. But as the Lord moved me to do this, I am humbled to have even touched such a project.

When the Infinite became Finite, without losing its Infinity, that is the Son of God becoming Jesus and forever being the fullness of the Godhead and humanity simultaneously as one.

The men and women whose sermons and writings are included in this book undoubtedly felt as I have. Yet, moved by the Holy Spirit, they dug and dug until they, too, were able to show the world just a single facet of an infinite diamond—Jesus Christ, the Jewel of Heaven.

The fact that they, too, discovered the comprehensive reality of "not I, but Christ" categorizes them as true Christian mystics. So how does the mystic differ from other Christians? A. W. Tozer (1897-1963, American pastor and writer) answers:

> The mystics experience their faith down in the depths of their emotional beings while the other does not. They exist in a world of spiritual reality. They are quietly, deeply, and sometimes almost ecstatically aware of the Presence of God in their own nature and in the world around them. Their religious experience is sometimes elemental, as old as time and

the creation. It is immediate acquaintance with God by union with the Eternal Son. It is to know that which passes knowledge (Tozer's comments are excerpted from a devotional on *www.immoderate.wordpress.com*).

I am certainly not in total agreement with all of the various positions that the many authors in this book held on every Christian doctrine, philosophy or experience. However, the Christian mystics I have selected meet that most basic quality that was true of each of them: They burned with a passion for a deep, intimate, unfiltered, and unfettered relationship with God — a synchronizing of hearts and minds with His. God's grace and love cover a multitude of sins!

As you will readily see, the readings in this book are dominated by the messages of one man — George H. Morrison. The Lord used his numerous sermons on many of the qualities of Jesus Christ to move me to undertake this project. No other preacher or teacher I have encountered took such a broad and clear-eyed look at so many aspects of Jesus Christ. Altogether, I have been blessed to find 135 brothers and sisters whose writing and preaching covered so much of who Jesus Christ is, and what His life means for believers and all of creation.

Overall, I have addressed 286 facets of Jesus Christ. However, I have taken the liberty of stretching some sermons and writings into two or three days' worth of readings, or have included additional material to amplify a particular facet. Even though there is a total of 286 facets presented, please know that this is only a small beginning in the process of coming to know Christ better — something that will take all eternity to complete.

The only way I could think of to organize this collection was to list the facets in alphabetical order. I discerned from Him no other means for organizing these. When I use the word "facets," I am including not only characteristics and qualities of Jesus Christ but also some of His vital roles, responsibilities, functions, relationships, and impact. Yes, this is a broad application of that word, but I believe it to be the best single word to capture the intent of this effort.

This quote by William H. G. Thomas (1861-1924, English/Welsh pastor) helps to amplify this point:

> Just as a diamond has several facets, each one contributing to the beauty and attractiveness of the complete stone, so Jesus Christ can be considered in various ways, and to the question, "What do you think of Christ?" different answers can be given.

And for any of you who do not like to read, may I encourage you to persevere in doing so anyway. To reinforce this, the following excerpt by John Henry Jowett (1863-1923, English pastor) provides advice that is both timely and highly applicable:

> How, then, can we become "lovers of God"? First of all, we must spend time with the God we desire to love. We must bring our minds to bear upon Him. Love is not born where there has been no closeness. There must be association and fellowship. And, in the second place, we must spend time with them that are lovers already. It is well that this should be through personal interaction, if such a happy privilege comes our way. But if this immediate fellowship is denied us, *let us seek their company through the blessed interaction of books.*

May the Lord be pleased to use this offering from my friends — the authors — and myself for His purposes, His glory, and for fulfilling the desires of His own heart in the lives of all who encounter and read any portion of this collection.

His Facets

Abiding	Abundance	Access
Activity	Advocacy	Agony
Anchor	Angels	Anger
Appeal	Appreciation	Ascension
Assurance	Astonishment	Authority
Balance	Baptism	Beauty
Beginning	Being	Beloved
Betrayer	Binding	Birth
Blessings	Blood	Boyhood
Brother	Building	Challenge
Character	Church	Churches
Claims	Commandments	Commission
Commonness	Compassion	Completeness
Confidence	Conforming	Consequences
Consolation	Constancy	Contention
Courage	Courtesy	Creation
Criticism	Cross	Cross-Bearer
Crown	Cry	Death
Decisiveness	Deity	Delays
Deliverance	Desire	Devotion
Difference	Directive	Doctrine
Doubter	Economy	Education
Emptying	Enemies	Enemy
Engagement	Everyday	Example
Expectation	Extravagance	Fact
Faith	Father	Feelings
Fellowship	Fires	Fleeing
Forerunner	Forgiveness	Foundation
Frankness	Freedom	Friends
Friendship	Fulfillment	Fullness
Gates	Genealogy	Gentleness
Gift	Giving	Glory
Grace	Growing	Guidance

Habit	Headship	Healing
Hearing	Heart	Hopefulness
Humanity	Humility	Hurt
Identification	Illumination	Immutability
Impartiality	Imperatives	Infinity
Influence	Inoffensiveness	Insight
Intercession	Intimate	Intolerance
Intrusiveness	Invincibility	Joy
Judgment	Keeping	Kingdom
Knocking	Knowing	Law
Leadership	Liberation	Life
Light	Likeness	Living
Loneliness	Love	Magnetism
Manifestations	Martyrs	Mastership
Meaning	Meekness	Mind
Miracles	Missions	Mother
Mourners	Mystery	Name
Nature	Nearness	Newness
Nourishment	Obscurity	Omnipotence
Oneness	Only	Originality
Overwhelming	Parables	Paradox
Partnership	Passover	Pastoring
Pastures	Patience	Peace
Permanence	Perspective	Philanthropy
Pledge	Politics	Poverty
Power	Praying	Priesthood
Priorities	Profession	Promises
Prophecy	Providence	Provision
Pruning	Punishment	Purchase
Purity	Purpose	Question
Quietness	Radiance	Radicalism
Rainbow	Reasonableness	Reckoning
Reconciliation	Redemption	Refining
Reflection	Refusals	Repetition
Reputation	Requirements	Resolve
Restfulness	Resurrection	Return
Revealing	Revelation	Riches

Righteousness
Salvation
Scars
Servants
Shepherds
Sight
Sonship
Star
Supper
Swiftness
Teaching
Terms
Thankfulness
Totality
Transcendence
Trials
Unattractiveness
Unselfishness
Victory
Visitation
Walk
Way
Wisdom
Word
Worshippers
Zeal

Sacrifice
Sanctification
Sermon
Severity
Sifting
Silence
Spirit
Strength
Surety
Sympathy
Tears
Terrors
Thoughtfulness
Touch
Transfiguration
Trouble
Unifying
Value
View
Visitor
War
Weapons
Withholding
Words
Wrath

Sadness
Saving
Servanthood
Shepherding
Sign
Sinlessness
Stability
Superiority
Sustenance
Tangibility
Temptations
Test
Timeliness
Touchstone
Transforming
Truth
Unity
Vessels
Visibility
Voice
Warning
Willingness
Witness
Working
Yes

My Suggestion for You in How to Begin

Personally, I have benefited immensely from what I call "immersion reading." I highly recommend it for this devotional as well. By "immersion reading," I mean that you read large quantities of these volumes straight through without stopping to understand or contemplate or figure out what any part of it means or how it applies or anything else. Instead, you push through with a straightforward reading of the material. Read them as traditional books as you would any other book, not as daily devotionals. Then, go back and read each day's devotional one at a time as scheduled.

What I pray happens in you is that the reality and the life and the love and the immensity of Jesus Christ will so move throughout your entire being so that, in a sense, your soul will have undergone a thorough plowing. You will be ready for the planting of the individual Facets of Jesus Christ to take deep root in your heart. These, by His grace, will be nourished by Him through the work of the Holy Spirit overseen by the Master Gardener, our Heavenly Father.

May the Lord be pleased to use these devotionals to fill you with His Truth, His Light, His Love, His Grace, and His Beauty!

Facets of Jesus Christ
Volume One: January - June

January 1
His Abiding

by Albert Benjamin (A. B.) Simpson (1843-1919) Canada

Excerpted from "Christ the Living Vine," *The Names of Jesus*, published by The Christian Alliance Publishing Company, New York, New York in 1892

"Yes, I am the vine; you are the branches. Those who [abide] in Me,
and I in them, will produce much fruit.
For apart from Me you can do nothing."
John 15:5 (NLTSE)

God has always used the vine as the symbol of the most sacred things, its juice being the type of Christ's blood, and its stems and branches the most perfect figure of the mystery of Godliness, Christ's union with His people. The Scriptures give us no profounder view of Christian life than these verses contain.

The first truth conveyed in the Master's teaching is that of union with Jesus. There are two sides to this. The first is "in Me," the second, "I in you." The first expresses our justification; the second our deeper union with Christ in sanctification. To be in Christ is to accept Him as our Savior, and to be justified through His blood and righteousness, accepted by the Father for His sake, and received into all His rights and privileges, as the children of God and the redeemed family of Christ. There are two races—the Adam race, and the Christ race. We are all born in Adam, and in Adam all die, but all who are in Christ shall be made alive. And so we came into Christ by receiving Him as our Head and our Savior, and being born again into His life through His Holy Spirit. Every believer is in Christ, and there is no condemnation to them that are in Christ Jesus, for we are made accepted in the Beloved.

To be in Christ has reference rather to our standing than our actual experience. It denotes the relationship between us and Christ, rather than the actual life, and realization of His presence and communion. Of course, it will bring an actual experience; but that is more fully described by the other phrase, "I in you." This is the other side of our union with Jesus. It is that which brings Him personally into actual touch with us, for this is the great mystery of redemption, that Christ actually comes to dwell in the heart that is in Him, making it His personal residence and chosen home, and filling it with His love and joy and purity. He declared that it would be the first result of the Holy Spirit's coming into the heart, that He should reveal it, consummate it, and make it intensely real to our consciousness. "At that day," He says (the day of the Holy Spirit's coming to abide with us), "you shall know that I am in My Father, and you in Me, and I in you." And still later He added, "If a person loves Me, they will keep My commandments, and I will love them and manifest Myself unto them." And then He adds still further, "My Father will love them, and We will come in unto them, and make Our abode with them." This is the glorious reality to which He refers in this figure, "I in you."

One of the attitudes implied in abiding is dependence. It is the habit of continually looking to Christ for everything, for He says, "Apart from Me you can do nothing." We are to continually distrust ourselves, and feel our utter inability to think a right thought, and to look to Him in utter helplessness, and yet in trustful reliance for every breath and thought and feeling, taking our life each moment from Him, both for soul and body, bringing every temptation to Him, every need, every desire, and living really by Him and on Him, as a baby upon its mother.

Another thought suggested by abiding is the momentary life. It is not a life of drift and impulse, not a life in which we act on general principles, but a moment by moment dependence upon Christ. It is simply finding that the life that can be maintained for one moment can be equally maintained for innumerable moments. It is just living out the simple word of Paul in Colossians, "As you have received Christ Jesus the Lord, so walk in Him."

January 2
His Abundance
by Adoniram Judson (A. J.) Gordon (1836-1895) USA
Excerpted from "Life and Life More Abundant," *Twofold Life*, published by Fleming H. Revell Company, New York, New York in 1883

It is an unhappy circumstance that so many Christians look upon the salvation of the soul as the goal rather than as the starting point of faith. We do not forget indeed that the Scripture uses the expression "receiving the end of your faith, even the salvation of your souls." But the connection clearly shows that it is the further end, not the nearer end which is here referred to, the perfecting and glorifying of the soul at the revelation of Jesus Christ, not its justification when it believes on Christ. "The one who believes on the Son has eternal life"—has it in life and principle. But Christ says, "I am come that they might have life, and that they might have it more abundantly." Christ for us, appropriated by faith, is the source of life; Christ within us through the indwelling of the Holy Spirit is the source of more abundant life; the one fact secures our salvation, the other enables us to glorify God in the salvation of others.

How distinctly these two stages of spiritual life are set forth in our Lord's discourse about the water of life! The first effect upon the believer of drinking this water is "they shall never thirst: but the water that I shall give them shall be in them a well of water springing up into everlasting life." That is, the soul receives salvation, and the perennial joy and peace which accompany salvation. But the second stage is this: "The one who believes on Me, as the Scripture has said, out of their belly shall flow rivers of living water. But this He spoke of the Spirit which they that believe on Him should receive." Here is the divine life going out in service and testimony and blessing through the Holy Spirit.

It is the last stage, the fullness and consequent outflowing of the influences of the Spirit, which needs to be especially sought in these days by Christians. There are so many instances of suspended development in the Church; believers who have settled into a condition of confirmed infancy, and whose testimony always begins back with conversion, and hovers around that event, like the talk of children who are perpetually telling how old they are. Now even our conversion, blessed event as it is, may be one of those things that are behind, which we are to forget in the pursuit of higher things. There is a deep significance in that expression of two-fold union which our Lord so often uses, "You in Me and I in you." The branch that is in the vine has its position; but only as the vine is in it, constantly penetrating it with its sap and substance, does it have power for fruitfulness. "If anyone is in Christ they are a new creature." They are regenerated. They are justified.

Here is the lesson, above all others, which this generation needs to learn. Do we mourn that ours is a materialistic age? Would that it were only so on the scientific and rationalistic side. But what we have most reason to fear is that subtle materialism which is creeping into our Church life and methods. How little dependence is there on supernatural power as all sufficient for our work! How much we are coming to lean on mere human agencies! — upon art and architecture, upon music and rhetoric and social attraction! If we would draw the people to Church that we may win them to Christ, the first question with scores of Christians nowadays is, what new turn can be given to the kaleidoscope of entertainment? What fresh novelty in the way of social attraction can we introduce; or what new flash of wit can be delivered from the pulpit to dazzle and captivate the people? Oh for a faith to abandon utterly these devices of naturalism, and to throw the Church without reserve upon the power of the supernatural! For Christian experience, if it is true and divinely inspired, is but the Bible translated and printed in illuminated text, scripture "written large," for the benefit of dim eyes that cannot read the fine print of doctrine.

January 3
His Access
by William M. Clow (1853-1930) Scotland
Excerpted from "The Rent Veil," *The Day of the Cross*, published by Hodder and Stoughton, New York, New York in 1909

And behold, the curtain in the Temple was torn in two from the top to the bottom.
Matthew 27:51 (KJV)

"By one offering He perfected forever them that are sanctified" (Hebrews 10:14). God was reconciled to man by an eternal redemption. The exclusion from the presence of God passed away in the tearing of the curtain. Now that great truth has found a sure place in the minds of men. To those who have accepted it in a clear consciousness of its grace, it has been the source of their peace and the wellspring of an unwearying devotion. It has made itself a power in the minds of all men who knew the revelation of God in Christ. The one truth today which all men accept, which sometimes blind men to other truths, is that God is love. Into every heart there has come the assurance that whatever may be a man's attitude towards God, He has been reconciled to man. That understanding is an indestructible possession of the consciousness of men in Christian lands, and it is as strikingly absent beyond them. And it is due, in a way some do not imagine, to the teaching of Jesus, consummated and verified on the cross. The curtain that hung between man and God—and that must hang between sin and holiness—has been torn in two by the one perfect, finished sacrifice of Christ.

That truth, however, seems to human hearts too great to be true, and there are two darkening departures from it in the teaching of men who profess to accept it. There is one large portion in Christendom which has not pondered the torn curtain. It has substituted the Mass for the Lord's Supper. Day by day, under a priestly consecration, we are told, the bread of the sacrament becomes the flesh, and the wine becomes the blood of Jesus. They are then lifted up to God in sacrifice by priestly hands. And the confessed purpose of this miracle, which honest eyes cannot see, and of this elevation of the host, which men with the New Testament in their hands know to be a vain oblation, is to represent what He is still doing in Heaven, and to continue the sacrifice of Jesus offered to an offended God. Peter and Paul and John knew nothing of this sacrifice. The accounts of the Lord's Supper distinctly deny it. It is a product of superstition and priestcraft. And it has forgotten the interpretation of the torn curtain. In the instant that the curtain was torn in two, all sacrifice passed away. "Christ entered once into the Holy Place, having obtained eternal redemption." He has offered one sacrifice for sins forever. God has been once for all, and by one final, decisive act, reconciled unto men. All that is needed now is to eat and drink in remembrance of Him. The curtain has been torn in two.

All of us have heard what has been called "the gospel preached," especially by men to whom has been given the gifts and the office of the evangelist. They have appealed to men to draw near unto God and He will draw near unto them, to come to Him with true repentance and confession, His anger will be turned away, to tear their hearts and humble themselves, and God will turn from His wrath and be reconciled to them. But that is not the gospel of the cross; that is a meager version of the Old Testament message. Underneath all such preaching there lurks—in subtle ambush that binds the souls of men—salvation by works. Its message is that as we turn to God, as we offer the sacrifice of our confession, or our repentance, or our humiliation, God will be reconciled to us. But God is now already reconciled to all men. Our repentance, our confession, our tears, even our faith, are only acceptances of the mercy of God. And therefore the preacher's gospel should be the story of the God and Father of Jesus Christ our Lord, who put away sins by the sacrifice of Himself, and the preacher's best figure may well be—the torn curtain.

January 4
His Activity
by John Charles Ryle (1816-1900) England
Excerpted from *Expository Thoughts on the Gospels: St. John,* published by Robert Carter & Brothers, New York, New York in 1879

Jesus replied, "I am the bread of life. Whoever comes to Me will never be hungry again. Whoever believes in Me will never be thirsty. But you haven't believed in Me even though you have seen Me. However, those the Father has given Me will come to Me, and I will never reject them. For I have come down from Heaven to do the will of God who sent Me, not to do My own will. And this is the will of God, that I should not lose even one of all those He has given Me, but that I should raise them up at the last day. For it is My Father's will that all who see His Son and believe in Him should have eternal life.
I will raise them up at the last day."
John 6:35-40 (NLTSE)

Our Lord would have us know that He Himself is the appointed food of people's souls. The soul of every person is naturally starving and famishing through sin. Christ is given by God the Father to be the Satisfier, the Reliever, and the Physician of our spiritual need. In Him and His mediatorial office — in Him and His atoning death — in Him and His priesthood — in Him and His grace, love, and power — in Him alone will empty souls find their needs supplied. In Him there is life. He is "the bread of life."

Do we know anything of spiritual hunger? Do we feel anything of craving and emptiness in conscience, heart, and affections? Let us distinctly understand that Christ alone can relieve and supply us, and that it is His office to relieve. We must come to Him by faith. We must believe on Him, and commit our souls into His hands. So coming, He pledges His royal word that we will find lasting satisfaction both for time and eternity. It is written, "Anyone who comes to Me shall never hunger, and anyone who believes on Me shall never thirst."

What did our Lord mean by saying, "I will never reject them"? He meant that He will not refuse to save anyone who comes to Him, no matter what he may have been. His past sins may have been very great. His present weakness and infirmity may be very great. But does he come to Christ by faith? Then Christ will receive him graciously, pardon him freely, place him in the number of His dear children, and give him everlasting life.

We are taught by these words that Christ has brought into the world a salvation open and free to everyone. Our Lord draws a picture of it, from the story of the bronze serpent, by which bitten Israelites in the wilderness were healed. Everyone that chose to "look" at the bronze serpent might live. Just in the same way, everyone who desires eternal life may "look" at Christ by faith, and have it freely. There is no barrier, no limit, no restriction. The terms of the gospel are wide and simple. Everyone may "look and live."

We are taught, furthermore, that Christ will never allow any soul that is committed to Him to be lost and cast away. He will keep it safe, from grace to glory, in spite of the world, the flesh, and the devil. Not one bone of His mystical body shall ever be broken. Not one lamb of His flock shall ever be left behind in the wilderness. He will raise to glory, in the last day, the whole flock entrusted to His charge, and not one shall be found missing.

Let the true Christian feed on the truths contained in this passage, and thank God for them. Christ the Bread of life—Christ the Receiver of all who come to Him—Christ the Preserver of all believers—Christ is for every person who is willing to believe on Him, and Christ is the eternal possession of all who so believe. Surely this is glad tidings and good news!

January 5
His Advocacy
by Charles S. Spurgeon (1834-1892) England
Excerpted from "The Sinner's Advocate," delivered on June 21, 1863
at the Metropolitan Tabernacle, London, England

*My little children, these things write I unto you, that you sin not.
And if any man sins, we have an Advocate with the Father,
Jesus Christ the righteous.*
1 John 2:1 (KJV)

The Apostle John presents us with a very clear and emphatic testimony to the doctrine of full and free forgiveness of sin. He declares that the blood of Jesus Christ, God's dear Son, cleanses us from all sin, and that if any man sins, we have an Advocate. It is most evident that John is not afraid of doing mischief by stating this truth too broadly; on the contrary, he makes this statement with the view of promoting the holiness of his "little children." The object of this bold declaration of the love of the Father to his sinning children is "that you sin not."

This is a triumphant answer to that grossly untruthful objection which is so often urged by the adversaries of the gospel against the doctrines of free grace—that they lead men to depravity. It does not appear that the Apostle John thought so, for in order that these "little children" should not sin, he actually declares unto them the very doctrine which our opponents call immoral. Those men who think that God's grace, when fully, fairly, and plainly preached, will lead men into sin, know not what they say, nor what it is they affirm.

It is neither according to nature nor to grace for men to find an argument for sin in the goodness of God. Human nature is bad enough—and far be it from me to flatter that leprous criminal, that reeking mass of corruption—but even a natural conscience revolts at the corruptness of sinning because grace abounds. Shall I hate God because He is kind to me? Shall I curse Him because He blesses me? I venture to affirm that very few men reason this way. Man has found out many inventions, but such arguments are so transparently abominable that few consciences are so dead as to tolerate them. Bad as human nature is, it seldom turns the goodness of God into an argument for rebelling against Him; as for souls renewed by grace, they never can be guilty of such infamy.

The believer in Jesus reasons in quite another fashion. Is God so good? Then I will not grieve Him. Is He so ready to forgive my transgressions? Then I will love Him and offend no more. Gratitude has bindings which are stronger than iron, although softer than silk. Think not, sirs, that the Christian needs to be flogged to virtue by the whip of the law!

Loved of God, we feel we must love Him in return. Richly, yes, divinely forgiven, we feel that we cannot live any longer in sin.

When the Spirit of God gives you a clearer view of your own depravity, mind that you hold to this: "If any man sins, we have an Advocate with the Father." It should be practically remembered, dear friends, at all times.

Every day I find it most healthy to my own soul to try and walk as a saint, but in order to do so, I must continually come to Christ as a sinner. I would seek to be perfect; I would strain after every virtue, and forsake every false way; but still, as to my standing before God, I find it happiest to sit where I sat when I first looked to Jesus, on the rock of His works, having nothing to do with my own righteousness, but only with His.

Depend on it, dear friends, the happiest way of living is to live as a poor sinner and as nothing at all, having Jesus Christ as all in all.

January 6
His Agony
by Frederic W. Farrar (1831-1903) England
Excerpted from "Gethsemane: The Agony and the Arrest," *The Life of Christ*, published by E. P. Dutton & Company, New York, New York in 1875

Jesus knew that the awful hour of His deepest humiliation had arrived — that from this moment until the utterance of that great cry with which He died, nothing remained for Him on earth but the torture of physical pain and the poignancy of mental anguish. All that the human frame can tolerate of suffering was to be heaped upon His shrinking body; every misery that cruel and crushing insult can inflict was to weigh heavy on His soul; and in this torment of body and agony of soul even the high and radiant serenity of His divine spirit was to suffer a short but terrible eclipse. Pain in its acutest sting, shame in its most overwhelming brutality, all the burden of the sin and mystery of humanity's existence in its apostacy and fall — this was what He must now face in all its most inexplicable accumulation.

"My soul," He said, "is full of anguish, even unto death. Stay here and keep watch."

Reluctantly, He tore Himself away from their sustaining tenderness and devotion, and retired yet farther, perhaps out of the moonlight into the shadow. And there, until slumber overpowered them, they were conscious of how dreadful was that outpouring of prayer and suffering through which He passed. They saw Him sometimes on His knees, sometimes outstretched in prostrate supplication upon the damp ground; they heard snatches of the sounds of murmured anguish in which His humanity pleaded with the divine will of His Father. The actual words might vary, but the substance was the same throughout: "Abba, Father, all things are possible for You; take away this cup from Me; nevertheless, not what I will, but what You will." And that prayer—in all its infinite reverence and awe—was heard, that strong crying and those tears were not rejected. We may not intrude too closely into this scene. It is shrouded in a halo and a mystery into which no footstep may penetrate.

And from where came all this agonized failing of heart, this fearful amazement, this horror of great darkness, this passion which almost brought Him down to the grave before a single blow had been inflicted upon Him—which forced from Him the rare and intense phenomenon of a blood-stained sweat—which almost bowed down body and soul and spirit with one final blow? Was it the mere dread of death—the mere effort and determination to face that which He foreknew in all its dreadfulness, but from which, nevertheless, His soul recoiled? Through all this He passed in that hour which, with a recoil of sinless horror beyond our capacity to conceive, He tasted a worse bitterness than the worst bitterness of death. It was the burden and the mystery of the world's sin which lay heavy on His heart; it was the tasting, in the divine humanity of a sinless life, the bitter cup which sin had poisoned; it was the bowing of Godhead to endure a stroke to which man's apostacy had lent such frightful possibilities. It was the sense, too, of how deadly, how frightful, must have been the force of evil in the Universe of God which could render necessary so infinite a sacrifice. It was the endurance, by the perfectly guiltless, of the worst malice which human hatred could devise; it was to experience in the bosom of perfect innocence and perfect love, all that was detestable in human ingratitude, all that was diseased in human hypocrisy, all that was cruel in human rage. It was to brave the last triumph of Satanic spite and fury, uniting against His lonely head all the flaming arrows of Jewish falseness and heathen corruption—the concentrated wrath of the rich and respectable, the yelling fury of the blind and brutal mob. It was to feel that His own, to whom He came, loved darkness rather than light—that the race of the chosen people could be wholly absorbed in one insane repulsion against infinite goodness and love.

January 7
His Anchor
by William L. Gaylord (10831-1882) USA
Excerpted from "The Soul's Anchor," *Sermons and Other Papers*, published by The Case, Lockwood & Brainard Company, Hartford, Connecticut in 1883

We have this hope as an anchor for the soul, firm and secure.
Hebrews 6:19 (NIV)

These words have the sound in them of the footsteps of God. There is a majesty in the very progress of the thought and in the movement of the sentences. There are two figures, apparently most unlike, brought together here—a refuge and an anchor. "Who have fled for refuge to lay hold upon the hope set before us, which hope we have as an anchor."

I think there is a wonderful unity in these figures that is not often seen. It is as if the writer of the book of Hebrews had seen the soul beset with great troubles like storms. Doubts and temptations blacken the air; the poor, driven soul flies for shelter, the very wind drives it; the peril of the elements and their terrible threat speed it to some shelter, and so it makes for the refuge. And then, in the universality of his imagination, he sees the storm not alone upon the land, but upon the sea; the mariner is swept with the wind and dashed with the overwhelming waves, and for his peril the anchor is the refuge. The storm is common to both figures; the refuge is for the land, the anchor for the sea; and both of them mean one thing, security. For what a strong house is in the one sphere, that a sure and steadfast anchor is in the other.

What, then, is the substance of the teaching? It is this: That there is a trust in God and a trustworthiness in Him, which can hold the soul in every emergency. This is not a consolation arising from a sense of one's own integrity or strength, nor from consciousness of achievement, even though these are effected by Divine help. There is no state of grace, there is no condition of affection, there is no amount of virtue or strength which, in extremity, can be a source of joy. No amount of experience, no steadfastness, no victorious power of resistance to evil, will inspire joy except for the first hours of victory. Nothing is more common than self-confidence in times of prosperity, but trouble strips a person.

There is nothing like real trouble to bring a person to the test, and then these vain self-confidences that were of some help, when they did not need them, become as nothing at all when they are in urgent need. Now the confidence expressed here arises simply from a trust in God. It is the feeling that springs up from our very helplessness. It is such a sense of the Divine nature as makes the thought of God just as inevitably a refuge as the sight of a tower or of a fortress to the fleeing and the pursued. Now it is the nature of God to take care of those who put their trust in Him. The very idea of God in His infinity is infinite care, infinite kindness, infinite goodness.

There are also times when God seems to remove from life all its light, and to change all things to darkness. He takes away all stability from things that seemed firm. He turns business into folly, all things are perishable, vain, and frivolous in our sight; nothing has any life or value but the eternal world. The only anchor for the soul is its hope in God.

There is a cup that everybody must drink; there is darkness for everyone; there is a Gethsemane for every human creature with or without Christ; there is a night, a period of sadness and sorrow. There is a time when the firmest hopes grow insecure, when the sweetest pleasures cease any longer to please. Have you made any provision for that hour? Is there between your souls and Christ a sacred union? Do you now call Him Savior and Lord? Have you laid your head upon His heart? Have you so given yourself to God that if He forgets you, He forgets Himself? Think of it!

January 8
His Angels
by George Campbell Morgan (1863-1945) England
Excerpted from "Angels," *The Teaching of Christ,* published by
Fleming H. Revell Company, New York, New York in 1913

We have our Lord's declaration that angel life is entirely different from human life; in that it is not terrestrial, nor can be; but that it is celestial, and must abide celestial. The angels are direct creations of God; each individual one is immediately created by God; and in that sense they are the "sons of God." That sweeps out all the ideas that bring angels at all into kinship with humanity. They are of a different order of being, of an entirely different nature, not to be thought of as we think of men and women today.

Of course the main point of Christ's teaching in this connection was that, in the life beyond, men and women will have come into the angel realm of life, and share in some sense their nature, but He separated the angels from the earth as to kinship. He showed that the angels are the ministers of God, touching the earth, visiting the earth, interested in the earth; but never of the earth. They are an entirely different order and race of beings; and they are never procreated, but are always the direct creation of God Himself. There is no light upon their nature beyond that. The mystery is not explained, because it cannot be explained to us in this life. There are things of which we in this present limited life can never come to full comprehension, or know the meaning.

Jesus spoke of them as the "holy angels." He called them holy, using that word which means quite simply, profoundly reverential; and yet which always stands for the reverence of sanctity, or separation; and which is always connected with the sanctity or separation of an absolute purity. Angels are still referred to as the armies of Heaven. It is still declared that they minister to the saints. We see them divided into ranks and orders, and yet united in service; and the worship of angels is emphatically condemned, forbidden.

In Hebrews 1:14, it says, "Are they [angels] not all ministering spirits, sent forth to do service for the sake of them that shall inherit salvation?" Thus we learn that angels are now occupied, under the government of God, in the service of humanity.

Their present ministry is that of the perpetual chorus, the offering of praise in the high places of the universe, whenever men turn home to God.

These are only gleams of light, but through them I see an order of being; every individual member of the great order created by God; belonging to the things celestial and having no natural contact with the things terrestrial; not mortal but immortal; not knowing all things, but learning, and receiving, and knowing the things revealed; sinless, absolutely pure, magnificent in their holiness, with the very holiness of God.

Our Lord also described the future ministry of angels; and here perhaps we are in graver difficulty; and yet the words of Jesus are perhaps more circumstantial than in any other application. He declared that He would come again, that He will once again be focused for earthly observation. He who came will come, and His next coming will be in glory; and the angels will be in attendance in the hour of His vindication. They who have been unseen ministers will be visible attendants upon His glory.

According to the teaching of Jesus, when we make our way from the sanctuary and into the life of every day, we receive ministries other than material, ministries other than the essentially spiritual; not only fellowship with the Father and with the Son and with the Spirit; but, to aid us in a thousand ways of which we do not dream, the touch of other creations upon our lives, whispers in language we cannot catch so as to repeat it, which has its influence upon us in the hour of danger.

January 9
His Anger
by Robert Law (1860-1919) Scotland/Canada
Excerpted from "The Anger of Jesus!", *The Emotions of Jesus*, published by Charles Scribner's Sons, New York, New York in 1915

And when He had looked round about on them with anger, being grieved for the hardness of their hearts, He said unto the man, "Stretch out your hand."
Mark 3:5 (KJV)

Jesus could be angry, and again and again displays anger. Anger flashed out of Him against temptation. Never, I think, was Jesus so hotly angry as at that moment when He heard the voice of carnal unbelief and worldly wisdom speaking to Him through the lips of the chief of His disciples to turn Him aside from the way of the cross, and when He met the shameful suggestion with the scathing rebuke, "Get behind me, Satan!" In many of the parables there is an undertone of wrath; but its full thunder breaks out in His denunciation of the sanctimonious formalism into which Jewish religion had so largely degenerated. If one would know with what passion of abusive human language may be charged, how words may be made to play like forked lightnings around the heads of self-satisfied hypocrites and evil-doers, let him read, in the twenty-third chapter of Matthew, the "woes" of Jesus against "scribes and Pharisees, hypocrites." And we not only hear anger in His words, but see it in His actions.

Jesus never resented circumstances, but trustfully accepted them as the Father's will. His meekness and lowliness of heart were armor of proof against all careless discourtesy and all studied insult. When men called Him a glutton and a wine-bibber, a Sabbath-breaker, and, deadliest of insults, an ally and regent of Beelzebub [Satan], He still met them with unruffled calm and dispassionate appeal to reason. And when, because they could not answer Him otherwise, they drove Him to the cross with bitter insults and unpitying mockery, His only reply is to intervene between them and the hand of an avenging God the one possible extenuation of their guilt, that word of eternal significance, still heard in Heaven and on earth, "Father, forgive them; they know not what they do." In all the manifestations of His anger there is no trace of personal resentment.

God is love; Jesus is love; the anger of Jesus and all holy anger is the anger of love. For love is not wholly sympathy and sweetness; love is full of indignation and wrath. Anger is the emotion produced by antagonism; and love by its very nature is antagonism to everything that works injury to life. Look at the anger of Jesus. In every case it is the anger of love. His love to God and zeal for God's worship makes Him indignant at whatever dishonors God, and compels him to cleanse the Temple courts of a profane and polluting traffic. He was angry as one might be angry at a sick man who in sheer perversity refuses the remedy in which lies his only hope. "He looked round about upon them with anger, being grieved for the hardness of their hearts." Did ever such anger and such sorrow perfectly meet except in the wonderful Christ?

There is nothing our Master so vehemently forbids and denounces as selfish anger—vindictive anger that makes it a pleasure to retaliate upon those who cause us injury or annoyance. Such resentment Jesus absolutely repudiates. So far as our own feeling is concerned we must be ready always to turn the other cheek. I do not say that it is not possible to feel a pure and righteous anger against a wrong done to ourselves, just as if it were done to another. But there we have a duty and a prerogative superior even to just resentment—the power and the duty of forgiveness. There we can set ourselves beside Christ on the cross, and say, "Father, forgive."

January 10
His Appeal
by George H. Morrison (1866-1928) Scotland
Excerpted from "The Winsomeness of Jesus," *The Afterglow of God*,
published by Hodder and Stoughton, London, England in 1912

And all…wondered at the gracious words which proceeded
out of His mouth.
Luke 4:22 (KJV)

Our text tells us that the words of Christ were gracious words, and in every sense of the word "gracious" that is true. But the exact meaning of the terms which are used here is a little different from what we commonly imagine. His hearers were not referring to Christ's message; they were referring rather to Christ's manner. They marveled, not at the grace *about* which He spoke; they marveled at the grace *with* which He spoke. In other words, what so secured their attention as they gathered around and listened to the Master, was what I would call the winsomeness [charm, appeal] of Jesus.

You will note that this appeal of Jesus was not by any means confined to His speech. It was in His speech that people felt the spell most powerfully, but it radiated out from His whole life. From the moment when He was baptized, on to the last agony on Calvary—at the marriage feast—at the table of Zacchaeus—out in the meadows where the lilies were—everywhere, in every different circumstance, people felt not only the holiness of Jesus; they were gripped also by His charm. It was indeed this very charm that was a stumbling block to godly Jews. It was so different from all that they had read of in the men whom God had sent to be His messengers. Had Christ been stern, and lived a rugged life, and dwelt apart in fellowship with Heaven, they would have been swifter to recognize His claims. It was in such form the ancient prophets lived. It was in such form that John the Baptist lived. He was a rugged man of fiery speech, and he lived coarsely, and loved to be alone. And then came Jesus moving with delight among the homes and haunts of common people, and what I say is that this very winsomeness was a perpetual riddle to the Jews. They could not understand His childlike interest in every flower that made the meadow beautiful. They could not understand His love for children nor His quiet happiness in common life. Reverencing the old prophetic character as that of the true messenger from God, they were baffled by the appeal of Jesus.

Now if you wish to feel the wonder of that appeal there are one or two considerations which are helpful. You have to think of it, for instance, in connection with the stupendous claims which Jesus made. One of the most common features of the charming character is a certain delightful and engaging modesty. It is extremely rare to discover charm in anybody who seems a stranger to the grace of modesty. And though of course not for a single instant would I suggest that Christ was such a stranger, yet the fact remains that there never lived a man who made such amazing and stupendous claims. "I am the way. I am the truth. I am the life." "No man comes unto the Father but by Me." The wonderful thing is that with a note like that ringing like a trumpet through the ministry, people should still have felt that Christ was appealing. The fact is that unless Christ had lived people would have called His character impossible. So to assert, yet all the while to charm, is almost beyond credibility psychologically. And it is just this glorious self-assertion sounding through the ministry of Christ that makes His winsomeness to thinking individuals such a baffling and amazing thing.

With words of grace His ministry began, and there were words of grace upon the cross. With a deed of grace His ministry began, and there were deeds of grace in the resurrection garden. I want you to feel as you have never felt before the magnificent persistence of Christ's winsomeness, that you may be ashamed at what the years have been plundering from you.

January 11
His Appreciation
by James Boardman Hawthorne (1837-1910) USA
Excerpted from "God's Appreciation of Humble Service," *An Unshaken Trust and Other Sermons*, published by American Baptist Publication Society, Philadelphia, Pennsylvania in 1899

"Whosoever shall give you a cup of water to drink in My name because you belong to Christ, verily I say unto you, he shall not lose his reward."
Mark 9:41 (KJV)

To me everything that belongs to Christianity is precious, but there is no feature of it which I admire and love more than its sympathy with the weak and lowly. When Jesus Christ entered upon His mission He sought neither favor nor recognition from men of authority and influence. Herod sat in his golden palace at Tiberias in depraved splendor, but of him He took no notice except to say to His disciples, "Go and tell that fox." He wanted Herod to understand that He neither courted his favor nor dreaded his frown. He despised him, not for the office he held, but for the corrupt life which he lived.

The Pharisees were the dominant religious party of Judea and were recognized as the religious aristocracy of their time. They swept through the Temple courts in their fringed robes with supreme haughtiness and with sovereign contempt for everybody who did not belong to their sect. For them Christ had no words but rebuke and condemnation. Their smiles and patronage He did not covet.

The dreaded emperor was all-powerful at Rome. To him Jesus sent no appeal; of him He sought no favor. He had no more regard for his influence than for that of the humblest subject of his empire. For worldly pride and display, for despotic power and cruelty, for extravagance and lust, He had nothing but frowns. But for suffering, weakness, and humble devotion, He had infinite compassion and love.

To the haughty and self-sufficient He was wrathful as the storm, but to the feeble and lowly He was gentle as the summer's breeze. He pitied and loved the sick and the poor. He loved children, He loved sinners, and of all sinners He loved most those who had suffered most and those who were divorced from human respect and sympathy.

True Christianity stretches out its hands, not to the mighty, but to the weak, and its victories have been won, not only without the help of the world's power, but in utter disregard of it. Christianity and not philosophy has taught us the inherent dignity of man.

Christianity and not philosophy has taught us to appreciate man for those faculties which connect him with God and a boundless future.

He who did not blush to sit at the banquet of the publican, who shrank not from the white touch of the leper, and who felt no pollution from the harlot's tears, has done more to secure for man the respect, sympathy, and affection of his fellows than all other people combined.

From the life and teachings of Christ we learn the lesson that each man is as great as he is in God's sight and no greater. This thought is full of consolation to those who are obscure and who feel that their individuality is lost in the multitude.

God appreciates everything for the purposes for which He gave it existence. Every drop of rain has its mission. God's eye is upon His humblest servant, that He accepts the most inconspicuous service, if inspired by generous motives, and that He will as truly reward the little gift of the pauper as much as the large gift of the millionaire.

January 12
His Ascension
by Alexander Maclaren (1826-1910) Scotland
Excerpted from "The Ascension," *After the Resurrection and Other Addresses*, published by American Tract Society, New York, New York in 1903

Here is an end which circles round to the beginning. "I came forth from the Father, and am come into the world; again, I leave the world, and go unto the Father." The Ascension corelates with and meets the miracle of the Incarnation. And as the Word who became flesh, came by the natural path of human birth, and entered in through the gate by which we all enter, and yet came as none else have come, by His own will, in the miracle of His Incarnation, so at the end. He passed out from life through the gate by which we all pass, and "was obedient unto death, even the death of the cross," and yet He passed likewise on a path which none but Himself have trod, and ascended up to Heaven, from where He had descended to earth. He came into the world, not as leaving the Father, for He is "the Son of Man which is in Heaven," and He ascended up on high, not as leaving us, for He is with us "always, even to the end of the world." Thus the Incarnation and the Ascension support each other.

But let me remind you how, in this connection, we have the very same combination of lowliness and gentleness with majesty and power which runs through the whole of the story of the earthly life of Jesus Christ. Born in a stable, and waited on by angels, the subject of all the humiliations of humanity, and flashing forth through them all the power of Divinity, He ascends on high at last, and yet with no pomp nor visible splendor to the world, but only in the presence of a handful of loving hearts, choosing some dimple of the hill where its folds hid them from the city. As He came quietly and silently into the world, so quietly and silently He passed. In this connection there is more than the picturesque contrast between the rapture of Elijah, with its whirlwind, and chariot and horses of fire, and the calm, slow rising, by no external medium raised, of the Christ. It was proper that the mortal should be swept up into the unfamiliar Heaven by the pomp of angels and the chariot of fire. It was proper that when Jesus ascended to His "own calm home, His habitation from eternity," there should be nothing visible but His own slowly rising form, with the hands uplifted, to shed blessing on the heads of the gazers beneath.

In like manner, regarding the Ascension as an end, may we not say that it is the seal of Heaven impressed on the sacrifice of the cross? "Wherefore God also has highly exalted, and given Him a Name, which is above every name; that at the Name of Jesus every knee should bow." We find in that intimate connection between the cross and the Ascension, the key to the deep saying which carries references to both in itself, when the Lord spoke of Himself as being lifted up and drawing all men unto Him.

And then this Ascension is also the culmination and the natural conclusion of the Resurrection. As I have said, the Scripture point of view with reference to these two is not that they are two, but that the one is the starting point of the line of which the other is the goal. The process which began when He rose from the dead, whatever view we may take of the condition of His earthly life during the forty days in between, could have no ending, rational and intelligible except the Ascension. Thus we should think of it not only as the end of a sweet friendship, but as the end of the gracious manifestation of the earthly life, the counterpart of the Incarnation and descent to earth, the end of the cross and the culmination of the Resurrection. The Son of Man, the same that also descended into the lowest parts of the earth, ascended up where He was before.

January 13
His Assurance
by William M. Clow (1853-1930) Scotland
Excerpted from "The Penitent Malefactor," *The Day of the Cross*, published by Hodder and Stoughton, New York, New York in 1909

"Jesus, remember me when You come into Your Kingdom."
Luke 23:42 (NIV)

We need not wonder at the brevity of the reference to the penitent criminal, although we understand the attempt to lift the veil which enshrouds him. Tradition and legend have been busy with his history. They will trace his life from his birth, tell you his name, and recount the romantic passages of his past. His conspicuous death, his unique experience, his intellectual strength, his noble self-control in the hour of dying, his chivalrous defense of Christ, his soaring faith, following upon a life of criminal wrongdoing, have made men eager to construct the story of his youth and manhood. But the Word of God rebukes by its reticence such wandering fancies. It sets him here for a few hours in the light and love of the dying Lord. It fastens our eyes, not upon the story of his past, but upon the experience of his soul. The one absorbing thought in the mind of this man who is moved by the Holy Ghost, is to show us a soul passing from darkness into marvelous light, from death unto life, from the power of Satan unto God.

But "where sin abounded, grace did much more abound." There is a way to Heaven from the very gate of hell. There is no soul so sunken in sin and so given over by the shallow heart of man but one glimpse of the mercy of God may restore him.

This criminal saw for one instant, and was saved. He hung upon the cross, at first in apathy, for the wine mingled with myrrh had done its stupefying work. But as his awful agony asserted itself, he fixed his eyes upon his fellow-sufferer. He marked His grace.

He saw a sight he never saw before. There, in loneliness, hung One on whose face was imprinted the indelible beauty of holiness. There He hung, and heard the taunts and derision of priest and ruler and passerby, yet He reviled not again. And as he looks, lo! like a soft, sweet music that rises and hushes every coarse and clamoring sound, His voice is heard in prayer, "Father forgive them for they know not what they do." The great, long-bound heart of this man stirred within him. Like the Arctic world, after the dreary winter, when the summer sun has come, a new life began to leap within him. You can trace in his words the very birth of his soul.

This villain was a noble theologian, the only discerning Christian thinker of his day, a man who knew with more than Peter's knowledge, and saw with more than John's vision. But we can make an even greater claim for him. He was justified by faith alone. He was snatched as a brand from the burning, and yet it can be made clear that in those few hours he hung beside Jesus, he grew into the ripest saint, the man on earth most ready for Heaven. For what makes a man a saint? A tender conscience, a deep reverence for God, a devout submission to His will, a heart lifted above the power of the world, scorning its gifts and advantages, a complete dependence on God, a vivid sense of the world unseen, a humble trust in Christ relinquishing all personal merit, a whole-hearted zeal for His honor, and an absorbing craving for His fellowship. These things make a saint wherever they are found, and all these grew to strength and beauty in the soul of this criminal in that short afternoon, while his life-blood ebbed away.

But the truth which engrosses all our hearts, as we read this amazing story is that there is hope for the worst of sinners. Here is the most unlikely man, under the most unlikely circumstances, saved by the grace of God in Christ. After a youth of waywardness, and a manhood of crime, he is seized and held when on the very edge of his doom. What a hope is born in a man when he realizes that grace has such possibilities!

January 14
His Astonishment
by Joseph A. Seiss (1823-1904) USA

Excerpted from "A Marvellous Believer," *Beacon Lights: A Series of Short Sermons*, published by General Council of the Evangelical Lutheran Church, Philadelphia, Pennsylvania in 1900

When Jesus heard this, He was astonished and said unto those following Him, "I tell you the truth, I have not found anyone in Israel with such great faith."
Matthew 8:10 (NIV)

Faith is the great thing in practical Christianity. The Scriptures everywhere assign it a most exalted place. We are justified by faith. "Without faith it is impossible to please God." And as our eternal salvation depends on our faith, all the doings and appointments of the Savior with reference to humankind look to the creation and development of it.

The text stands in connection with a case in which Jesus found faith so great as to command His special admiration. It is said that He "marveled" at it. This does not mean that it took Him by surprise, for He knew well what was in men and women. And whatever of the marvelous or the uncommon there was about it, it was worked by His Spirit. But it was so superior, in a case so unpromising, and produced under so many disadvantages, that He held it up as a marvel unto others, carrying in it a just rebuke to the disbelief and skepticism of the Jews and of all unbelievers.

People often greatly mistake what faith is. They have a notion that things must be positively demonstrated before they can be safely believed. Their philosophy is that "seeing is believing." But it is a mistaken philosophy. It is not the way they act in ordinary things. Faith does not rest on demonstration. It is a confident looking to an end which is not, and cannot yet be, a matter of demonstration.

The farmer who sows his seed for a future harvest believes, that is, he confidently expects that by these means the harvest will come; but he has no absolute proof that it ever will come. A merchant embarks in business believing, that is, confidently expecting that he can make it pay; but he has no certain guarantee that it will. A traveler takes passage on a ship believing, that is, confidently expecting that it will bring her safely to the point she wishes to reach; but she is without evidence that it will be so. In all such cases people adventure on probabilities, not upon demonstrated certainties. Having considered the nature and possibilities of the case and found the balance of probabilities in their favor, they have no hesitation in entering upon it. They trust that all will turn out as they hope; and this is their faith, which makes real to them for the time what is simply a thing of expectation.

And it is the same in matters of Christianity. We must trust for what we cannot see. We must rest on probabilities and promises. To demand and wait for absolute demonstration and infallible certainty as a condition of believing is an absurdity—a contradiction in terms; for what is thus made absolutely sure is knowledge, and no longer faith.

The faith referred to in the text certainly was not founded on absolute demonstration. It was simply the result of a contemplation of facts, and honest reasonings from those facts, producing in the man the strong persuasion on which he acted, and which he so splendidly expressed. And so it is in every case. The great central lesson for us all is to make diligent use of our opportunities; to embrace the Christ as He comes to us; to take Him as our Helper and glorious Lord; to look to Him in our need; to trust implicitly to His Word; and humbly to submit ourselves to Him as the great and merciful spiritual Caesar, whom none can neglect nor disobey without forfeit of all that is most precious to the soul, whether for this world, or that which is to come.

January 15
His Authority
by Charles Robert Hemphill (1852-1932) USA
Excerpted from "Jesus' Supreme Authority," *Southern Presbyterian Pulpit*, published by The Presbyterian Committee of Publication, Richmond, Virginia in 1896

"You call me Master and Lord: and you say well; for so I am."
John 13:13 (KJV)

Jesus and the twelve were assembled in the upper room of some unknown host in Jerusalem to celebrate the Passover. It was the same night in which He was betrayed, and while they were gathered about the table Jesus arose and laid aside His garments; took a towel and wrapped Himself; poured water into a basin, and washed His disciples' feet. He takes His garments and sits down again, and says to His disciples, "Do you know what I have done to you? You call me Master and Lord, and you say well; for so I am." The Son of God had abandoned His throne in Heaven; had laid aside the glory of His divinity; had girded Himself with the nature of man, and set Himself to the lowly service of cleansing and saving men. In a little while He is to return to Heaven from where He came, and to robe Himself with the glory which He had with the Father before the world was. The Son of Man is the Son of God. He that is among men as He that serves is also over men as He that rules. "You call me Master and Lord, and you say well; for so I am." These titles by which you address Me, says Jesus, are no mere conventionalities of speech; in their broadest importance they are true.

Master means teacher, Lord means owner or ruler; fusing these ideas together, the authority of teacher over pupil, of master over servant, of ruler over subject, we arrive at the understanding of supreme and absolute authority. The humble figure that a few moments ago was discharging so menial an office now assumes to

Himself a dignity and an authority none other of the sons of men have ever ventured to claim.

Many of His most familiar sayings carry with them the strongest assertion of His authority, and serve to display its nature. Here are some of them: "You believe in God, believe also in Me"; "I am the Bread of Life"; "If any man thirsts, let him come unto Me and drink"; "I am the Light of the world"; "Your sins are forgiven"; "The Son of Man shall come in the glory of His Father with His angels"; "The dead shall hear the voice of the Son of God"; "The Father has given Him authority to execute judgment." When one speaks in this fashion it is natural for him to add, "For one is your Master, even Christ." "I am the Way," He declares. Many are the roads, made smooth by the tread of many feet, over which men have traveled to find God. These paths end in darkness. Jesus is clothed with the authority to lead men into the knowledge of God, and to bring them into His presence; He is Himself the way. "No man comes unto the Father, but by Me."

Has Jesus traced limits within which He is to be supreme, and beyond which He is to be as other men? We discover none. His authority is coextensive with the faculties and acts and relations of man. The Lord Jesus is not a sovereign who commands obedience in certain spheres only; He is supreme over the whole man. He is the Lord of the reason. He comes within the realm of the intelligence, and requires subjection to Himself. He is to be "the master-light of all our seeing." The truths He utters are fixed points from which thought is to travel, and to which it is to return. The findings of the reason are to be construed in relation to His teachings, and corrected by them. He does not argue, He declares. "Verily, verily, I say unto you," is reason enough for our reason.

Loyalty to Jesus Christ is the need of the hour. For intellectual rest, for peace of heart, for guidance in duty, for enrichment of character, for motive and inspiration in the service of man, for bringing in the Kingdom of God, the Christian must, with emphasis and deep devotion, salute Jesus as his Master and Lord.

January 16
His Balance
by Alfred Rowland (1829-1902) USA
Excerpted from "The Heavenly Twin," *The Exchanged Crowns*, published by Robert Scott, London, England in 1910

"Be therefore wise as serpents, and harmless as doves."
Matthew 10:16 (KJV)

On this occasion our Lord was addressing the disciples whom He had chosen, and was for the first time sending them out as apostles. They were to be His representatives as well as His ambassadors, and therefore they required both integrity of character and wisdom in conduct. They were to be "blameless and harmless, the sons of God without rebuke, in the midst of a crooked and perverse generation." He would have them to be clean in life, simple in aim, gentle in disposition, stainless in reputation, "harmless as doves." At the same time they were to be prudent, not foolishly courting persecution and martyrdom, as some of their successors did, but exercising tact and discretion; for this is what He meant by saying, "Be wise as serpents."

These two creatures are referred to often in Scripture. The dove flew from the ark over the dreary waste of waters, which had drowned the world; and centuries afterward, in a time of equal hopelessness for the race, the Holy Spirit descended "like a dove" and rested on Him, who came to be our Savior, and from first to last was an emblem of peace and innocence. But the serpent, from the days of the Fall, had been an emblem of evil more often than of good, and it was characteristic of our Lord that He recognized its perceptiveness in avoiding danger rather than its harmfulness. The "wisdom" of our Lord was unfailing. How perfectly He read the characters of those Pharisees whom everyone else regarded as patterns of devotion. How readily He recognized the sincere repentance underlying the shameful life of the woman who was a sinner. How accurately He gauged the weakness of Simon Peter, and how gladly He saw the personal loyalty which was beneath it all the time. In every discourse, in every miracle, He adapted Himself with unfailing wisdom to the condition of those with whom He came into contact. But with all this He was as harmless as a dove. With power to overwhelm His foes, He would not even resist them; with possibilities of self-promotion and of self-indulgence open to none beside, He was holy, harmless, undefiled, and separate from sinners. The display of these combined qualities, in daily conduct, is looked for by our Lord, and nothing will do more to glorify Him. Like all His teaching, this touches both our thoughts and our conduct.

It is the combination of these qualities which is so rare, and yet so urgently instilled by our Lord. Quaint old Francis Quarles [English poet, 1592-1644] puts it well when he says, "Wisdom without innocence is dishonesty, innocence without wisdom is foolery; be therefore as wise as serpents, and innocent as doves. The subtlety of the serpent instructs the innocence of the dove; the innocence of the dove corrects the subtlety of the serpent." What God has joined together let no man separate. But in our days the tendency is the other way. The serpent is more popular than the dove. Intellect is more cultivated than earnestness. With knowledge of doctrines and of churches many Christians have no passion, no soul, no fervor in devotion. Their altar is heaped up, but no fire from Heaven consumes the sacrifice laid on it. This is where our deficiency lies, and the Lord, who knows all things, is compelled to say of some of us, "You search the Scriptures, but you do not come unto Me." To His feet let us make our way, that we may receive the gift of His Spirit, and are made willing to seek the world's salvation, though it means for us, as it meant for Him, a crown of thorns and a cross of agony.

January 17
His Baptism
by David James Burrell (1844-1926) USA
Excerpted from "The Baptism of Jesus," *The Morning Cometh: Talks for the Times,* published by American Tract Society, New York, New York in 1893

At that time Jesus came from Nazareth in Galilee and was baptized by John in the Jordan. As Jesus was coming up out of the water, He saw Heaven being torn open and the Spirit descending on Him like a dove. And a voice came from Heaven: You are My Son, whom I love; with You I am well pleased."
Mark 1:9-11 (NIV)

One day John was baptizing at the water's edge at Bethabara. The bank of the swift Jordan was lined with the eager multitudes who had come thronging from Jerusalem and Judea, the regions round about. "Repent! repent!" rang his voice above the roar of the swift-rolling, tumultuous river. "Cast up a highway for the coming of the King!" One and another of his hearers came down to the water's edge, saying, "I repent; baptize me." Then One detached Himself from the crowd and came down towards the river — a Man of the people in homespun garb, about whom the prophet of the wilderness cried, "Behold! behold the Lamb of God!"

And as Jesus came near, John said, "Not You, O Master. I am the unworthy one! I have need to be baptized by You." And Jesus answered, "Allow it to be so now, for thus it becomes Me to fulfill all righteousness." Then the heavens were opened above and a blessed commerce began — prayers ascending and blessings returning — which have never ceased. And down from above came the Spirit of God in form like a brooding dove, symbolizing the descent of peace to the sin-troubled world, and bringing to earth a blessing that passes all understanding. And a voice was heard, "This is My beloved Son." It was heard afterward, again and again. Some said, "It thundered," and they spoke well, for it was indeed a tremendous truth that was uttered, "This is My beloved Son." O friend, have you ever heard it uttered in reverberating tones from Heaven? "This is My beloved Son; listen to Him."

What was the significance of all this? What is the meaning of this baptism of Jesus? It was the formal induction into the active duties of His mediatorial office. He would return to the carpenter's shop no more. In vain shall the farmer bring his plow. Little children will look wonderingly at the closed door. The saw will hang against the wall, the dust lie thick upon the bench, the shavings be undisturbed on the floor. The Carpenter of Nazareth has left His lower tasks and entered upon His ministry. The hour has come.

Christ in this baptism pushes His way to a place beside us, lays His hand upon the sinner's shoulder, and bears the shame and sorrow with Him. Oh presently, up yonder, He will stand beside us; again we shall be silent and shamefaced, but He will speak: "You, Judge of all the earth, true and righteous altogether, the sentence has gone forth justly against this man; but I have borne his penalty; My heart broke on Calvary under the burden of his sin; for My sake let him go free." So it is written, "He was numbered with the transgressors; He bare the sins of many; the Lord has laid on Him the iniquity of us all."

He enters also in this inaugural ordinance into the fellowship of divine affiliation with us. "You," said the Voice from above, "are My beloved Son." We were alienated from the Heavenly Father; but in the Sonship of Jesus the way of restoration is opened unto us. He becomes the firstborn among many brethren; in Him we receive the spirit of adoption, whereby we cry, "Abba! Father!" Oh sweet and blessed fellowship! We are His humble brethren, and there is something more in Christ Jesus still before us: "Now we are the sons of God, and it does not yet appear what we shall be."

January 18
His Beauty
by George Elliott (1757-1817) USA
Excerpted from "The Beauty of Jesus," *The Beauty of Jesus*, published by Jennings and Pye, Cincinnati, Ohio in 1904

He had no beauty or majesty to attract us to Him, nothing in His appearance that we should desire Him.
Isaiah 53:2 (NIV)

No authentic portrait of the Master has reached us. Perhaps it is best that we have no picture. Each of us can frame for ourselves His likeness, and hang upon the walls of our imagination the face whose features are born of our own love's longing and our own inward communing with Him. How diverse are the images we form of Him! To the child, He still lies on His mother's breast, or with open-eyed wonder stands putting strange questions to the Temple sages; to the laborer, He is still the carpenter toiling in the Nazareth workshop; to the tempted, He still meets the hard testing of the will in the wilderness and vanquishes the tempter by His unshaken trust; to the weary, He still sits resting upon the wayside well; to the bereaved, He still weeps beside the mourners at the tomb; to the tortured heart, He still endures Gethsemane's agony and bears its bloody sweat. We have seen "the glory of God in the face of Jesus Christ," but it was the glory of "grace and truth," which bears for us the changing reflection of all our earthly variations.

The whole concept of the Christian life as found in the New Testament is most repellent to the unregenerate nature. Jesus makes the shadow of the cross fall across the whole of life. "Then He said to the crowd, 'If any of you wants to be My follower, you must turn from your selfish ways, take up your cross daily, and follow Me. If you try to hang on to your life, you will lose it. But if you give up your life for My sake, you will save it.'" We are called to be "crucified with Christ," called to the "fellowship of His sufferings." He has set up His cross in the pathway of our dearest longings and most passionate desires; our selfishness turns away from His sad features to the smiling welcome of the god of this world.

All beauty is at last the beauty of God, and Jesus Christ, the Son of God, is "the brightness of His glory and the express image of His Person." Was He a hungry peasant in working garb, tired, fatigued, lonely, with hands hardened at the carpenter's bench, and raiment dusty with weary wanderings? Still the glory at times shone through, until upon Mount Hermon, in transfigured splendor, Heaven breaks through the walls of earth and the chosen three beheld His glory. How the vision burned itself into their souls! They never could forget it, and a generation later Peter writes, "We were eyewitnesses of His majesty, for He received from God the Father honor and glory"; while, surviving two generations, the best beloved [Apostle John], who had laid on His bosom and seen deepest into His heart, cries, "We beheld His glory!"

Beauty is more than form and color; it lies deeper than the flesh, and its deepest life is in the soul. In this moral beauty, Jesus has no rival; He is the "fairest of the children of men." In the Human God and the Divine Man we find united the ideals of beauty and duty. They may be so united in our lives. The Cross and the Crown meet in the Christian understanding of life; for loving self-surrender and spiritual mastery are one. The beauty of Jesus—it may be ours. "Let the beauty of the Lord our God be upon us."

All heavenly ideals have left their lines of beauty in His perfect character and perfect life. This is the beauty of the glorified Lord, who, having been made "perfect through suffering," has now shined in human hearts through the outflow of the Spirit. It is the beauty and glory of God, and it shines for us in the face of Jesus Christ.

January 19
His Beginning
by John Charles Ryle (1816-1900) England
Excerpted from *Expository Thoughts on the Gospels: St. John,* published by Robert Carter & Brothers, New York, New York in 1879

In the beginning the Word already existed. The Word was with God, and the Word was God. He existed in the beginning with God. God created everything through Him, and nothing was created except through Him. The Word gave life to everything that was created, and his life brought light to everyone. The light shines in the darkness, and the darkness can never extinguish it.
John 1:1-5 (NLTSE)

The things which are peculiar to John's Gospel are among the most precious possessions of the Church of Christ. No one of the four Gospel-writers has given us such full statements about the divinity of Christ—about justification by faith—about the offices of Christ—about the work of the Holy Ghost—and about the privileges of believers, as we read in the pages of John. On none of these great subjects, undoubtedly, have Matthew, Mark, and Luke been silent. But in John's Gospel, they stand out prominently on the surface, so that he who runs may read.

The five verses now before us contain a statement of matchless grandeur concerning the divine nature of our Lord Jesus Christ. He it is, beyond all question, whom John means, when he speaks of "the Word." No doubt there are heights and depths in that statement which are far beyond man's understanding. And yet there are plain lessons in it, which every Christian would do well to treasure up in his mind.

We learn, firstly, that our Lord Jesus Christ is eternal. John tells us that "in the beginning was the Word." He did not begin to exist when the heavens and the earth were made. Much less did He begin to exist when the gospel was brought into the world. He had glory with the Father "before the world was" (John 17:5). He was existing when matter was first created, and before time began. He was "before all things" (Colossians 1:17). He was from all eternity.

We learn, secondly, that our Lord Jesus Christ is a Person distinct from God the Father, and yet one with Him. John tells us that "the Word was with God." The Father and the Word, though two persons, are joined by an indescribable union. Where God the Father was from all eternity, there also was the Word, even God the Son—their glory equal, their majesty co-eternal, and yet their Godhead one. This is a great mystery! Happy is he who can receive it as a little child, without attempting to explain it.

We learn, thirdly, that the Lord Jesus Christ is very God. John tells us that "the Word was God." He is not merely a created angel, or a being inferior to God the Father, and invested by Him with power to redeem sinners. He is nothing less than perfect God— equal to the Father as touching His Godhead—God of the substance of the Father, begotten before the worlds.

We learn, fourthly, that the Lord Jesus Christ is the Creator of all things. John tells us that "by Him were all things made, and without Him was not anything made that was made." So far from being a creature of God, as some heretics have falsely asserted, He is the Being who made the worlds and all that they contain. "He commanded and they were created" (Psalm 148:5).

We learn, lastly, that the Lord Jesus Christ is the source of all spiritual life and light. John tells us, that "in Him was life, and the life was the light of men." He is the eternal fountain, from which alone the sons of men have ever derived life. Whatever spiritual life and light Adam and Eve possessed before the Fall, was from Christ.

January 20
His Being
by George H. Morrison (1866-1928) Scotland
Excerpted from "The Way, the Truth, the Life," *Footsteps of the Flock*, published by Hodder and Stoughton, London, England in 1904

Jesus told him, "I am the way, the truth, and the life."
John 14:6 (NLTSE)

No one was more ready than Jesus to detect the anxieties of those He loved. We picture Him, as He taught the twelve, watching intently the expression on their faces to learn how far His words were understood. Jesus had noted, then, tokens of heart distress (John 14:1). The disciples felt His departure like a torture. And it was then that He consoled them with such simple and glorious speech that all Christendom is the debtor to their agony. They thought that His death was an unforeseen calamity. Christ taught them it was the path of His own planning. They thought that Heaven was very far away. Christ taught them it was but another room in the great home of whose many mansions this beautiful world was one. He was not stepping out into the dark. He was passing from one room to another in the house.

But the mightiest encouragement of all came when He told them, "I go to prepare a place for you." This, then, was the purpose of His going, that love might have all things ready when they arrived. When a child is born here, love has all things ready for it. It will be the same when we awaken in eternity. When a boy or girl comes home from boarding school, has not some heart at home been busy in preparation? There is someone at the station, and the bedroom is arranged, and the lights are lit, and the table is spread, and all day there has been happy excitement in the home because James or Mary is coming home tonight. So Jesus says, "I go to prepare a place for you. I go to have all things ready for your coming." And though there are depths in these words we cannot fathom and mysteries we cannot understand, they mean at least that love is getting ready to give the children a real welcome home.

Then Jesus says, "I am the Way." It was the very word that the disciples wanted, for they all felt like wanderers that night. So far, they had all walked with Jesus. Now, at the cross, that pathway seemed to cease. We can hardly grasp the depth of comfort in it when they heard that Christ was to be the Way forevermore. It was in Him they were to fight and conquer. It was in Him they were to live and die. It was in Him they were to reach the glory and stand in the presence of the Father at the end. So Jesus, our Redeemer, is still the Way. A thousand things have gone, but that remains. It is through His death, and His rising from the dead, and through our daily fellowship with Him that we walk heavenward and reach home at last.

Then Jesus says, "I am the Truth." He does not say, observe, "I speak the truth." There was a deeper meaning in His mind than that. I hope that every child will speak the truth; yet every child, as its experience grows, will discover with shame how untrue it is at heart. Christ is the sum and center of all truth. Where Christ is not, there is a false note always. And one of the great joys of knowing Jesus is the sweet assurance that truth is ours at last.

Then lastly Jesus says, "I am the Life." There is no book in any literature so filled with the message of life as the New Testament. If there is one word that sums up the gospel, it is life. And here we are taught that that life is in Jesus Christ. He is the source of it. It is treasured in Him. And there is no way to gain it and to keep it but by trusting and by loving Him.

January 21
His Beloved
by Charles S. Spurgeon (1834-1892) England
Excerpted from "The Bridegroom's Parting Sermon," *Sermons Volume XIV*, published by Funk & Wagnall's Company, New York, New York in 1883

> *"You that dwell in the gardens, the companions listen to your voice: cause me to hear it."*
> Song of Solomon 8:13 (KJV)

The last words of the Lord in this book remind me of the commission which the Master gave to His disciples before He was taken up, when He said to them, "Go into all the world, and preach the gospel to every creature." Then, scattering blessings with both His hands, He ascended into the glory, and "a cloud received Him out of their sight."

The bridegroom, speaking of his bride, says, "You that dwell in the gardens." The Hebrew is in the feminine, and hence we are bound to regard it as the word of the Bridegroom to his bride. It is the mystical word of the Church's Lord to His elect one. He calls her "inhabitress of the gardens"—that is the word. So then, dear friends, we who make up the Church of God are here addressed under that term, "You that inhabit the gardens."

This title is given to believers here on earth, first, by way of distinction—distinction from the Lord Himself. He whom we love dwells in the ivory palaces, wherein they make Him glad. He is gone up into His Father's throne, and has left these gardens down below. Jesus has not taken us up with Him; He will come another time to do that. But now He leaves us among the seeds and flowers and growing plants to do the King's work until He comes. He was a visitor here, and the visit cost Him dearly; but He is gone back unto the place where He came, having finished the work which His Father gave Him. Our life work is not finished, and therefore we must tarry awhile below, and be known as inhabitants of the gardens.

It is expedient that we should be here, even as it is expedient that He should not be here. God's glory is to come by our time here, else He would have taken us away long ago. He said to His Father, "I pray not that You should take them out of the world, but that You should keep them from the evil." He Himself is an inhabitant of the palaces, for there He best accomplishes the eternal purposes of love; but His Church is the inhabitress of the gardens, for there she best fulfills the decrees of the Most High. Here she must abide awhile until all the will of the Lord shall be accomplished in her and by her, and then she also shall be taken up, and shall dwell with her Lord above. The title is given by way of distinction, and marks the difference between her condition and that of her Lord.

Your portion is with the Lord's saints, yes, with Himself; and what can be a better portion? Is it not as the garden of the Lord? You dwell where the great Husbandman spends His care upon you and takes pleasure in you. You dwell where the infinite skill and tenderness and wisdom of God manifest themselves in the training of the plants which His own right hand has planted; you dwell in the Church of God, which is laid out in due order, and hedged about and guarded by heavenly power; and you are, therefore, most suitably said to dwell in the gardens.

Beloved, if you dwell in the gardens you have a double privilege, not only of being found in a fat and fertile place, but in living there continually. You might well forego a thousand comforts for the sake of this one delight, for under the gospel your soul is made to drink of wines that are well refined.

January 22
His Betrayer
by David James Burrell (1844-1926) USA
Excerpted from "Judas Iscariot: or the Flower, Fruit, and Ashes of Sin," *The Morning Cometh* published by American Tract Society, New York, New York in 1893

And Judas Iscariot, who betrayed Him.
Mark 3:19 (NIV)

What is in a name? Much every way. An army of lads have been called "John" and "Peter" and "James," but was ever a lad named for Judas Iscariot? The world abhors the memory of that man. And rightly so. As friendship is the most genial, gratitude the most humane, and loyalty the most heroic of the graces, so is treachery the vilest and meanest of crimes. In the three lists of the disciples this Judas is always mentioned with the stigma, "which also betrayed Him." He has come down through the centuries bearing that scarlet letter on his breast.

Let us not mistake, however, in thinking of this as an isolated crime. It was indeed a unique opportunity which came to Judas Iscariot in this way to betray the innocent Son of God. In that he stands alone, yet all sin has in it the essence of treachery against Christ. So the writer of the epistle to the Hebrews speaks of certain ones who by persistence in evil-doing "crucify the Lord afresh and put Him to an open shame."

Sin, when it is finished, brings forth death. The sentence of the traitor is recorded in the words, "It were better for him had he never been born." Once only has that inscription been put upon the tomb of a human being. In other similar cases the veil of the awful future is not lifted. Of this traitor it is said, "He went unto his own place."

In the brief portion of his life that followed his ultimate resolution to betray Jesus we catch three glimpses of his face: Once when he hurried from the upper chamber "and it was night." In the Wiertz gallery at Brussels there is a picture of this man wandering about on that dreadful night. He has come upon a group of workmen who, wearied by their labors, have fallen asleep. The light of the moon falls upon their quiet faces. The features of Judas are distorted with evil passion. He catches sight of the cross lying on the ground, the carpenters' tools beside them. He clutches his money bag and hurries on. Again, at the doorway to the Hall Gazith where the rabbis are in session. He may not enter. He pauses at the doorway for a moment, his face haggard and convulsed with an unspeakable despair. With the cry, "I have betrayed innocent blood!" he hurls the thirty pieces of silver down upon the marble floor. His heart and conscience are on fire. He hurries out again into the night. Once more, at the field Aceldama, the body of the traitor hangs from the limb of a tree over the deep abyss of Hinnom. We may not linger for a moment here. Sin, when it is finished, brings forth death.

Two words, by way of application. One is a word of warning. Let him who would avoid the mortal sin take heed and beware of the beginnings of it. The other word is one of glorious hope and promise. We have reason to believe that if Judas Iscariot, at any moment before his death, had sought God's mercy he would have found it. No matter, friend, how heavy the burden of guilt that weighs upon you, God is a great Forgiver. "Come now," He says, "and let us reason together; though your sins be as scarlet, they shall be whiter than snow; though they be red like crimson, they shall be as wool." He waits to be gracious. He waits to see you sobbing at His feet that He may speak the word of pardon, "Son! daughter! your sins are forgiven!"

January 23
His Binding
by Thomas Guthrie (1803-1873) Scotland
Excerpted from "Christ in Providence," *Christ and the Inheritance of the Saints*, published by Adam and Charles Black, Edinburgh, Scotland in 1862

In Him all things hold together.
Colossians 1:17 (NIV)

God's work of providence is "His most holy, wise, and powerful preserving and governing of all His creatures and all their actions." It has no Sabbath. No night suspends it, and from its labors God never rests.

If philosophy is to be believed, our world is but an outlying corner of creation; bearing, perhaps, as small a proportion to the great universe, as a single grain bears to all the sands of the seashore, or one small quivering leaf to the foliage of a boundless forest. Yet, even within this earth's narrow limits, how vast the work of Providence! How soon is the mind lost in contemplating it! How great that Being whose hand paints every flower, and shapes every leaf; who forms every bud on every tree, and every infant in the darkness of the womb; who feeds each crawling worm with a parent's care, and watches like a mother over the insect that sleeps away the night in the bosom of a flower; who throws open the golden gates of day, and draws around a sleeping world the dusky curtains of the night; who measures out the drops of every shower, the whirling snowflakes, and the sands of man's eventful life; who determines alike the fall of a sparrow and the fate of a kingdom; and so overrules the tide of human fortunes, that whatever befall him, come joy or sorrow, the believer says, It is the Lord, let Him do what seems good.

In ascribing this great work to Jesus Christ, my text calls you to render Him divine honors. In the hands that were once nailed to the cross, it places the scepter of universal empire; and on those blessed arms that, once thrown around a mother's neck, now tenderly enfold every child of God, it hangs the weight of worlds. Great is the mystery of godliness! Yet so it is, plainly written in the words. By Him all things consist. By Him the angels keep their holiness, and the stars their orbits; the tides roll along the deep, and the seasons through the year; kings reign, and princes decree justice; the Church of God is held together, riding out at anchor the rudest storms; and by Him until the last of His elect are plucked from the wreck, and His purposes of mercy are all accomplished, this guilty world is kept from sinking under a growing load of sins. "By Him all things consist."

More could not be said of God; and Paul will not say less of Christ. Nor great, and glorious as they are, do they stand alone. Certainly not. In language as lofty, and ascribing to Jesus honors no less divine, Hebrews 1:1-3 states, "Long ago God spoke many times and in many ways to our ancestors through the prophets. And now in these final days, He has spoken to us through His Son. God promised everything to the Son as an inheritance, and through the Son He created the universe. The Son radiates God's own glory and expresses the very character of God, and He sustains everything by the mighty power of His command. When He had cleansed us from our sins, He sat down in the place of honor at the right hand of the majestic God in Heaven." How wonderful! He left a grave to ascend the throne. He exchanged the side of a dying thief for the right hand of God. He dropped a reed to assume the scepter of earth and Heaven. He put off a wreath of thorns to put on a sovereign's crown. And, in that work of providence to which I would now turn your attention, you behold Him, who died to save the chief of sinners, made "Head over all things to the Church."

January 24
His Birth
by Clarence E. Macartney (1879-1957) USA
Excerpted from "Was Christ Born of the Virgin Mary?" *Twelve Great Questions About Christ*, published by Fleming H. Revell Company, New York, New York in 1923

The angel answered, "The Holy Spirit will come upon you, and the power of the Most High will overshadow you. So the Holy One to be born will be called the Son of God."
Luke 1:35 (NIV)

From the beginning, the Christian Church has held the doctrine of the supernatural understanding and Virgin Birth of Jesus Christ to be a true and essential portion of the faith once delivered unto the saints. To unbelief in all of its forms this doctrine has always been offensive. As early as the third century we find the opponents of Christianity centering their attack upon the narratives of the Virgin Birth, and from age to age, people who hate the Christian religion and wish that it was driven out of the world have bitterly attacked this doctrine of Christianity. There is therefore nothing strange in the present day revival of the ancient assaults upon the Virgin Birth.

Many declare that the credibility and significance of Christianity are in no way affected by the doctrine of the Virgin Birth, and some go so far as to say that the doctrine is a stumbling block to faith, and puts a barrier between Jesus and the human race, and that narratives of the Virgin Birth in the Gospels arose in much the same way as the old legends and myths about the supernatural births of famous personages of the pagan world.

That such utterances as these should be made by men within the Christian Church, and by men solemnly ordained to proclaim to the world the gospel of Christ, shows the necessity of reaffirming the doctrine of the manner of the Incarnation.

In discussing this article of Christianity let us remember that we are dealing with a great mystery. The beginning of all life is a mystery, over which science, which can tell us so much about the progress and change of things, has shed not even the feeblest ray of light. Paul goes on to define wherein the mystery consists—it is the mystery of the Incarnation: God manifest in the flesh.

God created one sinless man, sinless, though free to fall. That first man, created in God's image, fell, and after him all men have sinned and fallen. Then God sent forth a new creation, a second Adam, the pre-existent and eternal Son of God, manifest in the flesh, assuming human nature, not fallen and stained and corrupted human nature, but human nature as God created it in the beginning, in the image of God. Again the great experiment is to be tried, while men and angels and devils look on with breathless interest. Will the second Adam fall like the first? Will temptation bring His forehead, too, down to the dust? The result of that experiment is the record of the Gospels. Christ perfectly kept the law of God, and by virtue of that perfect obedience demonstrated and won His right to be our Redeemer and to make satisfaction for our sins. All the rivers of Christian theology become one great life-giving stream in the cross of Christ. But if Jesus was only the son of Joseph and Mary, then He was not free from the taint of sin, He was not separate from sinners. You have left in that manger-cradle at Bethlehem the child who may become a world's great prophet, leader, dreamer, reformer, but Jesus, the Savior, the Redeemer, is gone! Christ is lost to humanity! Star of Bethlehem, go out and leave this world in the blackness of darkness, forever groping in endless cycles with its lusts and its illusions, for Jesus is not that Holy thing which shall be called the Son of God, and shall save us from our sins. He was born of flesh and of the will of man, not of the will of God. Our Christ is gone, and with Him dies the hope of humanity.

January 25
His Blessings
by James Boardman Hawthorne (1837-1910) USA

Excerpted from "Receiving Divine Blessings," *An Unshaken Trust and Other Sermons*, published by American Baptist Publication Society, Philadelphia, Pennsylvania in 1899

Blessed be...the God of all comfort, who comforts us in all our tribulation, that we may be able to comfort them which are in any trouble.
2 Corinthians 1: 3-4 (KJV)

These are the words of the most thoroughly poised and symmetrically developed man, save One, the world has ever seen. The human heart has never cherished a nobler and holier feeling than that to which he here gives utterance. He thanks God for comforts which he had received in great trials—thanks Him, not so much for the relief which they gave him, as for the new strength which they imparted to him for the comforting of others in distress. He gloried in his tribulations, because in them he had experiences of God's presence and power which enlarged his capacity for instructing, comforting, and strengthening other men, and especially other Christians.

To covet gifts for the use we can make of them in promoting the world's welfare is the best proof of a regenerated heart and a Christlike character. So much more did this man Paul love others than himself, that he was willing to be accursed from God if by bearing a divine curse he might save the apostate Jewish people.

Blessed is the man to whom God has given the secret of rejoicing even in tribulation. Blessed is the man who can see and enjoy at all times what is good in the world, and who can transform what is evil in itself into elements of strength and happiness. It is the condition of a man's heart that makes the world what it is to him. He sees things as he is.

Every man in going through the world will find just what he takes with him. If he takes darkness he will find darkness, and if he takes light he will find light. If there is beauty in his soul he will find beauty in every spot and in every object on which his eye rests. If he is selfish and mean he will find selfishness and meanness everywhere. If he has a heart whose sympathies embrace the whole world, he will find a kindly sympathy and a sweet charity greeting him in every community that he enters.

If a man has music in his soul, he hears music everywhere. Some men can walk through a forest on a May morning and find more inspiration in listening to the warbling of the birds than some other men would get from the grandest music that human voices can make.

Give me the man who sees and enjoys all the good in his earthly allotment. Give me communion with the soul that extracts honey from every flower that blossoms along its homeward journey. Give me for a friend and companion the man who finds nuggets of gold in the rocks over which his feet stumble. Give me for a counselor and guide the man who beholds objects of beauty and loveliness all along the pathway of toil and conflict. Give me for a comforter in distress the man who sees angels in the disguises of earth, and gets a blessing from them before they spread their radiant wings for homeward flight.

Lying out on the very surface of revealed religion is the great truth that God enriches no man, temporally or spiritually, without laying upon him at the same time the obligation to use the blessings bestowed on him in supplying the needs of other men.

January 26
His Blood

by Robert Law (1860-1919) Scotland/Canada
Excerpted from "The Blood of Abel and the Blood of Christ," *The Grand Adventure and Other Sermons*, published by Hodder & Stoughton, New York, New York in 1916

The blood of sprinkling, that speaks better things than that of Abel.
Hebrews 12:24 (KJV)

God said to Cain, "The voice of your brother's blood cries unto Me from the ground"; and Cain did not need to have it told to him what that blood was crying for. Observe that it was "the voice of your brother's blood." Abel did not cry for vengeance. Abel, had he been permitted to speak, would have pleaded every reason why mercy should rejoice against judgment. "Poor, pitiable Cain!" he would have said, "it was hard for him to see his younger brother preferred before him. I know not whether, if so tempted, I might not have shown myself as envious as he." But—here is the terrible thing—while Abel forgives, his blood will not forgive. Abel could not silence his own accusing blood; he could not stop the wheels of Cain's destiny. And this dread truth is often repeated in the Bible, and in the same terms. "When He makes an investigation for blood," says the Psalmist, "He remembers them: He forgets not the cry of the humble."

The Old Testament speaks of a brother's blood which cries to high Heaven for vengeance. The New Testament speaks of a blood which has an opposite virtue, which cries for mercy, which does not stain but cleanse—the "blood of sprinkling," the blood of Christ, that speaks better things than that of Abel.

Here we come upon one of those wonderful, universal truths which are woven into the essence of all life, and which broaden out and deepen endlessly as we look at them. The history of the world is written in blood; and the blood in which it is written throughout is of these two kinds, the blood of Abel that curses and the blood of Christ that redeems and saves. In all human history we see these two powers contending, balanced one against the other—life that is selfishly taken and life that is unselfishly given. In all ages the blood of Abel and his successors has been shed; the life of the innocent, the weak and helpless has been in every way exploited and preyed upon. It has been crying to Heaven against the injustice and ruthlessness of man to man, against the pride and greed and lust that have used up the lives and drunk the blood of countless victims, against the callousness which uses Abel as a mere tool which, when it is blunt and worn out, it throws without a qualm upon the scrap heap. What a weight of curse the blood of all the long generation of Abel has laid upon the world! And terribly has it been paid for. But always blood of a contrary quality and effect has been flowing for the redemption of the world.

No doctrine is quite so familiar to us as that of the atoning death of Christ; and there is none upon which it is more difficult to rationalize. When we have done our utmost to explore its depths, we feel that there is still an unfathomed deep beneath. But the first thing that meets us in that death of Calvary is that in some way we are all directly related to it as to no other. We feel instinctively about Christ as of no other, that He tasted death for everyone. The sacrifice of Calvary is not a mere fact of history. Christ's cross is ours; His infinite sorrows and dying pangs are ours. That is the heart of Christianity. It is that faith, that consciousness of Christ, which created Christianity, and which is forever its life and the source of its power.

Christ atones for everything. Christ makes up for everything—makes up to God, to man, for everything.

January 27
His Boyhood
by George H. Morrison (1866-1928) Scotland
Excerpted from "The Boyhood of Jesus," *Footsteps of the Flock*, published by Hodder and Stoughton, London, England in 1909

And the Child grew, and grew strong in spirit, filled with wisdom: and the grace of God was upon Him. Now His parents went to Jerusalem every year at the fast of the Passover. And when He was twelve years old, they went up to Jerusalem after the custom of the feast.
Luke 2:40-42 (KJV)

One of the holiest doctors of the medieval Church, who was placed by Dante [Italian poet, 1265-1321] among the saints of Paradise, said a striking thing about the youth of Jesus: "Take notice," he said, "that His doing nothing wonderful was itself a kind of wonder. As there is power in His actions, so is there power in His retirement and His silence." In our Gospels there is not a whisper of a boyish miracle. Jesus grew and became strong in spirit filled with wisdom, and the grace of God was upon Him (Luke 2:40). Let us learn then that uneventful years need never be idle or unprofitable years. Give Me, said Jesus, the quiet valley of Nazareth, and the blue sky and the blossoming of flowers, and David and Isaiah, and My village home and God, and I shall be well prepared for My great work.

Now out of these thirty silent years one incident alone has been preserved: It is the story of Jesus in the Temple. We learn that when Jesus was twelve years old, He went up with Mary and Joseph to Jerusalem to keep the Passover. And how, when the feast was over, Mary and Joseph set out again for home, and how they missed their Child and went to search for Him and found Him in the Temple with the doctors—all that we have known since our days of Sunday school. Now, why do you think this story has been preserved?

First, let us try to realize the influence that this journey had upon Jesus. It is always a very memorable hour when a lad for the first time leaves his village home. He has dreamed of the great world many a night, and now he is going to see it for himself. Prior to this, his horizon has been bounded by the range of hills that encircles his quiet home. Now he is actually going to cross the barrier, and touch the mystery that lies beyond. There is a stirring of the heart in such an hour, a fresh understanding of the greater world; a journey like that will do what a death does sometimes, it awakens the childish spirit to the mysteries. And the lad may come home again, and live with his father and mother, but the world can never more be quite the same.

Next note that in this incident the character of Jesus is revealed. For a boy of twelve reared in a quiet village, Jerusalem at Passover must have been paradise. Many a time at home He had questioned Mary, and Mary had said: "Ah, Child! I do not understand; it would take the Temple doctors to answer that." And now the Temple doctors were beside Him, and Jesus forgot the crowds—forgot His parents—in His passionate eagerness to ask and know. Mary alone found Jesus in the Temple. Is it not a priceless glance into a Spirit whose consuming passion was the things of God?

This incident has been preserved because in it we have Jesus' dawning sense of His mission to the world. How far He had seen into the dark yet glorious future, we shall know better when we see Him face to face. But at least He was conscious that He stood apart, and felt, as man had never felt before, the nearness and the glory of God's Fatherhood, and knew that from this point forward, life was to be to Him an absolute devotion to His Father's will. Then He went back with Mary and with Joseph and came to Nazareth and was obedient to them; but His mother kept all these sayings in her heart.

January 28
His Brother
by Handley C. G. Moule (1841-1920) England
Excerpted from "The Lord's Brother," *Cathedral and University and Other Sermons*, published by Hodder and Stoughton, London, England in 1920

But I saw none of the other apostles except James, the Lord's brother.
Galatians 1:19 (KJV)

My text is a note, the simplest possible, of an incidental matter of fact, made passingly by the writer in the course of a series of personal recollections. This writer is a missionary, addressing a pastoral letter to a group of his converts. It happens to be important that he should remind them of certain events in his own life which have a bearing upon their estimate of the value of his spiritual message. So recollecting, so recording, he mentions a visit which he had once paid to Jerusalem, some three years or a little more after a supreme crisis in his spiritual history. In the holy city he had stayed for about two weeks, as the guest of Peter, with whom it had been his purpose to talk. As it happened, the other members of Peter's circle, John, Andrew, Philip, and the rest, did not cross his path. One person only besides Peter of the nearer disciples of Jesus of Nazareth he did meet; and this was James, the Lord's brother. That is all; the matter at once passes off. With a warm declaration of the truth of his statement that of the inner circle he saw no one else during that two weeks, the writer, to wit, Paul of Tarsus, goes on at once to other and more extended recollections.

Here is as brief a memento as could well be put down; as it were a small item in a diary. In itself it is a plain fragment of the dry prose of fact untouched, uncolored, by the faintest haze of imagination; different as anything thrown into words could well be from the poetical, from the mythical, from the mysterious, from what transcends the level of common life. And it is a note, a note of this ordinary character, from the incidents of a time dating not far from nineteen centuries ago. What can it have to say to the hearts of us today, as the motive of a message from the Christian pulpit?

Consider a little what this suggests as to the fact-character of the biography of Jesus Christ. This artless mention, made when it was made, of personal interaction at Jerusalem between two men, one of whom was familiarly known as James, the Lord's brother, carries us up, beyond all serious risks of intervening legendary accumulations or distortions, to the earliest days of Christianity. The writer's recollection here has to cover only a quarter of a century. That is a tract of time which, to a man in middle life, shows itself in retrospect under the broadest daylight of a conscious certainty in regard to its main contents. James and Jesus, in the common jargon of the place, on the lips of the Nazarene men and women, were just brothers. No word would have been more common among the neighbors, no fact of local homelife more plainly free from the glamor of romance. But then, all the while, the thing had another side. It involved a surpassing wonder. That cottage home had embraced in its membership two young men, called brothers all around the town. One of them was James. But who was the other? He was — the Lord.

But to my own soul, let me humbly affirm it, this sentence in the Galatian letter, written within easy memory of the date of the Resurrection of our Lord, speaks with a power peculiar and intimate concerning alike the solid sanity and the transcendent glory of the Christian's faith. It takes me up at one step to the morning and youth of Christianity. It displays to me there, with one hand, a rock-like surface of intelligible circumstance, seen in the broad light of common human experience. With the other hand it reveals to me, set upon that firm platform, moving and in action upon it, the calm splendor of a certainty that the Jesus of history is also the mysterious and gracious Sacrifice for my sins, Life of my life, Crown of my joy, and absolute Object of my love.

January 29
His Building
by James Scholefield (1790-1855) England
Excerpted from "Christ the Builder of the Church," *The British Pulpit: A Collection of Sermons by the Most Eminent Divines of the Present Day, Vol. I*, published by Thomas Tegg, London, England in 1844

Tell him this is what the Lord Almighty says: "Here is the Man whose name is the Branch, and He will branch out from His place and build the Temple of the Lord. It is He who will build the Temple of the Lord, and He will be clothed with majesty and will sit and rule on His throne. And He will be a priest on His throne. And there will be harmony between the two."
Zechariah 6:12-13 (NIV)

Observe, then, the circumstances of the prophecy, and see how undeniably they all point to Christ, the High Priest of good things to come, by a greater and more perfect tabernacle. What was the work which the Father had given Him to do? It was to build the Temple of the Lord. The typical image of this was represented in the work in which Joshua [high priest, not the successor of Moses] was at this time engaged; and the subordinate design of the whole transaction to which the text refers, was, to encourage Joshua in his important work. But the temple He built, being but a shadow of good things to come, was again to be removed, as Solomon's had been before, and its glory to be done away. It would make way, in the fulness of time, for that other tabernacle, which the Lord built, and not man; and this is the true and spiritual Church of God, which is spread over all ages and all nations, which consists of all believers, all faithful people, and sanctified persons, throughout the world, gathered out of the vast multitudes of humankind, and brought into one mystical body, the members of which, for the most part, are unknown to each other by face during their earthly pilgrimage, but will all be united in the worship of the heavenly sanctuary through all eternity. It is the glory of the

Son of God to be the builder of this Temple: "Even He shall build the Temple of the Lord."

The materials of which it is composed are sinners, who are by nature dead in trespasses and sins, and in that state are far off from God, alienated from the life of God, having the understanding darkened, the mind blinded, and the heart hardened and corrupt. Whether the gospel finds men in the polished society of a Christian land, or debased in the revolting mystery of the New Zealand savage, or led captive by Satan in the thousand chains of Hindu superstition, whatever difference there be in the outward form and circumstances of the case, there is none whatever in those essential elements of character with which the gospel has to deal. It finds him lost, guilty, and spiritually dead; it addresses its gracious invitations, its life-giving message, to his soul. But he is dead, and cannot hear; he hears indeed, but understands not. And can these dry bones live? And is God able of these stones to raise up children unto Abraham? Yes; when the great Master Builder sends forth the mighty energy of His Spirit, the dead in sins are quickened into life, the stony heart is taken away, the scales fall from the eyes, and the veil from the heart, and the gospel is made the power of God unto salvation.

Converted sinners are made living stones, and, coming in faith to Christ, the living foundation stone, they are built up into a spiritual house, a holy priesthood, to offer up spiritual sacrifices, acceptable to God through Jesus Christ. And such sacrifices of holy and spiritual worship have been offered up, and are offered up to God continually, in every place where the gospel has been preached in faithfulness and in simplicity, and combined, as in all such cases it will be, with the demonstration of the Spirit, and with power. And herein is exercised the power of our Redeemer's grace — that He can soften and subdue the most stony hearts, and use the most unpromising materials, and make them serve His purpose in building the Temple of the Lord.

January 30
His Challenge
by William A. Scott (1813-1885) USA

Excerpted from "The Great Question," *The Pacific Coast Pulpit Containing Sermons by Prominent Preachers in San Francisco and Vicinity*, published by Western Reporting and Publishing Company, San Francisco, California in 1875

"What shall I do, then, with Jesus, who is called Christ?"
Matthew 27:22 (KJV)

It is remarkable that this question concerning Jesus, who came into about nineteen hundred years ago, should still be the question which the greatest minds of this age are most earnestly engaged in endeavoring to solve. Ours is an age of materialism, of money making, of speculation, of racial and political experiments; yet the subject which most deeply engages the minds of the most thoughtful men today crystallizes on Pilate's question.

He has been presented from every point of view that learning, and research, and criticism, and even the imagination, could find or invent. His enemies have denied His personal existence. But history has lifted up its voice in too powerful a manner to dispose of the Man, Christ Jesus, in this way. Some have taught that He was mere phenomenon, denying His real humanity altogether; and some have received Him as an extraordinary man and nothing more. But somehow all such theories and substitutes for the Christ of the Gospels have failed to meet the demands of historic facts; they rise, flourish for a time, and vanish. The most eloquent tributes to His character and to the greatness of His doctrines have, indeed, been given by those who did not believe in Him as the Messiah; and yet they have not given Him His place in history which answers to the facts of His life and His influence on the human race.

The learned unbelieving world is quite satisfied to settle down in a general way upon some accepted views of Zoroaster, Confucius and Mohammed, and concerning the rise and fall of the Roman Empire and all other empires and cities of the past, but is not able to agree in assigning a satisfactory place to the Man, Christ Jesus, of history. Meanwhile, His religion has become the most vital and powerful, and the greatest fact of this world in this nineteenth century. This is undeniable. All the great progressive nations—those that by arts and arms and wealth control the world—are nominally, at least, believers in Him as the Son of God and the Redeemer of man.

Some may, indeed, say, "We are indifferent, and we will not be pressed into a corner. The only thing we have practically decided is that we will think as little of the subject as possible." I will say to all on that point that if this is your decision, you have answered it. Such a decision is against having anything to do with "Jesus, who is called Christ."

Now, there are many timid believers such as these of whom I have been speaking, who if they were pressed for an answer to our test question would answer, "Why do you ask me such a question? I am on principle His follower; I hold on to Him; I cannot say I enjoy that fullness which I desire, but I will tell you what I know of Him. As yet I am much dissatisfied with myself; I am a poor sort of a Christian at best; I am overwhelmed with sense of my shortcomings. I have only an occasional glimpse of His glory and character and offices. Sometimes I am full of hope and joy, and at other times I am almost overpowered at my lack of faith and trust, and a sense of my shortcomings."

The more matured believer, who has learned that there may be clouds over his head that obscure the sun and yet that the sun is still shining, will be more ready to say Christ is always precious. The thoughtful conviction of his mind is that the testimony of God concerning His Son is true: that He is all in all. He is the light and joy of life.

January 31
His Character
by Alexander Whyte (1836-1921) Scotland
Excerpted from "The Express Image of His Person," *The Walk, Conversation and Character of Jesus Christ Our Lord,* published by Oliphant, Anderson & Ferrier, Edinburgh, Scotland in 1905

The Son is the radiance of God's glory and the exact representation of His being, sustaining all things by His powerful word. After He had provided purification for sins, He sat down at the right hand of the Majesty in Heaven.
Hebrews 1:3 (NIV)

The Greek word for "character" is a most expressive and a most suggestive word. The artists and the craftsmen of Greece employed this word to describe the etching on the face of a seal and the engraving on the face of a stamp. And from that first use of this ancient word we find it widening out to embrace every kind of distinctive feature; every kind of special sign and symbol.

Now, what, exactly, is meant in the text by the character of God the Father? What does the writer point at when he speaks of the express image, or as it is in the original, the character of God the Father? Well, God's character, His express image, is just His divine nature. It is just His love, and His joy, and His peace, and His long-suffering, and His gentleness, and all His goodness. That is God's character. It is His fullness of all these things that makes Him God, and our God. Jehovah revealed His whole moral and spiritual character when He descended and proclaimed the name of the Lord to Moses on Mount Sinai. "The Lord, the Lord God, merciful and gracious, long-suffering, and abundant in goodness and truth." That is God's name and nature. That is God's express image. That is God's character. That is what makes Him the only living and true God. That is what makes all the psalmists praise

Him. And that is what makes Micah exclaim at the end of his life, and as the seal of his ministry, "Who is a God like unto You?"

And then the Son of God is set out to us in the New Testament as the brightness of His Father's glory, and the express image of His person. Or, as the original Greek has it, the Father's whole character is fully and forever stamped and sealed down upon His Son. While the eternal generation of the Divine Son is unapproachably beyond and above us; while the transmission of the Father's character to the Son is high, and we cannot attain unto it; at the same time the transmitting and the impressing of the Divine character of the Father and the Son on the human nature of our Lord is that supreme study, and all-satisfying contemplation, to which the New Testament on its every page invites us. From His birth to His death, we are enabled and we are intended to see the character of our Lord evident in every word He spoke, and in every act He did. The whole of the four Gospels are written, and have been put into our hands, in order that we may have continually before our eyes the character of Jesus Christ, both for our justifying faith in Him, and for our sanctifying imitation of Him.

First His character, and then your own, those are the two things that most concern you and me in all this world. Death, with one stroke of his hand, will one day strip us bare of all that we now pursue and possess. But the last enemy will not be able to lay a finger on our Christian character, unless it is to add on its finishing touches. Our Lord carried up to His Father's house a human heart, a human character, which was and is and will forever be a new wonder in Heaven. He carried up all His human nature with Him, with all the stamp and impression of His divine nature upon it; all His human meekness and humility and lowliness of mind; all His human love and pity and compassion; all His human sympathy and approachableness and likableness. And like Him, if we are found at last in Him and like Him, we also shall carry to the same place the same things that He carried. And they are the only things we possess here that are worth carrying so far.

February 1
His Church
by David James Burrell (1844-1926) USA
Excerpted from "The Church," *The Golden Passional*, published by
Wilbur B. Ketcham, New York, New York in 1897

You are no longer foreigners and aliens, but fellow citizens with God's people and members of God's household, built on the foundation of the apostles and prophets, with Christ Jesus Himself as the chief cornerstone. In Him the whole building is joined together and rises to become a holy temple in the Lord.
Ephesians 2:20 (NIV)

The Christians of Ephesus would instantly understand the reference here. They lived under the shadow of Diana's Temple, one of the seven wonders of the world. It was four hundred feet long and above two hundred feet wide, and was two hundred and twenty years in building. Its roofs were supported by sixty-seven columns of green jasper, eight of which of which may be seen today in the Mosque of St. Sophia. The dome of this magnificent building was surmounted by an image of Diana catching the sunlight in her golden shield. In sight of this temple, within the hearing of its elaborate worship, dwelt a humble body of believers in Christ. To them Paul writes in terms of encouragement: "You are the living parts of a grander fabric, whose glory shall endure when the walls of the temple of great Diana have crumbled to dust. You are built upon the apostles and prophets, Jesus Christ Himself being the chief cornerstone; in whom all the building, properly framed together, grows into a holy temple in the Lord."

Here is the theme, therefore, which engages our thought: I believe in the holy Church, a spiritual house, a house not made with hands, built by God. Observe, the cornerstone is Christ. The engineers of the Palestine Exploration Fund, by sinking shafts and opening galleries along the walls of the Temple [in Jerusalem], came upon the original foundations. They are seventy feet below the surface, and rest upon the rocky slopes of Mount Moriah. At the lowest angle of this Temple area they discovered the cornerstone. It was four feet thick and fourteen broad, and its fine finish was almost unimpaired. It is not improbable that the prophet Isaiah had this very stone in mind when he uttered the Messianic prediction, "Behold, I lay in Zion for a foundation, a stone, a tried stone, a precious cornerstone." The first place, deepest down, most rudimentary and fundamental, binding the walls together and upholding the whole—this is reserved for Christ.

The name of the Church is eloquent with this fact. "What's in a name?" Everything here. Call the Church whatever you please, it is Christian above all. All other names, Greek and Latin, Catholic and Protestant, Lutheran, Calvinistic and Wesleyan, are subordinate to that Name which is above every other that is named in Heaven or on earth. All tribal banners are furled under the banner of the Lion of Judah.

Here, also, is clearly indicated the purpose or intent of the Church. Why did Christ institute it? What is it intended for? To set up the Kingdom of Jesus Christ on earth. We believe that He came from Heaven to suffer and die for the children of humanity; we believe that He rose triumphant, and now sits upon His throne high and lifted up; we believe that by the power of His Spirit He is working through this great living organism, which we call "the Church," for the restitution of all things; and we believe that in the fullness of time the heavens will part and He will come to reign as King over all, and blessed forever. To this end the Church was instituted; to this end its ministry was commissioned, "Go into all the world and evangelize"; and to this end the injunction is laid upon all Christ's people, "Let your light so shine among people that they may see your good works, and glorify God."

February 2
His Churches
by Albert Benjamin (A. B.) Simpson (1843-1919) Canada
Excerpted from "The Vision of the Churches," *Heaven Opened or Expositions on the Book of Revelation*, published by Christian Alliance Publishing Co., New York, New York in 1899

"He who has an ear, let him hear what the Spirit says to the churches."
Revelation 2:7 (NIV)

There is something very touching and solemn about the personal aspect of the Lord's last messages to the churches. It is very much the same as if your pastor should arise in the pulpit some Sabbath morning and say, "I have a letter from the Lord Jesus which He sent an angel to deliver to me during the night, addressed particularly to this congregation and which He has commissioned me to read to you as His personal and final message." Such a message would produce a profound impression and thrill every hearer with a deep concern and holy earnestness.

Each of these epistles is really a letter from the Lord Jesus to a particular church, and the fact that they were addressed to the seven churches of Asia does not make them any less personal and appropriate for us, for the very fact of the number seven being used shows that it is symbolic and designed to represent every church in the whole body of Christ to the end of the age. The order in which these churches are named represents an exact geographical line, so that a messenger starting out with seven letters to deliver would naturally begin at Ephesus, then go to Smyrna, and thence in turn to Pergamos, Thyatira, Sardis, Philadelphia and end at Laodicea. They were selected from the great body of the churches at the time to represent every particular congregation and the whole Church of Jesus Christ throughout the Christian age.

We have already seen that the Apocalypse begins with the vision of the Lord Jesus Christ Himself in His ascended glory as our Prophet, Priest and King. It next proceeds to the vision of the churches and then passes on to the providential dealings of God with the world, as Christ cannot deal with the world in judgment until He has first dealt with His Church. He is Head over all things in the realm of nature and providence; but He is the Head of the Church which is His body, and He governs the world with sole reference to His own people, therefore the vision of the Church must precede the vision of the world. In this vision we have seven types of Church life and character.

All through these letters we behold a little minority in each of these corrupt churches to whom the Lord speaks His words of gracious promise and approval. There are some of them in Pergamos. There are some of them in Thyatira. There are some even in Sardis that have not defiled their garments, and He is trying to gather some of them even out of Laodicea; and while He does not expect the church to reform He is rescuing the individual believers who are willing to hear His voice and meet His claims. They are described as "He that has an ear to hear what the Spirit says unto the churches." They are the men and women that know the voice of God and are hearkening to His voice and meeting His call. They are described as "he that overcomes." The word in the Greek is more significant still. The conqueror would be a more expressive translation. They are men and women that have gone in for victory in an Apostate Age over both the sufferings and seductions that surround them, and, whatsoever others do, as for them they will be true and win the victor's crown.

He not only comes to judge, but to reward. How blessed the promises that He gives in these letters to the conquering ones. How rich and heavenly the exquisite symbolism by which our hearts are drawn to turn from earth's delusions and win the crown He brings.

February 3
His Claims
by William H. G. Thomas (1861-1924) England/Wales
Excerpted from "The Claim of Christ," *Christianity is Christ*, published by Zondervan Publishing House, Grand Rapids, Michigan in 1900

Just as a diamond has several facets, each one contributing to the beauty and attractiveness of the complete stone, so Jesus Christ can be considered in various ways, and to the question, "What do you think of Christ?" different answers can be given. Looking again at the Gospels' story of His life, we are conscious of one remarkable fact that stands out on almost every page from the beginning to the close of His ministry. This is the claim that He made for Himself. It was a five-fold claim of a very far-reaching nature.

He claimed to be the Messiah of the Jews. It is well known that the Old Testament is a book of expectation, and that it closes with the expectation very largely unrealized. The Jews as a nation were ever looking forward to the coming of a great personage whom they called the Messiah. He would fulfill all their prophecies, realize all their hopes, and accomplish all their plans for themselves and for the world. Jesus Christ of Nazareth claimed to be this Messiah. During His ministry He referred to many passages in the Old Testament, and pointed to Himself as the explanation and application of it. He took the Jewish law and claimed not only to fulfill it, but to give it a wider, fuller, and deeper meaning. "I came not to destroy, but to fulfill." It was this definite claim to be the Messiah that led in great part to the opposition shown to Him by the Jews.

He claimed to be in some way the Redeemer of Humankind. "The Son of Man is come to seek and to save that which is lost"; "The Son of Man came not to be ministered unto, but to minister, and to give His life a ransom for many." This description of people as "lost," i.e., helpless, useless, and in danger of future condemnation, and this statement about Himself as having come to "save" them, constitute a claim that implies uniqueness of relation to humanity.

He claimed to be the Master of Humankind. He said that He was the Lord of the Sabbath. He called for obedience from people by His definite, all-embracing command, "Follow Me." The earliest influence of Christ over His disciples was exercised quite naturally and simply, and yet the claim He made on them was absolute. It is recorded without any explanation or justification, as though He had a natural and perfect right to make it. "He that loves father or mother more than Me is not worthy of Me." "He that loses his life for My sake shall find it." This remarkable claim to control lives and to be the supreme motive in life is surely more than human. He preached the Kingdom of God, and announced Himself as the King. He claimed to alter the law in spite of the sanction of its ancient authority.

He claimed to be the Judge of Humankind. He said that His words should judge humankind at the last day, and more than once He depicted Himself as the Judge before whom all people should be gathered to receive their reward or punishment. He claimed to sum up all the past and to decide all the future.

He claimed nothing less than the prerogatives of God. He claimed to be able to forgive sins, eliciting from His enemies a charge of blasphemy, since "Who can forgive sins but God only?" He associated Himself with God and God's work when He said, "My Father works thus far, and I work." Is this not the New Testament picture of Jesus Christ? Can anyone doubt as they read the four Gospels that this, and nothing short of it, is the claim that Jesus Christ made for Himself as Messiah, Redeemer, Master, Judge and God?

February 4
His Commandments
by G. S. Hubbs (unknown DOB), USA
Excerpted from "The Decalogue: Introductory Words," *Here and Hereafter*, published by the author, Janesville, Wisconsin in 1887

"And the Lord spoke to you from the heart of the fire. You heard the sound of His words but didn't see His form; there was only a voice. He proclaimed His covenant–the Ten Commandments–which He commanded you to keep, and which He wrote on two stone tablets."
Deuteronomy 4:12-13 (NLTSE)

Our Savior quoted from the words written by Moses, a remarkable condensing of the Ten Commandments. As recorded in Matthew 22:35-40, the account reads: "Then one of them, which was a lawyer, asked Him a question, tempting Him, and saying, 'Master, which is the greatest commandment in the law?' Jesus said unto him, 'You shall love the Lord your God with all your heart, and with all your soul, and with all your mind. This is the first and greatest commandment. And the second is like unto it, You shall love your neighbor as yourself. On these two commandments hang all the law and the prophets.'"

This answer of the Master not only shows that there are two classes of duties, but it teaches that "love is the fulfilling of the law." Nearly all of the commandments are prohibitions; they state our duties negatively, by forbidding sins against God and man. Our Savior here states those duties positively, and the "second" commandment of the greatest two is "like unto" the first, for love is the essence of both. As John teaches in his first epistle, love to God and love to man are inseparable duties—devotion and morality are parts of one great whole, both being commanded by Divine authority. As he expresses it in 1 John 4:21, "This commandment we have from Him, that he who loves God loves his brother also."

The moral law, summed up in the Ten Commandments, is of universal and perpetual obligation. The ceremonial law was only for the Hebrew nation, and was designed to be fulfilled and "done away in Christ"; but the law that teaches the duty of love to God and man, is evidenced by its nature to be for all men and all time, yes, for eternity, because, without the observance of the "law of love," Heaven would be an impossibility. Moreover, the New Testament reenacts the moral law, not only giving it the solemn sanctions of the Son of God and His apostles, but amplifying its meaning, enlarging its scope, multiplying its applications, and revealing its deep spiritual significance. We are living in the Christian dispensation, and we cannot, if we would, limit the moral law to outward observance alone; we are enlightened, and the law is enlightened by the shining of Christ's teachings upon it. We must read the Old Testament in the light of the New; we must add the spirit to the letter; we must, in studying the Ten Commandments as to what it means for us, ask how Christ interpreted it.

We do not seek life by the study and the keeping of the law; we look to the law for a comprehensive statement of our duties, for the quickening of our moral faculties, for conviction of sin — because it is evident we "all have sinned and come short of the glory of God," when we measure ourselves by this perfect standard. The law is, as Paul said, a "ministration of death, written and engraved in stones," but the gospel is a "ministration of the spirit" and a "ministration of righteousness." We may, therefore, stand without fear by quaking Mt. Sinai, with its "blackness, and darkness, and tempest, and the sound of a trumpet, and the voice of words," if Christ, who "has redeemed us from the curse of the law," stands by us, and dwells in us as a saving power. "For the law was given by Moses, but grace and truth came by Jesus Christ."

February 5
His Commission
by Matthew Simpson (1811-1884) USA
Excerpted from "The Great Commission," *Sermons*, published by
Harper & Brothers, New York New York in 1885

Jesus came and told His disciples, "I have been given all authority in Heaven and on earth. Therefore, go and make disciples of all the nations, baptizing them in the name of the Father and the Son and the Holy Spirit. Teach these new disciples to obey all the commands I have given you. And be sure of this: I am with you always, even to the end of the age."
Matthew 28:18-20 (NLTSE)

These words are selected, not for the purpose of discussing the nature of the commission to preach the gospel, nor yet the work of preaching the gospel in its detail, but for the purpose of calling attention to the declaration which Christ made with regard to the gift of power which He had received, and to that as connected with the promise of His presence. I think, if we put ourselves in the place of the disciples, we shall see that a declaration of this character was exceedingly comforting and eminently necessary. The Shepherd had been killed, and the sheep were scattered. The Messiah, in whom they had trusted that He would be a conquering Redeemer, had been taken by the hands of wicked men and crucified and slain. They had seen Him on the cross; they had known of His being carried to the tomb; He had fallen under the power of the government, and yet they had put their trust in Him as the Lord of life and of glory. How necessary, then, was this declaration that though He had seemed to be weaker than the Jewish power, weaker than the Roman authority; that though He had sunk beneath the blows of His persecutors, yet now, since He had risen, all power was given to Him; that He was superior now to all opposition to the kingdoms of the world, and was able to care for and protect those who put their trust in Him.

I wish to call your attention now to a thought showing, as I think, the beautiful relations of this declaration to the life of Christ. I believe that I can see Him as He stood on the mountain surveying the scene of His agony and His suffering. Beneath Him lay the garden where, when He prayed, the sweat rolled from His brow as great drops of blood. There on the hill was the Temple in which He had taught, where He had met with foes; just by the right of the city wall was the place where He was crucified, where the thieves were executed with Him. Yonder was the place where the Jewish council met; here was Pilate's hall; there were the emblems of Roman authority, and from the mountaintop He looked over them all. The scene of His agony, of His sufferings, and of His death were vividly before Him. But, turning to His disciples who gathered around Him, He said: "Now, how changed! All power is given unto Me. I have dominion over Rome and Judea; I have dominion over life and over death; I am not now the suffering Jesus. I am the triumphant Messiah."

Christ proclaims Himself to be King of all nations, and He has the right to send people into all nations. He rules over Europe, and He has the right to send people into Europe. He is Governor of Asia, and He has the right to open every door. Here, then, comes the authority for our going to the very ends of the earth. People may seek to close doors; but Jesus says: "The power is Mine; I reign over the nations; go, therefore, into all places of My dominion, even to the ends of the earth. If China erects a wall or barrier, leap over it; if the ports of Japan are closed, find a way of entrance; if Africa's sands are burning, I will be with you to restrain the heat, and in the wilderness I will make springs to break forth. Go into all the world, for I am Ruler of all, and no power has the right to resist My sway." See the strength of His commission: "As I have all power, go; I have dominion everywhere, go everywhere."

February 6
His Commonness
by Henry Edward Manning (1808-1892) England
Excerpted from "The Holiness of Common Life," *Sermons*, published by James Burns, London, England in 1846

"Is this not the carpenter, the son of Mary, the brother of James, and Joses, and of Juda, and Simon? And are not His sisters here with us?" And they were offended at Him.
Mark 6:3 (KJV)

Now it cannot but appear very strange, that our Lord Jesus Christ should have been so like other men that they should not have discovered Him to be something greater than themselves. We should have thought that the events attending first the annunciation, then His birth, the revelations to the shepherds and to the wise men, the warnings of God to Joseph, should have in some way come abroad, and invested the Child Jesus with awe and mystery or, if these things were kept secret, yet we should have thought that there must have been in His very gestures and words some indications which should have made people expect from Him something more than from other men. Yet it would appear that for thirty years He lay hidden, living among them unheeded, speaking and acting in the common way of men, so that He passed for the carpenter's son, Himself a carpenter, dwelling among His kinsmen, brethren and sisters as they are here called. They treated Him as one of themselves. Not only in the Temple at Jerusalem, where He might be unknown, did they ask, "How knows this man letters, having never learned?" But here, in His own city, they asked, in surprise and disbelief, "How did this Man obtain wisdom?"

From all this it would seem plain that our blessed Redeemer did not greatly differ, in what may be called His private life, from those about Him, that He dwelt under the roof of Joseph and

Mary, in childhood subject to them, in manhood serving them with perfect familial duty, in plainness, poverty, retirement. He, in whom dwelt the fulness of the Godhead bodily, the brightness of His Father's glory, and the express image of His Person, lay so concealed in the paths of ordinary life that His own townsmen knew Him only as the carpenter, as an unnoted member of Joseph's household.

Firstly, it is the fact that the holiest of persons may to all outward eyes appear exactly like other people. For in what does holiness consist but in due fulfilment of the relative duties of our state in life, and in spiritual fellowship with God?

Secondly, we may learn what, indeed, is implied though not expressed in the text, that true holiness is not made up of extraordinary acts. But if there is anything true, it is that for the greater part of men, the most favorable discipline of holiness will be found exactly to coincide with the ordinary path of duty, and that it will be most surely promoted by repressing the wanderings of imagination, in which we frame to ourselves states of life and habits of devotion remote from our actual lot, and by spending all our strength in those things, great or small, pleasing or unpalatable, which belong to our calling and position.

Thirdly, we may learn, that any person, whatsoever is their outward circumstances of life are, may reach to the highest point of devotion.

It is impossible for us to live in fellowship with God without holiness in all the relative duties of life. If we were worthy of greater things, He would call us. If He does not, He bids us to know ourselves better, to mortify vanity, and high thoughts of our own powers to do Him service. Every state has its peculiar graces. There is discipline of humanity in the cares and burdens of life which mellows the hearts of the just.

February 7
His Compassion
by James W. Alexander (1804-1859) USA
Excerpted from "The Compassion of Christ to the Weak, the Sorrowing, and the Sinful," *Consolation*, published by Charles Scribner, New York, New York in 1852

In the character of the Lord Jesus Christ there is nothing of sporadic and sudden action. The greater portion of His life was spent in obscurity. The hills and valleys of Galilee, and the borders of the Sea of Galilee, witnessed the silent loveliness and rapt devotion of the Son of Mary. His precursor and kinsman after the flesh [John the Baptist], as he uttered the voice of Elijah in the wastes of Judah, seems never to have had a personal knowledge of Him whom he proclaimed. When John points Him out, he expressly adds, "There stands One among you whom you do not know." And when again he points Him out, as the great appeasement, the Lamb of God, not the thousands of Israel, but only two Galileans, follow Him. When the third convert, Philip of Bethsaida, makes known his discovery to his guileless friend, Nathanael answers: "Can any good thing come out of Nazareth?" What may have been the feelings of His near friends we do not know. At the wedding in Cana, where, by the "beginning of miracles," He "showed His glory," we are informed about the unguarded zeal with which His mother, Mary, would have drawn Him out to a premature development of His majesty. But His hour was not yet come. And after this sudden and fleeting flash of His divinity, He went back again into the shades of home: "He went down to Capernaum, He, and His mother, and His brethren, and His disciples" (John 2:12).

Even after the public manifestation of Christ, there is a singular reserve as to fuller disclosure of His greatness. His most explicit revelations are made in private and to humble individuals, as to the woman of Samaria, and the man that was born blind. Though our Lord must have come into contact with a very large portion of the inhabitants of Palestine, He retreated from public show, and the acclamations of the masses. "I do not receive honor from people." He did not covet the flamboyant conflict of the foolhardy martyr of fanaticism.

But from various passages we learn that the grand revelation of the body of evidence was postponed until a critical point in His mediatorial history—the resurrection from the dead. This, as it was in itself the visible seal of Heaven on His teaching, was that which brought to recollection, and so to public view, the tide of generous and supernatural wonders which had been flowing together for several years, as so many streams, to form a torrent of evidence, which at the appointed time should burst out with irresistible conviction.

There is here a transition of a natural and pleasing kind, from the gentleness of the Messiah's character to the feebleness and insignificance of His people. That feebleness and insignificance He will not despise or crush, but will uphold it as a means towards His victory. Though the King of Glory, at whose approach the everlasting gates are lifted up, He stoops to the lowest and most burdened. It is the same connection of ideas which occurs in that matchless invitation, "Come unto Me, all who labor and are heavy laden, and I will give you rest; take My yoke upon you, and learn of Me; for I am meek and lowly, and you will find rest for your souls." It is by reason of this meekness, this lowliness, this serene and retiring and silent compassion, that the shrinking and the self-condemned, the fainting and the unprofitable, are emboldened to draw near. The encouragement might be less cheering if it had not been inscribed centuries before the advent, on the very scroll of His prophetic and royal commission, and if we had not heard it among the ancient titles of his Messiahship: "A bruised reed He will not break, and smoking flax He will not quench."

February 8
His Completeness
by William L. Gaylord (10831-1882) USA
Excerpted from "Christian Completeness," *Sermons and Other Papers*, published by The Case, Lockwood & Brainard Company, Hartford, Connecticut in 1883

The completeness that Paul has in mind is not that which belongs to Christianity as a system of faith and salvation, nor simply completeness of character in a religious point of view, though both of these are implied in the union of the believer with Christ; but a thorough human completeness achieved in Him who first brought into our humanity, in His own person, the fullness of the Godhead, and then raised their humanity to headship over all principality and power. This completeness in Christ comes into direct contrast with the promoted perfecting of humanity through science and an external culture. By this contrast, however, Paul does not condemn speculative inquiry concerning God, nor using knowledge attained by reason in matters of religion. In opposing the pretentious philosophy by which he was surrounded, he takes exception not to the object at which it aims — the development of the Godlike in humanity — but to the medium through which it professes to accomplish this, as a spontaneous outgrowth of human intelligences; whereas Christ and Christianity fully, intelligently, and cordially embraced are alone completeness to man. It is completeness, therefore, in the broadest view, the completeness of the individual under every aspect of his being; the completeness of humankind in all true development.

In Christ, humanity becomes a brotherhood, without respect of race, or nation, or place, or time. In Christ, those narrower sympathies and affections that constitute the love of home, of people, of country, expand into the love of humankind; and this love becomes the universal law of commerce, of state, of society, while law, in its essential elements of justice, of order, of authority, is transformed into love. In Christ, liberty, for which humankind had yearned in thought, in religion, and in government, becomes the higher, wider freedom of the Kingdom of God — the soul made free by His truth becomes heir of all things; the children of the Kingdom are made possessors of life and of death; this inner Kingdom is above all outer kingdoms, and either through them all, or over them all, it shall yet assert the glorious liberty of the sons of God.

In Christ, the failures of the old religions and philosophies are compensated; the yearnings of the old poets and prophets are met; the lack of the old civilizations is supplied; the desire of all nations is fulfilled. Christ sums up in Himself the long exposition of humanity. The lines of conscience and of thought, the lines of culture and of hope, along which nations and ages had slowly and uncertainly worked their way toward a desired, but unknown good, are drawn together and coiled about this one historic human life; while all later lines of man's progress in a true civilization run back to that same life for impulse and direction. The cross binds the longings of the old world with the realizations of the new. Before Jesus came, religious thought had passed through many revolutions. Since He came, it has made great conquests; yet it does not go beyond, and it can never go beyond, the essential ideas that Jesus has created. He has fixed forever the idea of pure worship. He has created in religion pure sentiment. The foundation of the true religion is all His work. After Him there is nothing left but to develop and to make fruitful. And this great foundation was entirely the personal work of Jesus. To cause Himself to be adored to that degree He must have been adorable. Love does not go forth without an object worthy to kindle it; and if all we knew about Jesus was the passion with which He inspired His followers, we must still affirm that He was great and pure. We place, then, upon the highest summit of human greatness the person of Jesus — that magnificent Person who each day yet rules the destinies of the world.

February 9
His Confidence
by William L. Watkinson (1838-1925) England
Excerpted from "The Inspiration of the Master's Confidence," *The Supreme Conquest and Other Sermons Preached in America*, published by Fleming H. Revell Company, New York, New York in 1907

He will not falter nor be discouraged until He establishes justice on Earth. In His law the islands will put their hope.
Isaiah 42:4 (NIV)

Painful failure was the feature of the life of our Lord; yet He was sustained by the vision of the world that was to be, despite His failure, no, through His failure. "And the seventy returned with joy, saying, Lord, even the devils are subject unto us in Your name. And He said unto them, I beheld Satan fallen as lightning from Heaven." Amid the hostilities, humiliations, and seeming failures of His personal history, He beheld His ultimate triumph; saw against the dark background a world of light, knew the partial discord lost in the vaster music. Let us with Him look far and wide in days when the immediate environment is discouraging. "Surely You are a God that hides Yourself, O God of Israel, the Savior." Yet within the shadow He sweetly and effectively bends the crooked to His sovereign will. Despite unpleasant appearances, He walks amid the golden candlesticks; He rules in His Church, harmonizing all contradictions, subjugating His enemies and ours, and compelling all events to the supreme issue of universal truth and righteousness.

The presence and progress of the Kingdom of God are largely obscured by those worldly accompaniments through which it is developed. This is again a trial of our faith. We believe that the main motive and working of history are spiritual; but how little this appears to the carnal eye! How entirely is the Kingdom of God veiled by the kingdoms of this world, the spiritual forces masked by the mediums through which they play! Consider the morning paper, which is the mirror of the current world, and this fact is obvious enough. Parliaments, palaces, markets, armies, navies, crimes and carnivals, science, art, literature, storms, earthquakes, famines, and a thousand other tangible things and sensational events strike the eye and excite the imagination; we hardly get a glimpse, however, of that Kingdom of God which is the core of all things, the secret of history, the goal of the ages. Our mind and imagination are filled with the shapes, movements, colors, and voices of a world whose fashion passes away. The spiritual significance of contemporary history is hidden, except to the devout and reflective mind especially directed to the search. We see the cables, but not the message they flash; the body, but not the soul which activates and shapes it; the mechanism, but not the Spirit in the midst of the wheels; the scaffolding, but not the rising shrine it conceals. The personages, occurrences, and movements chronicled in the daily journal are, consciously or unconsciously, willingly or unwillingly, the mediums, agents, and instruments of the Kingdom of God; yet they nevertheless hide the Kingdom they serve to introduce and establish.

This is a trial to faith. We become faint-hearted because we and our work are so little in evidence. Let us be reassured. Our Master warned us: "The Kingdom of God does not come with observation." It belongs wholly to the invisible, the silent, the imperceptible, the inscrutable. Nonetheless, it comes. The unseen dominates the visible; the still small voice is more commanding than all trumpets, drums, and sirens; and the inscrutable movement that is so difficult to verify, the marching on the tops of the mulberry trees, inevitably works the salvation and sanctification of the race. "He shall not cry, nor lift up, nor cause His voice to be heard in the street"; yet He works like the indefinable, imponderable forces of nature until the kingdoms of this world and the glory of them are swallowed up in the excelling glory of His own.

February 10
His Conforming
by Hannah Whitall Smith (1832-1911) USA/England
Excerpted from "Conformed to the Image of Christ," *The God of All Comfort,* published by James Nisbet & Co., Ltd., London, England in 1906

For those God foreknew He also predestined to be conformed to the likeness of His Son, that He might be the firstborn among many brothers and sisters.
Romans 8:29 (NIV)

God's ultimate purpose in our creation was that we should finally be "conformed to the image of Christ." Christ was to be the firstborn among many brothers and sisters, and His brothers and sisters were to be like Him. All the discipline and training of our lives is with this end in view; and God has implanted in every human heart a longing, however unformed and unexpressed, after the best and highest it knows.

Christ is the pattern of what each one of us is to be when finished. We are "predestined" to be conformed to His image, in order that He might be the firstborn among many brothers and sisters. We are to be "partakers of the divine nature" with Christ; we are to be filled with the spirit of Christ; we are to share His resurrection life, and to walk as He walked. We are to be one with Him, as He is one with the Father; and the glory God gave to Him, He is to give to us. And when all this is brought to pass, then, and not until then, will God's purpose in our creation be fully accomplished, and we stand forth "in His image and after His likeness."

Our likeness to His image is an accomplished fact in the mind of God, but we are, so to speak, in the manufacturing phase as yet, and the great master Workman is at work upon us. "It does not yet appear what we shall be; but we know that, when He shall appear, we shall be like Him; for we shall see Him as He is."

The Scriptures tell us, "The first man, Adam, became a living person. But the last Adam, that is, Christ, is a life-giving Spirit." What comes first is the natural body, then the spiritual body comes later. Adam, the first man, was made from the dust of the earth, while Christ, the second Man, came from Heaven. Earthly people are like the earthly man, and heavenly people are like the heavenly Man. Just as we are now like the earthly man, we will someday be like the heavenly Man.

It is deeply interesting to see that this process, which was begun in Genesis, is declared to be completed in Revelation, where the "one like the Son of Man" gave to John this significant message to the overcomers: "The one who overcomes will I make a pillar in the Temple of My God; and they shall go out no more; and I will write upon them the name of My God, and the name of the city of My God which is new Jerusalem, which comes down out of Heaven from My God: and I will write upon them My new name." Since name always means character in the Bible, this message can only mean that at last God's purpose is accomplished, and the spiritual evolution of men and women is completed—they have been made, what God intended from the first, so truly into His likeness and image, as to merit having written upon them the name of God!

Words fail before such a glorious destiny as this! But our Lord foreshadows it in His wonderful prayer when He asks for His brothers and sisters that "they all may be one; as You, Father, are in Me, and I in You, that they also may be one in Us; that the world may believe that You have sent Me. And the glory which You gave Me I have given them, that they may be one even as We are one. I in them, and You in Me, that they may be made perfect in one." Could oneness be closer or more complete? If we would be conformed to the image of Christ, then we must live closer and ever closer to Him. We must become better and better acquainted with His character and His ways; we must look at things through His eyes, and judge all things by His standards.

February 11
His Consequences
by Baptist Wriothesley Noel (1798-1873) England
Excerpted from "The Consequences of Ultimately Rejecting Christ," *The British Pulpit: a Publication of Sermons by the Most Eminent Divines of the Present Day, Vol. II*, published by Thomas Tegg, London, England in 1844

Whoever believes in the Son has eternal life, but whoever rejects the Son will not see life, for God's wrath remains on him.
John 3:36 (NIV)

To receive Christ Jesus, then, is the indispensable condition of the salvation of the sinner. He came that He might, by His sacrifice, bring us into the favor of God; and by His renewing of the Holy Spirit, might prepare us for heavenly glory. These are the two great parts of our Redeemer's work.

To receive Christ, then, is heartily to consent to this His work; to depend on His merit exclusively for our acceptance with God; and to ask for the grace of the Holy Spirit, whom Christ sends forth to bless His people. To refuse this, and, on the contrary, to depend on our own righteousness, on our own moral strength, is to reject the work of Christ, and, by consequence, to reject Christ Himself: and the passage before us declares, that whosoever does reject Him, whosoever does "not believe on the Son, shall not see life, but the wrath of God abides on him." He must lie under the wrath of God, because originally deserving it, He has rejected the Savior by whom it may be removed. Unable to atone for his own ungodly life, he must, therefore, be exposed to that unchangeable doom. On the other hand, he must lie under the wrath of God, because his nature remains ungodly. It was through Christ alone that the renewal of the Holy Ghost was promised, or became possible; and Christ being rejected, the nature remains unrenewed by the Holy Spirit; and the course of the sinner, still fulfilling the desires of the flesh and of the mind, must, therefore, as long as his human life is preserved, be only heaping up fresh guilt before God. Finally, he must lie under the wrath of God, because he has, in rejecting Christ, poured contempt on the unparalleled love of his Maker, rejected God's highest gift. And if "he who despised Moses's law died without mercy, under two or three witnesses, of how much sorer punishment, do you suppose, shall he be thought worthy, who has trodden underfoot the Son of God, and has counted the blood of the covenant wherewith he was sanctified a common thing, and has scorned the Spirit of grace?" This, then, is the fearful condition of everyone who rejects the Savior.

My dear brothers and sisters, if you persist in rejecting Christ, this passage assures us that the wrath of God must abide upon you. You will die under the wrath of God. The Almighty God will then be opposed to your happiness; you will then be exposed to the wrath of One who is infinitely benevolent; whose anger is never fickle, never severe, never unjust, and by so much the more to be feared. You will be exposed to the wrath of One who has treated you with compassion and mercy all your life; One whom you continually ill-treated, slighted, and opposed; and under whose vengeance you must now suffer. Christ has become of no effect; you are exposed to the wrath of the Almighty; to the wrath of the gentle, gracious, infinitely condescending Savior. You are exposed to His wrath, whose love you trifled with all your life. Will He be your Mediator? When the very Savior who would have plucked you from the abyss of hell is now your Judge, and you see in Him, who would once have been so willingly your Advocate, nothing but your enemy—what, my brethren, will be lacking then to fill up the cup of your wrath? "Whosoever believes not the Son, the wrath of God abides on him."

February 12
His Consolation
by William L. Watkinson (1838-1925) England
Excerpted from "A Meditation for Easter," *Studies in Christian Character*, published by Fleming H. Revell Company, New York, New York in 1903

And when I saw Him, I fell at His feet as dead. And He laid His right hand upon me, saying unto me, "Fear not; I am the first and the last: I am He that lived, and was dead; and, behold, I am alive for evermore, Amen; and have the keys of hell and of death."
Revelation 1:17-18 (KJV)

We have here not only teaching concerning the law of death, but also precious doctrine touching the lawgiver. Jesus Christ is the Lord of death. By virtue of His divinity He holds the mystic keys. "I am the first and the last, and the Living One." "I am the Alpha and the Omega, says the Lord God, which is and which was and which is to come, the Almighty." It is the prerogative of Almighty God to give life, to sustain it, and to take it away. But Christ is also Lord of death by virtue of His own death and resurrection: "I was dead, and behold, I am alive."

Here, then, is the grand teaching of the text: The law of death is the active will of Jesus Christ. It is the glory of Christianity that it consistently exhibits law not as metaphysical rule, impersonal force, or abstract order, but as the action of a personal, intelligent, loving Ruler. In the days of our termination, when our heart and flesh fail, we shall need consolation and strength, and, thank God! we may have it. He who ever sympathizes with His people will be able to comfort us. He who walked the waves of Galilee rules also the swellings of Jordan, commanding strength and peace in the trying hour. Wearied with the burdens of life, we go to Him and find sympathy, for He too was a son of hardship and toil; fainting under temptation. He strengthens us, for He also was led into the wilderness to be tempted by the devil; and so amid the anguish and mystery of death we have a tender and faithful helper in Him who tasted the sharpness of death when He "opened the Kingdom of Heaven to all believers."

He knew death under its most terrible form, in the most revolting place, and in its grimmest power. But none of the ransomed ever knew how deep were the waters crossed, nor how dark was the night that the Lord passed through, before He found His sheep that was lost. "He laid His right hand upon me." John knew the touch of that vanished hand; he had felt its wondrous virtue in days long past, its softness, its warmth, its energy, and it was with unspeakable joy that he felt again the touch that thrilled his whole frame with abounding life and power. "Saying unto me, Fear not." John was a young man when he last heard that voice so full of strange tones; now he is a very old man, but he immediately recognizes the accents of Infinite Truth and Love.

"Precious in the sight of the Lord is the death of His saints." In the light of this text death becomes transfigured; the keys are in the pierced hand; the keys are golden, they open a door into Heaven. The text inspires deep consolation touching the issues of death. "I am alive for evermore." There is a limit to the power of death. It does not destroy the personality; the dead may live again, live in new power and splendor. There is a limit to the range of death. "Alive unto the ages of the ages."

In the face of those oriental systems which threatened men with endless deaths, transmigrations, and metamorphoses, systems which modern paganism seeks to revive, Christianity holds that the faithful pass through one eclipse only into personal, conscious, immortal life. The law of death is not the law of all worlds; there are spheres where it has no place, golden ages undimmed by its shadow. The Christian knows that death's sting cannot harm him, but an instinct within him causes him to shrink whenever he comes into contact with the ghastly thing. But in this shrinking there is no terror or despair.

February 13
His Constancy
by John Ker (1819-1886) Scotland
"Christ Absent and Present," *Sermons: Second Series*, published by David Douglas, Edinburgh, Scotland in 1888

"...I am with you always..."
Matthew 28:20 (NLTSE)

His words, "Surely I am with you always" remind us that we have a Savior who is also divine. How the shrinking fears of His humanity were reconciled with His true divine nature is not for us to say. There are other great chasms across which our thought cannot step, and some of them in our own history. We cannot say why our body, with the feelings and fears that belong to it, should so often fall far short of the confidence in a higher life sometimes gained by our spirit. But it is possible for us to hold fast to both. So in the memory of the death of Christ we must seek to realize His divinity.

The promise to be with us always is not completed in the continuance of His words with us, or of His example, or His influence, or of His death memorials going down from age to age. It has a deeper meaning, the promise of a presence which implies an omnipresence; so that at every communion He is divinely repeating the words, "This is My body: This is the new covenant in My blood," and bringing home to the heart which looks to Him and His nearness in the spirit and the life. And, if in this communion, then always and everywhere. No sacrament should cut off the Lord Jesus Christ from communion with the rest of our life, but should remind us how He can be present with us through it all.

"Surely I am with you always" is a promise to be constantly beside us. We fondly dream at times of our departed friends, that though unseen they may be near us, permitted to look in as witnesses, or as ministering spirits with the angels to whom they are joined. Who can tell? But here is something more helpful to us, a Friend who does not say I will visit you, but I shall be with you, with you always, and whose presence means that infinite power and wisdom and love are beside and around us to protect and guide and comfort to the end, true Man to sympathize, and very God to save to the uttermost. And we put our fingers in the print of the nails, and know Him to be human, and look up and embrace Him as our Lord and our God.

But still this other word must be spoken by one who is to be a complete Savior, "Surely I am with you always." It is the word of life, of life which has conquered death and sin which is the sting of death. The New Testament constantly connects the resurrection of Christ with the death of Christ, as the seal and assurance of its success, as God the Father's answer to Christ's own word, "It is finished," the sun rising on Him after the night of struggle, when He saw God face to face, and He and His were preserved. Had it not been for His risen life, the Lord's Supper would have been a memorial of defeat. We cannot see how the cross of Christ could ever have been ground for glorying had it not been followed by an event like this. His disciples would have struggled to forget and hide it; and that they did not is evidence that they had a strong conviction which counterbalanced it and turned the darkness and shame of His death into something which they could proclaim with joy: "Who is the one who condemns?" "It is Christ that died, yes rather, that is risen again." And so we may take these truths, a crucified and a risen Savior, and bring them together into our thought of Christ. We have two monuments of them which stand side by side: The Lord's table and the Lord's day. We can follow up their history, link by link, until we fasten it to the very rock of the tomb; and through space and through time, as it were, put our hand on Him who was delivered for our offenses and raised again for our justification.

February 14
His Contention
by Adolphe William Monod (1834-1916) France
Excerpted from "God's Controversy with His People," *Pulpit Eloquence of the Nineteenth Century*, published by Dodd & Mead, New York, New York in 1874

For the Lord has a case against His people; He is lodging a charge against Israel. "My people, what have I done to you? How have I burdened you? Answer me. I brought you up out of Egypt and redeemed you from the land of slavery. I sent Moses to lead you, also Aaron and Miriam."
Micah 6:2b-4 (NIV)

What is this controversy between God and His people; and what is this plea which the Almighty uses? It is not a controversy which God has begun with Israel, but, rather, a controversy which Israel has begun with God. It is a plea in justification, offered by the Almighty, who regards Himself as accused by His people. It is man who is the plaintiff in this astonishing process; and it is God who appears as the defendant to argue in His own behalf.

Israel has, thus far, said nothing; and we are at a loss, at first, to understand how God should regard Himself as the accused. Israel has complained neither of the severity of His laws, nor of the severity of His judgments. But God has perceived in the conduct of His people something equivalent to a formal accusation — something proving that, while they honored Him with their lips and their sacrifices, they had no sincerity, and they regarded His service as grievous and fatiguing.

For this reason, God begins His plea: "What have I done unto you? and how have I wearied you? Testify against Me." He summons Israel to an explanation; He bids the people to show what He has done to merit their ill treatment, and how His service is wearisome to them. He summons them, not as the sovereign Judge of the universe, but as a Friend who complains of the coldness of one still cherished—as a husband who complains of a wife to whom he is devoted, and upon whom he does not cease to bestow the most tender names. He speaks as with a consciousness of His innocence, and as if determined to do all in His power, not to triumph over His accusers, but to appease them, avoiding all that can wound them, and reminding them of none of their wickedness, except with evident regret that He is compelled to do it. In pleading against them, He does not fail to call them His people: "O, My people, what have I done unto you; and how have I wearied you? Testify against Me."

Do you understand this language, my brethren? It signifies that, from the first moment of His connection with the people of Israel, God made Himself known to them as a God of love, and that the establishment of His alliance with them, was a work of love; that He drew them from slavery, and gave to them as leaders not tyrants, but prophets full of gentleness, charged with guiding them toward the land of promise; that it was by this commencement, and by this work, that the people of Israel ought to judge their God; and that neither His word nor His dispensation can contain anything that does not proceed from this same love.

The people are ourselves—are Christians in general; for the people of Israel have been, throughout all their history, a prophetic image of the Christian world, or of the Christian Church. The plea of the Almighty is that of God manifest to us in Jesus Christ, who complains that we seem willing to fall out with Him, as if we found fault with what He has done, and as if we were weary of His service. He summons us to specify our complaints, and wishes to justify Himself against us. This is the justification which I am about to pronounce in the name of God. I plead His cause. I plead as He has done, not to triumph over you, but to convince you of His love, and to gain your love by His love.

February 15
His Courage
by Charles Kingsley (1819-1875) England
Excerpted from "The Courage of the Savior," *Twenty-Five Village Sermons,*
published by H. Hooker, Philadelphia, Pennsylvania in 1854

*Then He said to His disciples, "Let us go back to Judea." "But Rabbi,"
they said, "a short while ago the Jews tried to stone You,
and yet You are going back there?"*
John 11:7-8 (NIV)

If you want to see true fortitude, think of what has happened thousands of times when the heathen used to persecute the Christians. How delicate women, who would not venture to set the sole of their foot to the ground for tenderness, would submit, rather than give up their religion and deny the Lord who died for them, to be torn from husband and family, and endure nakedness, and insult, and tortures which make one's blood run cold to read about, until they were torn slowly to pieces, or roasted in burning flames, without a murmur or an angry word—knowing that Christ, who had borne all things for them, would give them strength to bear all things for Him, trusting that if they were faithful unto death, He would give them a crown of life. There was true fortitude—there was true faith—there was God's strength made perfect in woman's weakness! Do you not see, my friends, that such a death was truly brave? How does bulldog courage compare beside that courage—the courage which conquers grief and pain for duty's sake, instead of merely forgetting them in rage and obstinacy?

And do you not see how this bears on my text? How it bears on our Lord's whole life? Was He not indeed the perfectly brave Man—the Man who endured more than all living men put together, at the very time that He had the most intense fear of what He was going to suffer? And, stranger still, endured it all by His own will, while He had it in His power to shake it all off any instant, and free Himself utterly from pain and suffering.

Now this speech of our Lord's in the text is just a case of true fortitude. He was beyond Jordan. He had been forced to escape there to save His life from the mad, blinded Jews. He had no foolhardiness; He knew that He had no more right than we have to put His life in danger when there was no good to be done by it. But now there was good to be done by it. Lazarus was dead, and He wanted to raise him to life. Therefore He said to His disciples, "Let us go into Judea again." They knew the danger; they said, "Master, the Jews of late sought to stone You, and You go there again?" But He would go; He had a work to do, and He dared to bear anything to do His work. Yes, here is the secret, this is the feeling which gives a man true courage — the feeling that he has a work to do at all costs, the sense of duty. This is fortitude; this is true courage — this is Christ's likeness — this is the courage which weak women on sick beds may have as well as strong men on the battlefield. Even when they shrink most from suffering, God's Spirit will whisper to them, "It is your duty, it is your Father's will"; and then they will find His strength made perfect in their weakness, and when their human weakness fails most, God will give them heavenly fortitude, and they will be able, like Paul, to say, "When I am weak, then I am strong, for I can do all things through Christ, who strengthens me."

The Son of God knows what fear is. He who said that His soul was troubled — He who at the thought of death was in such agony of terror that His sweat ran down to the ground like great drops of blood, He who cried in His agony, "Father, if it is possible, let this cup pass from Me," He understands my pain; He tells me not to be ashamed of crying in my pain, like Him, "Father, if it is possible, let this cup pass from Me," for He will give me strength to finish that prayer of His, and in the midst of my trouble say, "Nevertheless, Father, not as I will, but as you will."

February 16
His Courtesy
by John Summerfield (1807-1842) England
Excerpted from "Christian Courtesy," *Sermons and Sketches of Sermons*, published by Harper & Brothers, New York, New York in 1864

Courtesy is, strictly speaking, a Christian grace. It is a plant of heavenly origin. This present evil world, like the ground which the Lord has cursed, is utterly incapable of yielding anything so excellent and lovely. Courtesy cannot grow in selfish nature's soil. It is never found except in the garden of God. It is a fruit of the Spirit, and not a work of the flesh. It is the offspring of love. And since it derives its being from Divine grace; since it is made the subject of a Divine command; since it is especially calculated to smooth those little severities which sometimes hinder even "the living stones of the Temple" from being so perfectly joined and so properly framed together as they should be; since it powerfully tends likewise to remove the prejudices and to dispel the enmity so generally entertained by the world towards the Church; above all, since, in combination with other causes, it may contribute to win souls to God, we surely should make it the subject of our specific and attentive consideration.

But the courtesy of a Christian is not a mere form. It is not the illusion of a feeling which has no real existence. It is the outward expression of an inward disposition, the conduct which a compassionate mind will on all occasions instinctively suggest. It is the natural and unconstrained operation of sincere love. Let us only love our neighbor as ourselves, and it will be morally impossible to violate the laws of courtesy; for love works no harm to our neighbor. It will teach us cautiously to avoid whatever might unnecessarily wound their feelings; it will move us to diligently study their inclination, ease, and convenience; it will make us anxious to interpret their very looks, that we may even anticipate their requests; it will enable us cheerfully to make a sacrifice of our own gratifications with a view to theirs. All this is perfectly easy; it is even delightful where love exists without disguise; but let this heavenly principle be lacking, take away from the form of courtesy the power, and it becomes a grueling and tiresome task, a yoke grievous to be borne.

The courtesy of those who follow Jesus is the unaffected expression of a poor and contrite spirit. He who has learned of Christ goes and sits down in the lowest place, not to indulge in reflections upon others, or to obtain the admiration of others, but because he really feels it is the place which properly belongs to him. He esteems others better than himself, and therefore, without artificial restraint, he can submit to become the servant of all in everything consistent with a conscience "void of offense towards God and towards men." For such will never attempt to ingratiate themselves by flattery or worldly conformities. It is the honorable subjection of a servant of Christ; it flows from a gracious nobility of soul, directly opposed to that despicable policy which involves a sacrifice of principle to the pleasure and will of others. This courtesy shrinks from no shame but that of evil. It is ambitious for no dignity but that of being conformed to the image of God's Son. While it despises the scorns of an evil and adulterous generation, and would "resist unto blood, striving against sin," yet it manifests an obliging readiness of mind to perform the lowest services for the chief of sinners, if it can just administer to their comfort in body or soul.

Our Lord's conduct in the house of Simon displays a fine example of real courtesy. On the one hand, see Him meekly submitting to occupy a place at the table of a man who, by the omission of every customary form of hospitality, had treated Him with marked discourtesy and neglect. On the other hand, we behold Jesus manifesting the most tender regard towards a woman that was a sinner, though well aware He was submitting to the utmost humiliation and contempt in the eyes of His self-righteous host.

February 17
His Creation
by Charles S. Spurgeon (1834-1892) England
Excerpted from his sermon entitled, "Christ the Creator," delivered Sunday evening, September 7, 1873, in Metropolitan Tabernacle, London, England

All things were created by Him and for Him.
Colossians 1:16 (KJV)

There can be no mistake as to the Person concerning whom Paul is writing under the inspiration of the Holy Spirit—it is Jesus of Nazareth, the Incarnate Son of God who was crucified on Calvary for, writing concerning the same Person in the 14th verse, Paul says, "In whom we have redemption through His blood, even the forgiveness of sins." It is, therefore, that Savior whose blood was shed for His people's redemption who is here declared to be the Creator of all things and by whom all things consist!

The first verse of the Book of Genesis tells us that, "in the beginning God created the heavens and the earth," so someone may ask, "How do you reconcile that statement with Paul's declaration that all things were created by Christ and for Him?" No reconciliation is needed, for the two statements are identical, as Jesus is God, and "in Him dwells all the fullness of the Godhead bodily." Jesus said, "I and My Father are One," and so they are! We know not how it is, but the Father, the Son and the Holy Spirit are distinct Personalities, yet there are not three Gods, but only one, as the Apostle John writes, "There are three that bear record in Heaven, the Father, the Word and the Holy Spirit; and these Three are One." The one God of Abraham, Isaac and Jacob is the Father, Son, and Spirit—Three in One and One in Three!

So, first, Heaven itself was created by and for Christ Jesus. Then there is such a place, as well as such a state, and of that place Jesus is the center! Next, all angels were created by Jesus and for Him. However great and strong and swift they are, there is not one angel that ever flies from Jehovah's Throne that was not created by Christ!

As for the fallen angels who rebelled against God and who have sunk forever into hopeless alienation from Him — even these were created by Christ and for Him! And though they hate Him, they shall be compelled to obey Him and to acknowledge that He is Lord over all! Even their malice against the people of God shall only draw out His love toward them and manifest His vigilance, wisdom, and power on their behalf.

And even Hell itself, terrible as it is, was created by Christ as a necessary part of the moral government of the universe so that sin might not go unpunished. Even there Christ reigns! His Sovereignty is supreme down to its lowest depths. He has the keys of Hell and of death — and when the appointed time comes, He will send an angel with the key to the bottomless pit and bid him lay hold on "the dragon, that old serpent, which is the devil and Satan," and bind him for a thousand years and cast him into the bottomless pit.

And then, after the Millennium, and Satan has been again loosed for a little season, he shall be "cast into the Lake of Fire and brimstone, where the beast and the false prophets are — and shall be tormented day and night forever and ever." Christ is King even over that dark, sad part of His domains! And amidst all the confusion and tumult of the Pit, His enemies shall "confess that Jesus Christ is Lord, to the Glory of God the Father."

Jesus is the key to the universe — its center and its explanation. Creation and history are mysteries which can only be understood in the light of the cross. Try, beloved friends, wherever you are, to see all things in the light of Christ.

February 18
His Criticism
by David James Burrell (1844-1926) USA
Excerpted from "The Outside of the Platter," *The Golden Passional and Other Sermons,* published by Wilbur B. Ketcham, New York, New York in 1897

"Now then, you Pharisees clean the outside of the cup and dish…"
Luke 11:39 (NIV)

The reference is to the superficial devotion of the Pharisees. They had more regard for the outside of the cup than for the wholesomeness of the drink within it. They were much given to external rites and ceremonies. The most important of the six books of the *Mishna* is devoted to purifications. The washing of the hands is prescribed with utmost meticulousness: One and one-half eggshells full of water must be used; the hands must be lifted in a certain position when the water is poured upon them; then the right must rub the left, and the left the right; then they must be held at a downward incline so that the water may drop off. And the towel must be properly held. The schools of Hillel and Shammai were prone to discuss with great earnestness the holding of the towel. Furthermore, there were thirty chapters bearing on the cleansing of cups and platters.

How the Lord Christ hated all shams! The Pharisees stood before Him in their frontlets and phylacteries [religious adornments], as if to say, "Behold how fair!" He tore away the covering and exposed the dismal fraud: "Woe unto you, you hypocrites! you are as whited sepulchers, fair without, but within full of dead men's bones and all uncleanness."

But the Pharisees are dead. We have to do, not with the faults and follies of long centuries ago, but with the superficial devotion of today. God sees us through and through. It is monstrous trifling to be tithing mint, anise and cumin, while neglecting the weightier matters of law. The form of godliness without the power thereof is but the decoration of death. Man looks on the outward appearance, but God looks on the heart.

Let us hear then the conclusion of the whole matter. The only religion which can fully meet the divine requirement is that which takes hold of our entire nature. It is not enough that it shall touch us at a single point. It must reach the heart as well as the reason, and the conscience as well as the heart. It must take possession of mind, conscience, heart, and will; eyes and ears; hands and feet. It must so penetrate us through and through, so permeate us, that our whole life and character and being shall be full of light.

Furthermore, the religion which meets the divine requirement must not only give God possession of the entire mind, but must place the mind in possession of the entire Christ. It is not enough that I shall "come to Jesus"; I must come to the Lord Jesus Christ. He is Jesus, my Brother. Yes, and more. He is Messiah the Christ. Yes, and more still. He is Christ Jesus my Lord; my Lord, to protect, command, rule over me.

To accept Him is to receive Him into my life as Prophet, Priest and King. As Priest, He atones for me; as Prophet, He instructs me, sitting at His feet, so that His word becomes my creed; as King, His command is ultimate law to me, and every thought is brought into subjection to Him.

Two words in conclusion: "Pure religion and undefiled before God and the Father is this: To visit the fatherless and widows in their affliction, and to keep one's self unspotted from the world." And again, "If any man will come after Me, let him deny himself, take up his cross, and follow Me."

February 19
His Cross - 1
by James Stalker (1848-1927) Scotland
Excerpted from "The Cross and Offences," *The Ethic of Jesus*, published by
Eaton & Mains, New York, New York in 1909

In evangelical preaching it is common to implore sinners to be reconciled to God; and for doing so with overflowing affection and urgency there is high authority. But it is possible to carry this to excess, and to plead and press to a degree unworthy of the dignity of the gospel. The Savior Himself did not press any to follow Him unconditionally. On the contrary, He held some at arm's length; and some who pressed their fellowship upon Him He sent about their business. To one enthusiast He said, "Foxes have holes, and the birds of the air have nests, but the Son of Man has nowhere to lay His head." To a lukewarm heart, who asked, before following Him, to be allowed to go and say farewell to his friends, He answered, "No man, having put his hand to the plow and looking back, is fit for the Kingdom of Heaven."

He did not, then, wish to be followed merely because of an impulse of enthusiasm, nor did He press anyone unduly. On the contrary, He called upon all to sit down and count the cost, employing extreme images to depict what the consequences might be if they came after Him without doing so. The figure cut by a man who, without calculation, begins to build a house but is not able to finish it, or by a general who with five thousand men goes to meet an enemy who comes against him with fifty thousand, is not more unenviable than may be that of the man who, under a sudden impulse towards religion, begins to follow Christ without sufficient reflection. Jesus never said that it is easy to be a Christian—He called people to follow Him. But He warned them that if they did so, they would have to face a variety of hardships; and the term in His mouth for all these put together was the cross.

To Him the cross was two things: First, the last step of submission to His Father's will; and secondly, the last act of opposition to Him on the part of humanity. That which distinguished the Man Christ Jesus from all the other children of humanity was that at every step He perfectly fulfilled the will of God. But God's will was not for Him, any more than for the other sons of Adam, easy to fulfill. It led Him in a way that was very difficult and that, as He advanced, became dark and intricate, until He cried out that He whose will He had always followed had forsaken Him. In Gethsemane He groaned amidst His tears, "Not My will, but Yours be done," and the next and last step was the cross. Such was the cross from one point of view.

Now what the cross was to Him, it is also to those who follow Him. First, it is the pain involved in doing the will of God: "Whoever does the will of My Father which is in Heaven, the same is My mother and sister and brother." This is the path for all disciples; but for them, being what they are, it cannot be an easy one; because their thoughts are not God's thoughts nor their ways His ways. Accordingly, they have to give up their own thoughts, ways and wills. But what are a person's thoughts, ways and will but of themselves? So that they have to give up themselves. Thus exactly did Jesus read the case when He said, "Let him deny himself"; and, because the occasions for such self-sacrifice are occurring every hour, He added "daily." "Let him deny himself and take up his cross daily and follow Me."

Although Christ never concealed the cross, He did not doubt that it was wise to carry it, because the compensation would be far greater than the sacrifice.

Connection with His person, preoccupation with His image, and the anticipation of future union with Him will always be the essentials of Christian experience. In these is generated the virtue on which the moral victory depends.

February 20
His Cross - 2
by David James Burrell (1844-1926) USA
Excerpted from "The Wondrous Cross," *The Wondrous Cross and Other Sermons*, published by Wilbur B. Ketcham, New York, New York in 1898

From then on Jesus began to tell His disciples plainly that it was necessary for Him to go to Jerusalem, and that He would suffer many terrible things at the hands of the elders, the leading priests, and the teachers of religious law. He would be killed, but on the third day He would be raised from the dead. But Peter took Him aside and began to reprimand Him for saying such things. "Heaven forbid, Lord," he said. "This will never happen to You!" Jesus turned to Peter and said, "Get away from Me, Satan! You are a dangerous trap to Me. You are seeing things merely from a human point of view, not from God's."
Matt. 16:21-23 (NLTSE)

We believe in two great powers who contend for the sovereignty of this world, but they are not co-equal. One is infinite; the other — though of immense guile and resource — is finite. And the end is to be seen from the beginning. God is always and everywhere getting the upper hand on Satan.

There never was a moment, from the beginning of the eternal ages, when God did not intend to save this world. All things were included in His foreknowledge. Sin, suffering, salvation, the casting down of iniquity, and the restitution of all things in the fullness of time, were from eternity present before Him.

In one of the boldest and most picturesque portions of Scripture we are introduced into the councils of the indescribable Trinity. The three Persons are represented as in solemn conference respecting the deliverance of our sin-stricken race. The cry of the erring and perishing has come up into Their ears. The inquiry is heard, "Whom shall We send, and who will go for Us?" Then the only-begotten Son offers Himself: "Here am I; send Me!" He girds himself with omnipotence, binds upon His feet the sandals of salvation, and goes forth as a knight-errant to vindicate and rescue the children of humanity. When next we behold Him, He is a child, wrapped in swaddling-clothes and lying in a manger. The incarnation is the first chapter in His great undertaking, and a necessary part of it. As Anselm of Canterbury [1033-1109, Italian monk] says in *Cur Deus Homo*, "He must become man in order to suffer, and He must continue to be God in order that He may suffer enough for all." In thus assuming our nature He laid aside the form of His Godhood and "the glory which He had with the Father before the world was"; but He never lost sight of His benevolent purpose. He realized constantly that He had come to redeem the world by dying for it.

We are now ready for our proposition, which is this: The vicarious death of Jesus is the vital center of the whole Christian system; and any word which violates it is in the nature of a satanic suggestion. There is one truth before which all other truths whatsoever dwindle into relative insignificance, and that is that our Lord Jesus Christ was wounded for our transgressions and bruised for our iniquities, that by His stripes we might be healed. The person who grasps this by faith is saved by it.

And inversely, any denial of this truth is mortal heresy. The first satanic suggestion made to humans was a denial of the law, when the tempter said to Eve, "You shall not surely die." The last satanic suggestion is a denial of grace: "It is not necessary that Christ should die for you." The first ruined the race, and the last will destroy anyone who entertains it. To deny this doctrine of the vicarious atonement in any of these ways or otherwise, is to set one's self crosswise against the whole trend of Scripture.

February 21
His Cross-Bearer
by William M. Clow (1853-1930) Scotland
Excerpted from "Simon of Cyrene," *The Day of the Cross*, published by Hodder and Stoughton, New York, New York in 1909

And they compelled one Simon a Cyrenian, who passed by, coming out of the country, the father of Alexander and Rufus, to bear His cross.
Mark 15:21 (KJV)

Here is this stranger, who has pressed in through the crowd, and now looks on in pity at the sight. This unknown man, this pilgrim from the South, will serve the purpose. The soldiers' strong hands seize him, he is dragged from his place in the crowd, the beams are laid upon his shoulders, and, with soldiers before and soldiers behind, within lines of flashing steel, Jesus and Simon march on — and Simon of Cyrene bears the cross of Jesus.

How singular that this man of Cyrene, this stranger in Jerusalem, should play so conspicuous a part in its most historic deed! How captivating is it that this man, going up with joyous heart and shining eyes, should be suddenly thrust into this tragedy! God leads us by paths that are not known. Those who looked upon Simon that day thought that an evil circumstance had come upon him. Rude jests fell from the soldiers' lips as he was numbered with the transgressors. Very certainly he deeply pitied himself. But this is what is beating in the minds of the writers of the Gospels as they place his name on their page, that to no man was there ever given a higher honor than to Simon of Cyrene.

There is more than a picture here, there is a parable for the soul. Let us understand not only the honor of the deed, but its blessedness. No one can ever do for Jesus precisely what Simon did. And yet in spirit, in the words and deeds of our daily lives, and pre-eminently in the greater hours of trial and sorrow, what we are called upon to do is this very thing—to walk in the way after Jesus, and to carry His cross.

There is such a predestined moment in every life. The urgent need of many souls, and the peculiar opportunity of God's Holy Spirit, is that they know themselves to be alone with Jesus. In this busy life, when the world is too much with us, when the old silences and privacies seem to be impossible for many, there are many souls who are never alone with Jesus. God makes the opportunity for them. For some it is made by a low, easily-hushed call in their unblemished youth; for others it is reached in the gentle providences of God; for others it is gained by the compelling words of some persuasive counsel. It is a blessedness, which is a joy forever, for a person to know themselves compelled to be alone with Jesus through these simple and easy devices of God. But others, like Simon of Cyrene, do not reach it until some cross is laid upon their shoulders, and they are compelled to walk in the *via dolorosa* [the path of Jesus and His cross in Jerusalem] with Jesus.

Is there any person who has been suddenly thrust into some tragedy, any person whose life purpose has come to nothing, any person who has found overwhelming circumstances breaking life in two, any person who is dazed with a stroke of sorrow? What is the meaning of it? Your cross is laid upon you, that it may give you the great opportunity of your life; that you may realize, although you walk one of life's busiest ways, that you are alone with Jesus, and you have only to look up and meet the Divine look of longing and appeal, to carry your cross, as Simon did, with heroic faith, after Jesus. How will you use this predestined moment in your life? Do not writhe under your cross, do not escape from it, do not become hardened by it. Take it up, and as you bear it, be sure that One is looking upon you, seeking the answering look, and eager to bestow upon you that blessing which is the germ of all the greatness God can give here and hereafter.

February 22
His Crown
by George H. Morrison (1866-1928) Scotland
Excerpted from "The Crown of Thorns," *The Return of the Angels*,
published by Hodder and Stoughton, London, England in 1909

...and twisting together a crown of thorns, they put it on His head...
Matthew 27:29 (ESV)

Among all the sufferings which Christ had to endure in the last and terrible days of His humility, none has more deeply moved the heart of Christendom than His wearing of the crown of thorns. We have never felt the agony of nails, nor the cruel piercing of a Roman spear. And therefore, we can only dimly realize the physical pain of such experiences. But in the torment of sharp and biting thorns we reach the more common lot of our humanity; within our own remembrance we have that which interprets this experience of our Lord. To us who have never known the stab of wounds, the wound of the spear is but a faint imagining. It would take a soldier, gashed and bleeding on the field, to have fellowship with Jesus Christ in that. But in a world so thick with tangled briers, the crown of thorns is like a touch of comradeship in a scene of lonely and exalted sorrow.

But there is something in that coronation that reaches deeper than any homely anguish. There is a meaning more profound than that, more vital in the purposes of God. They twisted together a crown and put it on His head, and He was the Second Man, the Lord from Heaven. He was not one man more amid the thousands who suffered and slept under that Eastern sky. In Him was the very essence of humanity. In Him the race was gathered and united. In Him was every child who ever played and every woman who ever wept in secret. All human life was hidden in that form whose face was disfigured more than any man's; all joy that shares its secret with the stars; all passion that hears its echo in the winds. And

Him they crowned—Him the representative—Him the embodiment of all humankind, and they crowned Him with a crown of thorns.

They did it as we know in merry jest, for they were brutal men and loved a brutal sport. And one of them went out into the night and plucked the twigs from the garden of the palace. And he rejoiced in being a clever person, and he knew how his quick wit would be appreciated, and he never dreamed he was a fixed messenger in the hand of an ordering and sovereign God. Here was a jest, and yet it was reality. Here was a mockery, and yet the truth. Here was the coronation of humankind, and on its brow, there was a thorny crown. And that is the deep and universal meaning of it, worked out by soldiers in their beastly sport, that on the brow of humanity there is a crown, yet always it is a crown of thorns.

I think of Jesus Christ who loved us so, and who was mocked and beaten and slain, who found in love the pathway to His joy and equally the pathway to His cross. Love has its triumph and has its torture. Love has its paradise and has its pain. Love has its mountain of transfiguration, and its olive garden where the sweat is blood. Love is the secret of the sweetest song; love is the secret of the keenest suffering. Love is the very crown of life and it is a crown of thorns. "And they twisted together a crown of thorns and put it on His head." That is what God is doing with all of us. And shall I tell you why He treats us so, and stabs us in our coronation? It is so that, looking upon the brow of Christ, we may all feel we have a Brother there. It is so that, watching His patience and His courage, we may be patient and courageous too. It is so that we may lift our eyes today to where the Lamb is standing at the throne, where there is no more pain; where there is no more curse, where the thorn has vanished from the crown forever.

February 23
His Cry
by Robert Law (1860-1919) Scotland/Canada
Excerpted from "Why Hast Thou Forsaken Me?" *The Grand Adventure and Other Sermons*, published by Hodder & Stoughton, New York, New York in 1916

And about the ninth hour Jesus cried with a loud voice, saying, "Eli, Eli, lama sabachthani?" that is to say, "My God, My God, why have You forsaken Me?"
Matthew 27:46 (KJV)

This is one of those passages of scripture which a preacher approaches with a hesitancy amounting almost to reluctance. For preacher and hearers alike one feels that it requires that distinctly devotional atmosphere we breathe when we are gathered around the Lord's Table. On the other hand, this word from the cross is a revelation so unique and amazing of the inner experience of our Lord that it not only deserves but demands our most reverential study, even though the result is to make us feel that here we stand upon the verge of an inscrutable abyss, or can enter only a little way into the shallows near the shore.

From the hour of noon, we are told, and for three hours thereafter, a great darkness came down upon Calvary and the surrounding country. Now, in the Gospels, the history of these three hours is a complete silence. It would seem as if the pall of gloom which turned midday to midnight stopped all movement and held men rooted to the spot where they stood. All the babel of voices which had surged around the cross, all the chatter and the laughter, suddenly died on the lips of the mockers. All was still, soundless as the grave. And there, in the heart of that solitude, curtained in from all the world, alone, Jesus hung for three hours of mortal agony upon the cross. And how grateful, as we might think, must that solitude have been to Him. Now, like a dying man who has bidden farewell to the world and turns his face to the wall to await his summons, now might Jesus forget friend and foe alike and be alone with God, to strengthen and comfort Himself in His Father. But what is our amazement and almost our dismay to discover? that with Him it is midnight within as well as without, and that the one voice which breaks that unearthly silence is the cry of the soul in conflict with despair: "My God, My God, why have You forsaken Me?"

And yet more than this is present in His experience. The last victory of faith is to rise superior to feeling, to triumph over the direct consciousness of the soul itself. It is very possible, as the records of religious faith so often show, for a man to be made a mark for all the "slings and arrows of outrageous fortune," to seem "stricken of God and afflicted," and for that man to feel assuredly in his heart that God loves him, and even with such a heightened assurance that in this one great happiness he possesses all things. But when all a man feels, all he is conscious of, is darkness, and yet he stretches out his hands and struggles towards the light, this is faith in the highest degree. And this is one of the many crowns upon Christ's head — the crown of Faith. He feels despair, only despair, yet He exercises faith. Feeling forsaken by God, He calls only the more upon God.

Think how through that awful gloom and desolation of feeling the faith of Jesus stretches forth both its hands to the God whose love He could not feel, and cries, "My God, My God." All God's billows go over Him and bury Him in darkness, yet in the depths He clings to the Rock. "As one in deep water, feeling no bottom, makes a desperate plunge forward and stands on solid ground, so Jesus in the very act of uttering His despair overcomes it. Feeling forsaken of God, He rushes into the arms of God; and these close around Him in loving embrace" [James Stalker, Scottish pastor, 1848-1927]. The darkness passed away; the last moments were full of God's perfect peace. The last victory of Faith was won.

February 24
His Death
by James Stalker (1848-1927) Scotland

Excerpted from "The Seventh Word from the Cross," *The Trial and Death of Jesus Christ*, published by Hodder and Stoughton, London, England in 1910

"Father, into Your hands I commit My spirit."
Luke 23:46 (NIV)

While all the words of dying persons are full of interest, there is special importance attached to the last of them. This is the last word of Jesus; and both for this reason and for others it claims particular attention.

Not all the words from the cross were prayers. One was addressed to the penitent thief, another to His mother and His favorite disciple, and a third to the soldiers who were crucifying Him; but prayer was distinctly the language of His dying hours. It was not by chance that His very last word was a prayer; for the currents within Him were all flowing toward God. Natural as prayer is it is only so to those who have learned to pray before. It had long been to Jesus the language of life. He had prayed without ceasing—on the mountaintop and in the busy places of people, by Himself and in company with others—and it was only the bias of the life asserting itself in death when, as He breathed His last, He turned to God.

It is worth observing in what manner Jesus made this quotation taken from Psalms. He added something at the beginning and He omitted something at the close. At the beginning He added, "Father." This is not in the psalm. The new consciousness of God which Christ introduced into the world is embodied in this word, and, by prefixing it to the citation, He gave the verse a new coloring. We may, then, do this with the Old Testament: We may put New Testament meaning into it. Indeed, in connection with this very verse we have a still more remarkable illustration of the same treatment. Stephen, the first martyr of Christianity, was in many respects very like his Master, and in his martyrdom closely imitated Him. Thus on the field of death he repeated Christ's prayer for His enemies, "Lord, do not lay this sin to their charge." Also, he imitated Jesus' final word, but he put it in a new form, "Lord Jesus, receive my spirit"; that is, he addressed to Christ the dying prayer which Christ Himself addressed to the Father. The other alteration which Jesus made was the omission of the words, "for You have redeemed me." It would not have been appropriate for Him to employ them. But we cannot omit them; and if, like Stephen, we address the prayer to Christ, how much richer and more meaningful are the words to us than they were even to David who first penned them. These same words were the dying words of many. When John Hus [Czech theologian, 1372-1415] was being led to execution, there was stuck on his head a paper cap, scrawled over with pictures of devils, to whom the wretched priests by whom he was surrounded consigned his soul; but again and again he cried, "Father, into Your hands I commend my spirit." These were also the last words of Polycarp, of Jerome of Prague, of Luther, of Melanchthon, and of many others [famous Christians from history]. Who could wish their spirit to be carried away to God in a more glorious vehicle?

It is to Christ we have to go. He has the words of eternal life. He spoke on the subject without hesitation or obscurity. His dying word proves that He believed for Himself what He taught to others. Not only, however, has He by His teaching brought life and immortality to light: He is Himself the guarantee of the doctrine, for He is our immortal life. Because we are united to Him we know we can never perish; nothing, not even death, can separate us from His love; "Because I live," He has said, "you shall live also."

Do not close this book without breathing, "Father, into Your hands I commend my spirit."

February 25
His Decisiveness
by George H. Morrison (1866-1928) Scotland
Excerpted from "The Decisiveness of Christ," *The Weaving of the Glory*, published by Hodder and Stoughton, London, England in 1913

"But I say unto you..."
Matthew 11:22 (KJV)

There is one element in the character of Jesus which is very worthy of our consideration. It is the element which, in default of a better word, one might describe as His decisiveness. In other people, even the greatest, you catch continually the note of hesitancy. Even in the most dogmatic person you have the occasional sense of possible mistake. But in the Jesus given us in the Gospels there is not the faintest trace of such a hesitancy. There is an absolute and instantaneous certainty in the face of every problem and perplexity. In other lives, if such certainty is found, it is found generally in exalted hours. It is found in those rare and elevated moments when the mists are scattered somehow, and we know. But with Jesus this decisiveness was normal. He did not have to wait for any glorious hours. It never seems to have left Him for an instant as He moved among the villages of Galilee. From the first recorded utterance of His boyhood, "Do you not know that I must be about my Father's business?" on to the last glad triumph on the cross, when He reveled in the thought that it was finished, there is not visible one shadow of perplexity, nor any halting as of uncertain feet, nor any clouding, even for a moment, of the calm decisiveness of Christ.

We catch that note of decisiveness in many spheres, and first in regard to the long past of Israel. There is nothing more striking in the Gospels' record than the attitude of our Savior to that past. How He viewed the glorious past of Israel, with its song of the psalmist and the oracle of the prophets, all that is written so that all may read. For Christ that story of Israel was divine. It was the revelation of His God. One jot or tittle of the law was not to pass until everything had been fulfilled. And even though He respected it with a far deeper reverence than any scribe who sat in Moses' seat, He judged it with unfaltering decision. He utters His judgments of these old actions with the perfect freedom of a full authority. He moves among these glories of the past not as a subject who has no right to question, but as a King who has the power to abolish, as certainly as He has the power to endorse. Moses said unto you so and so, but I say unto you so and so. He has the fullest authority to ratify, and He has the fullest authority to cancel.

The same striking feature of decisiveness is seen again in regard to His own person. Christ never seems to have doubted for an hour that He was supremely and extremely significant. No one doubted that He was meek and lowly. Everyone saw that He would not strive nor cry. There was a loving gentleness about this Man of Nazareth which drew the burdened and the broken to Him. And yet this loving, gentle, lowly Man said, "I am the way— I am the truth—I am the life," and "before Abraham was, I am." And now comes Jesus, and to men and women burning with passionate convictions such as these, He quietly says, "I am greater than Solomon," and "a greater than the Temple is here." The same decisiveness is very obvious again in our Lord's handling of the character of others. There is a ring of finality in all His judgments which is very striking and impressive. There is not one trace that He was ever baffled by the haunting problem of human personality. Then this decisiveness of Christ comes to its climax regarding the future. Whenever Christ speaks about a day of judgment, it is He Himself who is the central figure. It is He who separates the sheep and goats. It is He who says "Depart, I never knew you." And that magnificence of royal authority, which is interwoven with the whole gospel story, is the climax of the decisiveness of Christ.

February 26
His Deity – 1
by Thomas De Witt Talmage (1832-1902) USA
Excerpted from "The Superhuman Jesus," *Every-Day Religion*, published by
Funk & Wagnalls, New York, New York in 1886

Christ came, who is over all, God blessed forever. Amen.
Romans 9:5 (KJV)

Paul was a reckless man in always telling the whole truth. It mattered not who it hit, or what theological system it upset. In this one sentence he makes a world of trouble for all those who deny the eternal deity of Jesus Christ, and gives a cud for skepticism to chew on for the next thousand years. We must proceed skillfully to twist this passage of Scripture, or we shall have to admit the Deity of Jesus Christ. I roll up my sleeves for the work, and begin by saying, perhaps this is a wrong version. No, all the versions [of the Bible manuscripts] agree—Syriac, Ethiopian, Latin, Arabic. Perhaps this word "God" means a being of great power, but not the Deity. It is "God over all." But perhaps this word God refers to the first person of the Trinity—God the Father. No, it is "Christ came, who is over all, God blessed forever. Amen." Whichever way I take it, and when I turn it upside down, and when I try to read it in every possible shape, I am compelled to leave it as all have been compelled to leave it who have gone before me, an incontrovertible proof of the eternal and magnificent Godhead of the Lord Jesus Christ. "Christ came, who is over all, God blessed forever. Amen."

About the differences between the evangelical denominations of Christians I have no concern. If I could by the turning over of my hand decide whether finally all the world shall be Methodists, or Baptists, or Episcopalians, or Congregationalists, or Presbyterians, I would not turn over my hand; but between Unitarianism, which denies the Deity of Christ, and Trinitarianism, which argues for

His divine nature, there is a difference as wide as eternity. If Christ is not God, then we are base idolaters. If Christ is God, then those who deny it are blasphemers.

I suppose we are all willing to take the Bible as our standard. It requires as much faith to be an infidel as to be a Christian; but it is faith in a different direction.

The Bible says, "All things were made by Him." Stop! Does not that prove too much? He did not make the Mediterranean, did He? not Mount Lebanon? not the Alps? not Mount Washington? not the earth? not the stars? not the universe? Yes, all things were made by Him. And unless we should be so stupid as not to understand it, Paul concludes by saying, "Without Him, was not anything made that was made." Why, then, He must have been God. The Bible says, "At the name of Jesus Christ every knee shall bow, of things on earth and things in Heaven." See all Heaven coming down on their knees—martyrs on their knees, apostles on their knees, confessors on their knees, the archangel on his knees. Before whom? A man? No, God. The Bible goes on to say that "every tongue shall confess that Jesus Christ is Lord." Malayan, Indonesian, Mexican, Persian, Italian, German, Spanish, French, English—every tongue shall confess that Jesus Christ is Lord. He must be a God. The Bible says, "Jesus Christ, the same yesterday, today, and forever." People change; the body changes entirely in seven years, the mind changes, the heart changes; but "Christ the same yesterday, today, and forever." He must be God.

Do you think only a man could have made an atonement for millions of the race? Does your common sense teach you that? I tell you if Christ is not God, the redemption of our race is a dead failure. We want a divine arm to lift our burden. We want a divine atonement to take away our sin; and "Christ came, who is over all, God blessed forever. Amen."

February 27
His Deity - 2
by Gregory T. Bedell (1817-1892) USA
Excerpted from "The Fact of the Trinity in the Godhead," *Sermons*,
published by William Stavely-John C. Pechin,
Philadelphia, Pennsylvania in 1835

"...baptizing them in the name of the Father and of the Son and of the Holy Spirit..."
Matthew 28:19b (NIV)

The doctrine of the Trinity is that in the unity of the divine essence there were three persons; or, in perhaps better words, that the Father, the Son, and the Holy Spirit, are the one living and true God; and yet with such a personal distinction as to justify, as applied to each, the personal pronouns I, You, and He; and that divine attributes are applied to each.

Now there are passages in which the three are mentioned together in such a way as to show both their distinction and their equality: "The grace of the Lord Jesus Christ, and the love of God, and the communion of the Holy Spirit, be with you all. Amen." "And I will ask the Father, and He shall give you another Comforter, that He may abide with you forever; even the Spirit of truth whom the world cannot receive, because it does not see Him, neither knows Him: but you know Him, for He dwells with you, and shall be in you. But the Comforter, which is the Holy Spirit, whom the Father will send in My name, He shall teach you all things, and bring all things to your remembrance, whatsoever I have said unto you."

It appears to me that these require no comment. I will only mention one more passage to the same effect. It is the one placed at the head of this discourse: "Baptizing them in the name of the Father, and of the Son, and of the Holy Spirit." I make a brief commentary upon it merely to show the great importance which it has as connected with this subject. It cannot, I understand, but capture the attention of every individual, that at the very entrance and porch of Christianity, the Son and the Holy Spirit are placed on the same level with the Father. That they are placed in this relation shows their equality, and the utter absurdity of any other supposition can be thus shown.

You will of course have observed that I have made no attempt to explain the doctrine. I have simply stated what the doctrine is, and then have gone on regularly to prove it in the only way in which it is capable of proof—by proving that each of the persons—Father, Son, and Holy Spirit—are represented as God; and as there is but one God, so these three Persons are the one living and true God. This is the doctrine. Now the truth of the doctrine stands upon the proof which is brought to support it. It has no necessary connection whatever with the possibility or the impossibility of explaining it.

There are thousands and millions of facts, which, like this, depend entirely on evidence. Explanation is out of the question; explanation is not required. For if a fact could be rejected, though it was supported by evidence, merely because the rationale, if I may so speak, cannot be explained, there is no resort but to universal skepticism. No one, under such circumstances, could believe even their own existence. A principle which leads to such conclusions can have no claim to confidence; and no objection, founded on such a principle is worthy of a serious and enlightened mind. The only question to be decided is this: Do the Scriptures, interpreted according to the ordinary principles of language, teach that in the divine nature there is the distinction of Father, Son, and Holy Spirit; three in the distinction which we call Person, and yet but one in essence? If the Scriptures do teach this, there is no alternative but to admit the fact, or to deny the Bible.

February 28
His Delays
by George H. Morrison (1866-1928) Scotland
Excerpted from "The Doctrine of Delays," *The Unlighted Luster*, published by Hodder and Stoughton, London, England in 1909

For some time He refused.
Luke 18:4 (NIV)

This parable, as the Scripture itself tells us, was meant to teach us persistence in prayer. Christ, who was tempted in all points like as we are, and who had wrestled through many a stern hour of intercession, knew well how the heart is prone to give up when the Heaven we pray to is as brass [silent]. The judge in this parable is a corrupt and villainous creature, and anyone but Christ might well have hesitated to compare His actions with those of the Almighty. But a Son can take large liberties sometimes; He will run the risk of being misunderstood. I know of no parable [Luke 18:1-8] that so assures me of the perfect freedom that Christ had with His Father.

So to our text then, "for some time He refused." That is to say, this judge delayed to act. And that at once suggests to me the great problem of divine delay. We find it everywhere and in every sphere; there are many hearts that have been torn and tried by it. The delays of people may be infinitely frustrating, but they are nothing compared to the delays of God. We find it in nature, when people may be emaciated with famine, yet God will not hurry the harvest by one hour. We find it in life where all that a person has toiled for seemingly reaches them an hour too late. We find it in judgment when wrongdoers live and flourish until the cry from the altar rings in Heaven, "How long?" Above all, we find it in the sphere of prayer. How many patriots have prayed for their country's wounds, yet the years rolled on, and there was no arm to save. How many mothers have prayed for their sons or daughters, and been nearly brokenhearted by delay. What a world of experience there is and how the centuries vanish when we hear the cry of the psalmist, "O God, make haste to help me!" It is as if his faith was flickering out into its ashes, under the torment of delay.

But the very fact that the psalmist prayed that prayer shows that the problem is a very old one. And we are so knit together in this strange humanity, so touched into strength and courage by companionship, that often just to know the world-old pressure of a burden gives a certain ease in our own bearing of it. Now in this matter of delay it seems to me that many of God's people are still children. They think that God has some quarrel with them personally. They forget that the problem is as old as time. Noah felt it when he built his ark and the sun still shone in a sky of unclouded blue. Abraham felt it when the promise of Isaac was given to him, yet the summers passed and the hair of Sarah turned grey, and there was no sound of childish laughter in his tent. David felt it—had he not been anointed to be king? Yet here he was hunted as an outlaw on the hills. Paul felt it when he prayed and prayed again that the Lord would take away the thorn out of his flesh, yet he awoke in the bright morning to his work; and for all his prayer, the thorn was still with him. Do not say, then, "God has forgotten me," because the burden of delay weighs heavy on you.

It is good to remember, too, that the higher we rise, the more intense the difficulty becomes. Delay, then, tends to become more pronounced the higher you rise in the Creator's purposes. Great delays in the mystery of Providence are the highway for the chariot of great blessing. God is not idle when He does not answer us; He is busier preparing the answer than we think. I think it is wiser to pray on, struggle on, casting all doubts to the devil who inspired them; believing in a love that never mocks us, and that will give us our heart's desire in His own time.

February 29
His Deliverance
by James Boardman Hawthorne (1837-1910) USA
Excerpted from "Deliverance from Evil," *An Unshaken Trust and Other Sermons*, published by American Baptist Publication Society, Philadelphia, Pennsylvania in 1899

"Deliver us from evil."
Luke 11:4 (KJV)

Why God permitted evil to come into the world is a secret which He holds in the infinite depths of His own bosom. Neither in His written revelation nor in the volume of nature has He given the faintest clue to this mystery. While it is an insoluble mystery, it is a tremendous reality. We cannot ignore it. It stands out distinctly before us in a thousand different forms. In the Bible we have the record of the entrance of evil into the world, an epitomized history of its progress through a period of four thousand years, and prophecies of its future career up to the time when the great globe itself and all that it inherits shall dissolve and pass away. All about us today are faces lettered with sorrow and stamped with shame. Nothing but the fear of the iron fist of law keeps a large element of the very best of communities from riot and sedition. The existence of three or four hundred dens of vice in the city in which I speak is enough to convince us that devils still reside in human flesh and that much of this world's territory is under Satanic dominion.

Our daily newspapers are chronicles of current evil. Their chief business is to tell us how nations defraud nations, how politicians victimize each other by unrighteous trickery, how huge business monopolies enslave the toiling masses, how lust clamors for unrestrained freedom, how bank vaults and State treasuries are depleted by embezzlement, how drunken husbands murder their wives, how women despise motherhood, and how by assassination governments are deprived of their executive heads.

Christianity recognizes the reality of evil and utters no word of protest against those natural emotions which are excited by contact with it. When from the brow of Olivet Christ looked down upon Jerusalem and foresaw its destruction, He wept. To Him the suffering and slaughter of half a million human beings was evil—a stupendous evil—and He could not contemplate it without the deepest emotions of sorrow. He believed, and He taught, that death was an evil. Hence we see Him weeping at the grave of Lazarus. He pitied the sick, the poor, and persecuted, because He believed sickness, poverty, and persecution to be evils. He denounced lying, hypocrisy, theft, adultery, and tyranny, because He knew them to be evils.

How does Christ deliver us from evil? Not by removing evil from the world in which we live. He has nowhere promised to remove it. Until the end of time there will be disease, famine, strife, war, persecution, tribulation, and anguish. Christ does not deliver us from evil by removing us from contact with it, but by uniting us to Himself by a living faith, by letting His life into our life, and thereby raising us above the dominion and power of the evil one. Delivered from Satanic power nothing that is evil can overcome us or prevent us from being peaceful and happy.

To the wicked and godless man persecution is unmitigated evil. There is nothing in him to pacify the anguish of it; but when the Christian is "persecuted for righteousness' sake," he can rejoice and be exceedingly glad. The joy which comes to him from his union with Christ, and from the consciousness of Christ's supporting grace, more than compensates him for the wrongs which he endures.

March 1
His Desire
by William Henry Green (1824-1900) USA
Excerpted from "Christ's Desire for His People," *Princeton Sermons*, published by Fleming H. Revell Company, New York, New York in 1893

"Father, I want those You have given Me to be with Me where I am, and to see My glory, the glory You have given Me because You loved Me before the creation of the world."
John 17:24 (NIV)

If our minds were in perfect harmony with the mind of Christ our views would in many respects be greatly altered. Many things that we now desire and long for would lose much of their attractiveness, and other things that we dread and shrink from would cease to be unwelcome.

The great Redeemer is in this chapter giving utterance to the desires of His heart on behalf of His people. And the closing petition, the crowning one of all, is that they might be with Him to behold His glory. He had been with them here in His humiliation and life of toilsome sorrow. But the termination of His work on earth was now rapidly approaching, and He was shortly to leave the world and enter into His glory. The anticipated departure of their Lord, whom they loved and upon whom they leaned for more, far more, than any merely human friend or teacher could have brought them, had filled their hearts with sadness and grief. How lonely, cheerless, helpless would they be in this world if Jesus were taken away from them! But the separation, which grieved them so much, shall not last forever. It is His will that they should be with Him where He is. The last and highest blessing that He asks for them is their removal from earth to Heaven.

When Jesus prays that His people may behold His glory, He means something more than that they should witness a spectacle, even with the added thought that this spectacle should produce a beneficial and transforming effect upon them. He means not to have them stand like Moses on the top of Pisgah to view afar the enchanting prospect of the Canaan he should never enter. To "see death" is in Scripture phrase not merely to witness it but to experience it; to "see corruption" is to become a prey to corruption; to "see sorrow" is to be sorrowful; to "see good days" is to have a glad and joyful time; to "see the Kingdom of God" is to partake of its benefits; and to "behold Christ's glory" is to be a sharer of that glory. "The glory which You have given Me," says Jesus, "I have given them." "To the one who overcomes will I grant to sit with Me in My throne, even as I also overcame, and am set down with My Father in His throne."

It is the glory of their Redeemer and their Savior, achieved by Him for them, bestowed by Him upon them. They are one with Him, and all that He has is theirs. This is the end which Jesus seeks for all His followers; this is the result which He has contemplated from the beginning; this is the design of all His work for them, His work in them; this is the burden of His intercessions on their behalf. Is this what we are living for, and striving after, and reaching unto—the center of our hopes, the object of our desires, the mark toward which our struggles are directed?

Is our heart fixed not on an earthly but a heavenly aim, and does this enter into our daily and constant thoughts and plans, so that Heaven seems to us not a violent rupture of all that precedes, a sudden stop to our pursuits, an abandonment of cherished plans, a reversal of all that we were engaged in, but rather its legitimate, expected, longed-for consequence, the last step forward in the direction that we have been urging our way, and which puts the proper finish to our whole lives. Is our treasure in Heaven, or is it on the earth? The answer to this question will reveal to which world we belong, and in which world we shall take our portion.

March 2
His Devotion
by George F. Pierce (1811-1884) USA
Excerpted from "Devotedness to Christ," *Pulpit Eloquence of the Nineteenth Century*, published by Dodd & Mead, New York, New York in 1874

For none of us lives to himself alone and none of us dies to himself alone. If we live, we live to the Lord; and if we die, we die to the Lord. So, whether we live or die, we belong to the Lord.
Romans 14:7-8 (NIV)

Living unto the Lord may be considered as implying that we distinctly recognize the will of God as the rule of life. If I may so express it—as the natural subjects of the Almighty, we are bound to serve Him to the full extent of the powers He has given us. He has an unquestionable right to our obedience. This results from our relation as creatures. He made us and He preserves us. This original obligation, instead of being relaxed and impaired, is confirmed and intensified by purchase and redemption.

To live for Christ, and to live for ourselves, is utterly impractical. The union is a moral impossibility. We love a good name; but they that will live godly in Christ Jesus shall suffer persecution. We are rich; but the command is, "Sell all that you have, and give to the poor, and come follow Me." We love home and friends; but Christ calls to absence, and labor, and sacrifice. Religion is popular—you embrace it; the church is fashionable—you join it. The people shout Hosanna, and Jesus is escorted by a worshiping multitude—you say, "Lord, I will follow You wherever You go." The Master replies: "The foxes have holes, and the birds of the air have nests, but the Son of Man has nowhere to lay His head." What will you do now? Go away sorrowful? or, having counted the cost, go on to build? "Choose you this day whom you will serve"; or have you settled this question long ago in favor of duty and Heaven?

Are you living unto the Lord? You are making a fortune—is it that you may do more good? You are rising in the world, seeking title, and honor and influence—is it that you may enlarge your sphere of usefulness? O brother, if the carnal affection grows along with the carnal interest, your prosperity may destroy you. Or if you are seeking your own pleasure, gratification, and advancement, you have fallen from grace. Even Christ pleased not Himself. Paul obeyed the heavenly vision immediately, conferring not with flesh and blood. And every man who would fulfill the great purposes of His creation and redemption, must make God's approving judgment the motive of all his actions, and the goal of all his efforts. O, how the saints of the Bible basked in this element of devotion! "One thing have I desired of the Lord, that will I seek after: That I may dwell in the house of the Lord all the days of my life, to behold the beauty of the Lord and to inquire in His Temple." "I count all things but loss, for the excellency of the knowledge of Christ Jesus my Lord." These examples illustrate our subject. They lived unto the Lord. In His favor was life. "A day in His courts was better than a thousand elsewhere." They felt that they did not live at all except as they lived unto the Lord.

Let us live unto the Lord—let us live unto the Lord more than ever; let us be more prompt, self-denying, and laborious. Let us be steadfast, unmovable, always abounding in the work of the Lord, forasmuch as we know that our labor is not in vain in the Lord. What we lay out He will repay. Amid our toil, inconveniences, and trials, let this be our consolation: "We are the Lord's." If we live until our physical powers decay, the dim eye may still read our title clear. On Jesus' bosom we may lean the grey head, and in death's sad struggle feel our kind Preserver near. "Whether we live, therefore, or die, we are the Lord's." Living and dying, dead and buried, we are His—His when we rise, His when Heaven and earth are fled and gone, His in the New Jerusalem, forever and forever!

March 3
His Difference
by Henry A. Stimson (1842-1936) USA
Excerpted from "The Challenge of Christ," *The New Things of God*, published by Fleming H. Revell Company, New York, New York in 1907

"Do not believe Me unless I do what My Father does. But if I do it, even though you do not believe Me, believe the miracles…"
John 10:37-38a (NIV)

The great difference between Jesus and other leaders of humanity lies in the harmony between His life and His teaching. He alone could appeal with unquestioned force to what all people could see of His character and His works. In every instance it was this appeal which silenced His critics.

When we turn to Jesus, all changes. From that day to this, He has held the world by what the Gospels call His "works." The beauty, the generosity, the consistency and the sweetness of His life impressed the people of His day, even in the face of their bitter hostility. The very soldiers turned without executing the order for His arrest, awed by the unmistakable character of the Man upon whom they could not venture to lay hands.

His gospel was new, and for this reason it gave life, because it was life. It takes a soul to win a soul; and only a life so consistent, so perfect, can win and inspire, and remake other lives. His speech was the speech of the people: The lilies of the field, the birds of the air, the shepherd at his humble task, the fisherman on the sea of Galilee drawing his nets, furnished the metaphors and the terms in which His spiritual message was delivered. And that message is as charming in those terms today as it was in the ears of the people who first heard it.

But it was not the novelty of the speech that won for Him acceptance or that made His gospel new. He turned to the Old Testament and found no fault with its ancient history and its archaic phraseology, but He interjected into it a new meaning, and He drew out of it that precious content of Divine Truth which had made it a living gospel to the people of the generations before Him, and which makes it a live book for the people of today. He was not troubled as we are about the old doctrines and old forms of speech. The great truths which had possession of Him made all things new and all speech serviceable. The revelation of God in the past was gathered up into the new and greater revelation of God that filled His heart, and His life and spirit were what they were because of the power of that truth upon Him.

He came from His Father. He did the will of His Father. The life of His Father was manifested in Him, and when the hour came to return to that world out of which He had come, His promise was that as it was expedient for Him to go away, He would send the Comforter, the Spirit of Truth, who would abide with His disciples forever. This supreme revelation of the Godhead in which lies all the possibility of the Divine love, and the Divine purpose and plan of the Divine will, and all the perfection of Divine existence, was given to Him, and through Him to the world. It has been the central truth in the possession of His Church from that day.

It was a new gospel, but not new because of the speech in which it was uttered or the power of eloquence in the people who proclaimed it, but new because of the lives it everywhere produced.

Here then is the method of the gospel for today. It is the old method that is ever new. It begins in prayer to God for help in trusting in Him and not in one's self, and then leads on in doing right for Christ's sake and in His name, that you may so be a witness to Him.

March 4
His Directive
by David James Burrell (1844-1926) USA
Excerpted from "Search the Scriptures," *The Golden Passional and Other Sermons*, published by Wilbur B. Ketcham, New York, New York in 1897

"Search the Scriptures; for in them you think you have eternal life: and they are they which testify of Me. And you will not come to Me, that you might have life."
John 5:39-40 (KJV)

There is the Book. What shall be done with it? "Search it," the Master says. But first a preliminary inquiry. Before we search the Scriptures, we must know whether they are worth searching or not. They claim to be inspired with an inspiration which gives them a unique place in the literature of the world. "All Scripture is given by inspiration — is divinely breathed. Holy men of God spoke as they were moved by the Holy Ghost." Here is a book that makes a tremendous claim — it predicates its truth on its divine authorship. Let us determine at the outset the validity of this claim. Turn on the lights, pour on the acids. Call in your Higher Criticism. Let the severest tests of hostile as well as friendly scholarship be applied. Inquire if its doctrines are true, if its ethics are right. Test its science, test its philosophy, test its accuracy at every point.

"Search it." Thank God that we can! An open Bible is the greatest privilege of these days. It is accessible to all. It is no longer chained to the altar, as I have seen it in the Cologne Cathedral, closed with golden clasps and locked. All praise to the noble men of Reformation times, who gave their lives to secure this great privilege for us. "There is no hope," said William Tyndale [1494-1536, English Bible scholar and martyr, Reformation leader], "for the unshod except as they shall have access to God's Holy Word." And again he said, "If God spares my life, I will, before many years, cause that a boy who drives the plow shall know more of the Scriptures than many a learned ecclesiastic knows in these days." The prophecy has come to pass. The Bible is an open book for the lofty and lowly, for the learned and unlearned, for all sorts and conditions of men.

Search carefully. Read the Scriptures with dutiful regularity. Search them in the morning for the strength needed to face the tasks and obligations of the busy day. Read them at night for the comfort you need on entering the unknown country of sleep and for the joy that shall come in the night watches as you reflect upon the sweetness of God's Word.

Search systematically. Let the Scriptures be read consecutively. Not all portions are for public reading, not all are even appropriate for the uses of the family altar; but all Scripture is profitable for personal use, for doctrine, for reproof, for correction, for instruction in righteousness. This is profitable work. It is like mining; it is digging out gold.

Search prayerfully. We shall make little progress in our quest unless God shall illuminate the pages of the Book and then open our eyes to behold it. It is one function of the Holy Spirit to guide us into the truth.

Search experientially; that is, with the purpose of applying the truth and testing its quality in the conduct of your daily life. The Bible is full of truth, but, after all, your search will be unprofitable unless the truth you acquire shall be used in your walk and conversation; used for your personal upbuilding and character, and for the betterment of the world about you. The man who thus delights in the law of the Lord, meditates on it day and night, and uses it constantly, is said by the Psalmist to be "like a tree planted by the rivers of water, that brings forth his fruit in his season; his leaf also shall not wither; and whatsoever he does shall prosper."

March 5
His Doctrine
by James Boardman Hawthorne (1837-1910) USA
Excerpted from "Power of a Despised Doctrine," *An Unshaken Trust and Other Sermons*, published by American Baptist Publication Society, Philadelphia, Pennsylvania in 1899

We preach Christ crucified, unto the Jews a stumbling block, and unto the Greeks foolishness; but unto them which are called, both Jews and Greeks, Christ the power of God, and the wisdom of God.
1 Corinthians 1:23-24 (KJV)

It was not so much the Christ as Christ crucified that offended the Jews and Greeks. The Jews looked for a Messiah, and their dearest hopes were centered upon his mission; but a Messiah who would submit to arrest, insult, and scourging, and who would allow Himself to be crucified between two thieves, they would not have. The Greeks would not have objected to a Messiah if he had come as a great statesman, warrior, and philosopher; but to call a peasant Jew, who had died like other criminals on a Roman cross, the Messiah, was an insult to their pride and intelligence. This despised doctrine was the one great theme of Paul's preaching. It was the very heart and soul of the faith for which he contended and suffered so heroically and died so gloriously. The opposition of those ancient Jews and Greeks to this feature of the gospel has been reproduced in every subsequent generation; but it has survived every assault, and today is the banner of a host which defies the world and the very gates of hell.

Jesus, when unfolding the way of salvation to Nicodemus, said: "As Moses lifted up the serpent in the wilderness, even so must the Son of Man be lifted up." Only a week before His crucifixion He said, "And I, if I be lifted up from the earth, will draw all men unto Me"; and John declares that Jesus said this to signify "what death He should die."

"The Son of Man must be lifted up." The lifting up was an absolute necessity. It was in God's eternal plan of redemption, and if Jesus Christ had not been lifted up on the cross, not a human being could be saved. It was not essential to the scheme that Christ should preach a definite number of sermons and perform a definite number of miracles, but it was essential that He, "the just, should die for the unjust." Of this necessity He was profoundly conscious. He said to His disciples that He must go up to Jerusalem and be crucified and rise from the dead.

It is this lifting up of the Son of Man, His humiliating death on the cross, which renders the gospel we preach "foolishness" to some and a "stumbling-block" to others. They cannot see why a God of infinite resources should adopt such a scheme for redeeming the world. I suppose that the bitten and dying Israelites had about the same thought concerning the bronze serpent that was lifted up over their camp. "The Lord said unto Moses, Make a fiery serpent, and set it upon a pole: and it shall come to pass, that everyone who is bitten, when they look upon it, shall live."

Paul stood in the midst of Jews and Greeks and said, "That despised being, who hung upon that instrument of shame and torture, is the world's only hope. He is the only Being in all the universe who can pardon your sins and save your guilty souls. Whosoever believes on Him shall not perish, but have everlasting life." But you will never know His saving power and feel His divine life communicated to your secret soul until you see Him crucified. You will never know the joy of salvation until you see Him lifted up to the malice of earth, the fury of hell, and the wrath of Heaven. It is only in such a vision of Him that you see your own sins in all of their hideous vileness. Beholding Him there, as the victim of your iniquity, you see your guilt not only condemned, but forgiven and obliterated forever.

March 6
His Doubter
by Louis Albert Banks (1855-1933) USA
Excerpted from "Thomas, the Doubter, Reclaimed," *The Fisherman and His Friends,* published by Funk & Wagnalls Company, New York, New York in 1896

Then [Jesus] said to Thomas, "Put your finger here, and look at My hands. Put your hand into the wound in My side. Don't be faithless any longer. Believe!" "My Lord and my God!" Thomas exclaimed. Then Jesus told him, "You believe because you have seen Me. Blessed are those who believe without seeing Me."
John 20:27-29 (NLTSE)

We do not know why Thomas was absent from the meeting of the disciples on the first occasion of Christ's appearance to them after His resurrection. It is quite probable, however, that he was not with them because he had fallen into a state of religious despondency. His faith that they were to see anything more of the Lord was not very strong, and therefore he stayed away from the meetings. If Thomas had expected that the Lord was going to meet with them, nothing could have kept him away. The reason he is with them at this time is, no doubt, because he has been so influenced by the testimony of the disciples that Jesus had appeared unto them and broken bread with them on the former occasion, that he has determined not to miss another chance. He would not receive their testimony, and declared unequivocally to them that unless he should put his finger in the nail prints in the Savior's hands, and touch the wound in His side, he would never believe in the resurrection.

Yet, notwithstanding all these statements, no doubt honestly made, the joyous enthusiasm of the other disciples had its effect on Thomas, and while he thought they were deluded, and had only seen an unsubstantial vision, he could not help but feel that they were a good deal happier than he was, and that something very remarkable must have happened to lift the terrible load of gloom off their hearts and fill them with such joyous assurance that their Master had triumphed over death and was at that very moment a living Person. Whatever may have been the working of Thomas' mind, he had evidently come to the conclusion that in the future he would stick close to the rest of the friends of Jesus, and if anything good did happen to them he would be on hand for a share in it. Thomas never came to a wiser conclusion than that.

In this picture we are studying there is another suggestion that is exceedingly comforting to our hearts—the gentleness and patience of Jesus in specially singling out Thomas and lovingly meeting his doubts and using every method possible to dissipate them forever. The whole history of God's dealings with the world is in harmony with the divine gentleness illustrated in Christ's lovingkindness toward Thomas. He enables us to sing, with all confidence, "When other helpers fail, and comforts flee, Help of the helpless, O abide with me!"

When the need is great and despair rises within us, as it did in the mind and heart of poor Thomas, God does not go away, but remains near and precious to the broken and contrite spirit. Even when we have tried to go our own way and failed, God does not reproach us or cast us off; but by tender revelations of Himself, by gentle promise and the inspiration of hope, He quiets our restless spirits, and heals them with a deepened trust. We all need some heart to lean upon in which there is both strength and tenderness. Jesus Christ is, to everyone that will open his heart to receive Him, such a heart, that will never fail us, that never scorns us, that deals with us as gently as a mother with her child, that stoops to our own level, and in stooping lifts us up into a life more beautiful and precious than anything we could have ever known without His tender love and sympathy. Christ has made God real to us.

March 7
His Economy - 1
by Alfred Rowland (1829-1902) USA
Excerpted from "God's Recompense to Givers," *The Exchanged Crowns*, published by Robert Scott, London, England in 1910

"Give, and it shall be given unto you; good measure, pressed down, shaken together, running over, shall they give into your bosom. For with what measure you measure it shall be measured to you again."
Luke 6:38 (KJV)

The general truth in this dictum is that, according to God's good and wise law, expenditure brings return, so that when we pour out our love, our gifts, our powers of any kind, these are not wasted, but increased. Our Lord would have us apply this to Christian life and work. I say advisedly to Christian life, because it is only where life is that it holds good.

The Pharisees and Scribes recited laws which were true enough, and did acts, like almsgiving, which were right enough, and the priests in the Temple performed all things according to the law, but these doings did not increase the number or the fervor of true worshippers, because the Searcher of hearts was compelled to say, "You have no life in you." Only life can propagate life, and it is when we share the life of our Lord, and give it generously, in teaching, in gifts, and in prayers, that we shall share the reward promised here. The blessing which comes to a man who puts forth the powers which make him what he is, is exemplified in various spheres of activity. The fact is that all living creatures and all communities of living men develop by giving of themselves.

There is not a church, by whatever name it may be known, in which the same law does not hold good. If you, professing Christians, are content to cultivate a dignified ease, a serene self-complacency, thinking that you have adequately served God when you have lounged through a weekly service, if you are unconscious of any responsibility to the miserable and sin-stained around you, and even to the ignorant heathen who are far away from you, then you will lose the sense of our Lord's presence, your own spiritual life will become anemic, and you will bring on you the curse which ultimately falls on every wicked and slothful servant.

How few realize their responsibility for helping to enthrone Him. Let me beg you all to give of yourselves in the belief that you will be enriched in soul, though you may have no visible return for your service.

In the first place, let me remind you that some definite Christian work will increase your unselfishness, your decision of character, and your moral greatness. It is an advantage of Christian service that it brings us into associations which are likely to elevate us, and this also is an element in God's reward to givers. It is another advantage to those who give out of the life that is in them that they share their Lord's Spirit, as they face the sins and sorrows of the world.

Further, those of us who are thus seeking to give of our best find that prayer is necessary to our continuing success in it. Anything which will make our lives more devotional should be welcomed, for no rebukes which we receive from others, or administer to ourselves, will conquer prayerlessness. And there are nominal Christians whose hearts are voiceless towards God, with whom prayer is a mere memory of childhood days, and not a present reality. But those who truly serve Christ Jesus feel that they must speak to Him. Pour out your hearts before Him, and God will pour out His blessing on you, in nobler powers, in deeper devotion, and in holier and more effective service.

March 8
His Economy - 2
by James R. McGavin (1810-1887) Scotland

Excerpted from "The Principles of Christian Economy," *Modern Scottish Pulpit Sermons by Ministers of Various Denominations*, published by Robert Carter & Brothers, New York, New York in 1880

"To what purpose is this waste?"
Matthew 26:8 (KJV)

There is a wide and irreconcilable difference between common opinion and the estimate which God, in His gospel, forms of men and things. What the world despises, God esteems; what the world forgets and overlooks, God records and perpetuates. Thus, in the sacred narrative, deeds and persons are brought into prominence, and divinely applauded, when this is what we would least expect; and Scripture calls that noble, heroic, and blessed, which multitudes would pronounce mean or low-spirited—just because the wisdom of this world is foolishness with God, and "He has chosen the weak things of the world to confound the mighty, yes and things that are not, to bring to nothing things that are, that no flesh should glory in His presence."

We have a marked example of this great truth in the uniform action of our blessed Savior. His whole career lay far away from the walks of the world's admiration; and the individuals whom He admitted into His confidence, and the actions He approved, as well as the principles of morality and obedience which He taught, were a grand protest against the hollow selfishness and painted hypocrisy around Him. When He called children to His arms, while the world frowned and rebuked; when He commended the Canaanite woman, the Samaritan, the Centurion, the poor widow casting her mite into the treasury; while He ignored the needless show of the rich, and scorned the false pretenses of the Pharisee—you mark the essential contradiction between the world's shams and the Savior's sincerity, and the glory with which He adorns the modest but genuine principle, which lies concealed from the world's notice, because, like the largest and brightest gems, it is overlaid beneath the mass of the worthless materials around it.

If we ask why Mary brought this alabaster box, the readiest answer is because she had nothing else so precious. Hers was a love that must honor the presence of the Lord, and nothing was sufficiently costly to express her obligations to Him who had done everything for her soul. Every sacrifice was too little. This might have been her whole life's savings; and, in parting with it, she may have exposed herself to poverty for all her future career; but, to express her love for the Redeemer, she poured out her heart along with it. It was the tribute of a soul that gave itself up along with its offering, which, more than all the perfume of the ointment, was precious to Christ, and caused Him to vindicate and applaud her, as He said, "I tell you the truth, wherever this gospel is preached throughout the world, what she has done will also be told, in memory of her."

Now, how should you and I express our obligation to Christ as this woman did? We owe Him as much, if He is indeed our Savior; and we cannot serve Him with love which costs us less, if we are partakers of her spirit. May we not make sacrifices to Him of our money, our time, our talents, our life? Is there no sweet reward in the approval of Him who has done all for us? Ah! not one effort of the loving is lost. All shall be rewarded at the resurrection of the just.

What was counted waste here is fragrant with the love of Christ, and turns into treasure which is stored up in Heaven. Be assured, therefore, that the real waste of life is in the world's service.

March 9
His Education
by George H. Morrison (1866-1928) Scotland
Excerpted from "Our Lord as a Student," *Highways of the Heart*, published by George H. Doran Company, New York, New York in 1926

"How did this Man get such learning without having studied?"
John 7:15 (NIV)

What our text implies is this: That our Lord gave the impression of a student. The Jews as they listened to Him recognized the accent of a cultured, educated man. Our Lord stood up in the Temple and spoke, and whenever the Lord spoke a crowd would gather. There was something about Him that compelled attention, though nobody could say just what it was. The one question that sprang to every lip was, "How did this Man get such learning without having studied?" He had never been at any Rabbinical school, never graduated from any university, and was evidently only a common man from the province of Galilee. Yet as they listened to Him they recognized the student, the cultivated, educated Man.

It is also a very striking thing that the nearer people got to Him the more they recognized His scholarship. It was when people were in closest contact with the Lord that they found to their cost His scholarly precision. There are people who, from a little distance, give the impression of admirable scholarship, but whenever you get near enough to them you are sadly disillusioned. But nobody who came right up to Christ was ever sadly disillusioned; what happened was that they were overcome. Think for a moment of the Rabbis. They had given their lives to the study of the Scripture. They had scorned delights, and lived laborious days, poring over the sacred word of Scripture. Yet never one of them encountered Christ but was beaten disgracefully from the field; our Master was the master of them all. "What," He would say to them, "have you never read?" How the very question must have infuriated them. Never read! They had been doing nothing else since they entered the Rabbinical university. Yet the proudest scholar of them all invariably was convicted of incompetence by this strange Person from Galilee.

Nor did our Lord create that deep impression by any elaborate display of learning. All pretense was abhorrent to His soul. Among the Pharisees learning was largely dogma, with endless citation of authorities. It had passed out of touch with all reality in its meticulous exposition of the law. And over against that pharisaical formalism, which was the despair of common people, stands the perfect simplicity of Christ. With what perfect and unfaltering ease He used to handle the most obscure of themes! With what homely and familiar figures He would lighten what was dark! Where others stumbled, groping in the mists, lost in large multisyllabic words, our Lord moved just like a little child. The last thing the Lord would ever suggest to me is that of a man groping. There is such perfect mastery about Him, such ease of conscious and consummate power. His intellectual processes were beautiful, because His life and character were beautiful. He says, "I come to do Your will, O God."

I like to notice, too, that this so perfect student had always the quiet courage to be Himself, and the quiet courage just to be oneself is one of the finest kinds of courage in the world. And one of the glorious things about this student was that He never saw things through other people's eyes; He always had the courage to be Himself. Trained in the home at Nazareth, steeped in the teaching of the synagogue, with what tremendous pressure the learning of His day must have been brought to bear on Him. And His refusal to be overborne by the tradition of His time is one of the features of the gospel story. How fresh His expositions were! How He found the truth that everyone else had missed!

March 10
His Emptying
by David James Burrell (1844-1926) USA
Excerpted from "The Kenosis," *The Golden Passional and Other Sermons,*
published by Wilbur B. Ketcham, New York, New York in 1897

Let this mind be in you, which was also in Christ Jesus: Who, being in the form of God, thought it not robbery [a prize, a thing to be jealously cherished] to be equal with God: But made Himself of no reputation [literally, emptied Himself], and took upon Him the form of a servant, and was made in the likeness of men: And being found in fashion as a man, He humbled Himself, and became obedient unto death, even the death of the cross. Wherefore God also has highly exalted Him and given Him a name which is above every name: That at the name of Jesus every knee should bow, of things in Heaven, and things in earth, and things under the earth; and that every tongue should confess that Jesus Christ is Lord, to the glory of God the Father.
Philippians 2:5-11 (NIV)

The Lord Jesus Christ came into the world to accomplish a definite purpose, and He fully accomplished it. His last word was, "It is finished!" If we would attain to the highest success, therefore, we must catch His spirit; or, as Paul puts it, "Let this mind be in you that was also in Christ Jesus."

But this mind that was in Christ Jesus, what is it? The matter is made clear in these words, "He, being in the form of God, thought it not a matter of supreme importance to be equal with God; but emptied Himself and took upon Him the form of a servant, and was made in the likeness of men." There must have been a fulness before there could be an emptying. This leads us to consider the preexisting glory of Christ, which is fully set forth John: "In the beginning was the Word, and the Word was with God, and the Word was God." Christ was "in the beginning." Here is a separating gulf between Him and all the children of men. He was the pre-existent. Our life is without end; the life of the Son of God is without beginning and without end. He is Alpha and Omega; the beginning and the end. He said, "Before Abraham was, I am"; not "I was," but "I am," thus taking to Himself the incommunicable name by which God expresses His self-existence, "I am that I am." He was in the beginning "with God." That is, He had a distinct personality. He was in the company or by the side of God. The same truth is expressed in many ways: The Father is the Sender, Christ is the Sent; the Father is the Giver, Christ is the Gift—the unspeakable Gift. He "was God." Or, as the Nicene creed puts it, "Very God of Very God."

It must have been a great day in Heaven when the Second Person of the Godhead set out for earth to accomplish His great work. How angels and archangels, who had been used to veiling their faces before the display of His glory, must have sent blessings after Him! He vanished; and when He next appeared, lo! it was as a Child wrapped in swaddling bands and lying in a manger. Between the gate of Heaven and Bethlehem, something had fallen from Him. Not His Godhood; it is unthinkable that He should cease to be God. But He had lost the outward form of deity. There was no halo about the Christ-child. There was no form, nor comeliness, nor any beauty that we should desire Him. He had emptied Himself of the form of God, and taken upon Him the form of a man. He was exclusively neither God nor man; but *theanthropos*, the God-Man. He stooped to conquer.

He who has learned this truth and is willing to entertain the mind that was in Christ Jesus, shall win for himself, as Jesus won, a new name and shall be partaker of His glory. As it is written, "To him who overcomes...I will also give him a white stone with a new name written on it, known only to him who receives it."

March 11
His Enemies
by George Campbell Morgan (1863-1945) England
Excerpted from "Satan and Demons," *The Teaching of Christ,* published by Fleming H. Revell Company, New York, New York in 1913

The references of Jesus to Satan are too many and too explicit to need any argument to prove His belief in the existence of a spiritual personality of great subtlety, and of great power, who is actively engaged in evil operations producing evil results. The word "Satan" was in its first use a title rather than a name; but in the process of the history of Hebrew theology it had become a definite name attached to one person. The simple meaning of the word is adversary. He was a spiritual being, of vast wisdom and tremendous power, who was at war with the purpose of God. Our Lord took that name, and used it in His references to His personality.

He also used the name which we translate as "the devil," the Greek word "diabolos," which means the slanderer, the false accuser; and necessarily in that word there was always the thought and suggestion of evil which was not at first associated with the other word, adversary. Upon two occasions only, our Lord made use of the word by which this being was designated by the Pharisees, Beelzebub.

When dealing with the relation of Satan to the Kingdom of God, and its establishment in the world, He used the terms, "the evil one" and "the enemy." "The evil one" is sometimes rendered "the evil." The term, "the evil one," suggests that Satan is the origin, the fountainhead of evil; and our Lord employed it when dealing with his relation to the Kingdom.

"The enemy" means, quite literally, the hater, and therefore the one hostile to every purpose of benevolence and of love. In explanation of the parable of the tares, the Lord said, "the enemy that sowed them is the devil"; and in His address to the Seventy, "I have given you authority over all the power of the enemy."

Our Lord made use of one term only in describing the relation of this person to Himself: "the prince of this world." When Jesus spoke of Satan as the prince, the ruler of this world, it was always in connection with something He was saying of Himself.

There is also to be found in the teaching of the Lord a constant recognition of multitudes of evil beings, all acting under the direction of this one ruler. We shall examine that teaching by considering the common name used for these beings, and two defining terms. The common name is "demons." There are two defining terms of which He made use in connection with demons. He called them spirits. In describing the condition of a man from whom they were cast out, He said "the unclean spirit when he is gone out of the man, passes through waterless places, seeking rest, and finding it not."

This teaching reveals our enemies in the spiritual world, as it sets before us the fact of one personality, the *archon*, the ruler, who is the prince of this world; and reveals to us multitudes of spiritual beings under his control, following his command, cooperating with him in a persistent fight against the Kingdom of God, against righteousness, and holiness, and love. But the teaching reveals the Master as perfectly knowing them, persistently opposing them, and constantly triumphing over them. After those days of supreme temptation as a Man in the wilderness, we never find our Lord entering into any discussion with evil spirits, but always addressing them in terms of perfect mastery and perfect command; until at last He triumphed over them in His cross, putting them off from Him, making a show of them openly in the universe of God.

March 12
His Enemy
by Frederick Dan Huntington (1819-1904) USA
Excerpted from "Satan Transformed," *Sermons for the People*, published by Crosby, Nichols, and Company, Boston, Massachusetts in 1857

And no marvel; for Satan himself is transformed into an angel of light.
2 Corinthians 11:14 (KJV)

In the real Satan, we must look for a shrewder cunning, a more subtle diplomacy, a more prudent disguise. Whatever he may have been to the superstitious fears of cruder ages, to try the spirit of the nineteenth century he takes on the address of a courtier, the self-possession of a man of the world, the royal dignity of a prince, the beauty of an angel, and the manners of a gentleman. If you meet him now—and meet him you certainly will tomorrow and today—he will be transformed into an angel of light. It is the policy of the tempter to steal upon us by degrees, little by little, and by roundabout approaches, until we are taken in his net.

The peculiarity of temptation that I would fix your thoughts upon now is the indirectness of it—the circumventing policy by which it carries us to reefs of shame, and into a vortex of tempests, while we are all the while flattering ourselves that we are making a prosperous voyage.

Satan does not march his victim up to face hell pointblank. He leads him to it by easy stages, and through a labyrinth that shows no danger. Round and round go those circling currents of the Northern Sea that swallow the ship; and by the same winding coil goes the spiritual decline that ends in spiritual death. It is merriment, not the grave, that youth is seeking, when it steps inside the circle of forbidden pleasure. It is for social cheer, for good companionship, because he would not be gloomy, because he would scatter his misery, that the drunkard drinks damnation, not for damnation's sake. It is to pay his debt, the gambler urges, that he plays—to pay one debt that he forfeits all his credit. The first falsehood of a practiced liar may have been told to save a friend's reputation—a generous motive he thinks—Satan transformed into an angel of light!

Satan never plays a bold game. He wins by not showing his worst at first, by concealing his tricks, transformed into an angel of light. It takes a great deal of effort to put us thoroughly on our guard against his wiles; but when it is done, it is worth the pains. Says the Apostle Paul: "If Satan himself is transformed into an angel of light, it is no great thing if his ministers also be transformed as the ministers of righteousness—whose end shall be according to their works." All our sins creep on us under concealment, creep on us indirectly. Our first lesson of resistance is to learn that Satan is a deceiver, transforms himself, looks like an angel. Ever since the first mother gave her ear to the serpent, his approach to his victim has been "with tract oblique"; "encircling spires, fold above fold, sidelong he works his way."

But your temptations hover about you in wary ambush. They are not in great emergencies, heralded by horrid threatenings, but in the little things of your daily life, and hidden under unsuspected appearances. They lurk in the luxuries on which you rest; in the pillows of comfort on which you lay your thoughtless heads; in the imitation where you mistake the pride of excelling for the love of wisdom, and superiority for scholarship; in the common labor where the world gambles for your soul; in the merchandise where you are offered gain for falsehood; in the social fellowship where criminality corrupts under the name of cordiality. Here are your tempters. They are disguised; they take circuitous paths; they carry gifts in their hands, and place crowns on your heads; they are clothed like angels of light. No harm can come near you, but through the gate of your own yielding heart, set open by your own perverted will.

March 13
His Engagement
by Hannah Whitall Smith (1832-1911) USA/England
Excerpted from "Is God In Everything?" *The Christian's Secret of a Happy Life*, published by Willard Tract Repository, Boston, Massachusetts in 1885

One of the greatest obstacles to living unwaveringly this life of entire surrender is the difficulty of seeing God in everything. People say, "I can easily submit to things which come from God; but I cannot submit to man, and most of my trials and crosses come through human instrumentality." Or they say, "It is all well enough to talk of trusting; but when I commit a matter to God, man is sure to come in and disarrange it all; and while I have no difficulty in trusting God, I do see serious difficulties in the way of trusting men."

This is no imaginary trouble, but it is of vital importance, and if it cannot be met, [it] does really make the life of faith an impossible and visionary theory. For nearly everything in life comes to us through human instrumentalities, and most of our trials are the result of somebody's failure, or ignorance, or carelessness, or sin. We know God cannot be the author of these things, and yet unless He is the agent in the matter, how can we say to Him about it, "Thy will be done"?

Besides, what good is there in trusting our affairs to God, if, after all, man is to be allowed to come in and disarrange them; and how is it possible to live by faith, if human agencies, in whom it would be wrong and foolish to trust, are to have a predominant influence in molding our lives?

Moreover, things in which we can see God's hand always have a sweetness in them which consoles while it wounds. But the trials inflicted by man are full of bitterness.

What is needed, then, is to see God in everything, and to receive everything directly from His hands, with no intervention of second causes. And it is just to this that we must be brought, before we can know an abiding experience of entire abandonment and perfect trust. Our abandonment must be to God, not to man, and our trust must be in Him, not in any arm of flesh, or we shall fail at the first trial.

Our trials may be our chariots. We long for some victory over sin and self, and we ask God to grant it to us. His answer comes in the form of a trial which He means shall be the chariot to bear us to the longed for triumph. We may either let it roll over us and crush us, or we may mount into it and ride triumphantly onward. Joseph's chariots, which bore him on to the place of his exaltation, were the trials of being sold into slavery, and being cast unjustly into prison. Our chariots may be much more insignificant things than these; they may be nothing but irritating people or uncomfortable circumstances. But whatever they are, God means them to be our cars of triumph, which shall bear us onward to the victories we have prayed for.

If we are impatient in our dispositions and long to be made patient, our chariot will probably be a trying person to live in the house with us, whose ways or words will irritate our very souls. If we accept the trial as from God, and bow our necks to the yoke, we shall find it just the discipline that will most effectively produce in us the very grace of patience for which we have asked. If the will of God is our will, and if He always has His way, then we always have our way also, and we reign in a perpetual Kingdom. He who sides with God cannot fail to win in every encounter; and whether the result shall be joy or sorrow, failure or success, death or life, we may, under all circumstances, join in Paul's shout of victory, "Thanks be unto God, who always causes us to triumph in Christ!"

March 14
His Everyday
by James Russell (J. R.) Miller (1840-1912) USA
Excerpted from "Christ in Our Everydays," *The Lesson of Love*, published by Thomas Y. Crowell & Co., New York, New York in 1903

Some people seem to miss altogether the thought of bringing Christ into their common, everyday life. When a Christian young man was talking about what calling he would choose, expressing much uncertainty and perplexity on the subject, he was asked if he had prayed about it. He was astonished and said he could not think of troubling the Lord with such a matter as that. There are many good people who have the same thought. They suppose that God is interested only in their spiritual affairs and not in their secular matters.

But that is not the true thought of God's care for us. He is interested in everything that concerns us. There is nothing in all the range of our life which we may not bring to Him. There are none of our affairs in which religion does not have its place. We may make the most common things of business as beautiful and as holy as a prayer.

There is nothing in all our life, however lowly and commonplace, however mundane and secular, on which we may not put the name of Christ, something of the beauty of Christ. There are not two departments in life—one religious and one with which religion has nothing to do. The Sabbath is meant to bring us more consciously into the divine presence than the other days, that we may worship God, look into His face, and get fresh cheer and strength; but we are in God's presence as really on Monday and Tuesday as on Sunday, and we should do the work of the week just as religiously as we do our praying and Bible reading. Our business should be as devout as our worship. "Whatsoever you do, in word or in deed, do all in the name of the Lord Jesus."

We may do the most common, simple things in the name of Christ, and this brings the lowliest occupation as near to Christ as that of the minister or the deaconess. Jesus was just as holy in His life and lived just as near to God the first thirty years when He was a carpenter as the last three years when He was engaged in the great work of His Messiahship. We may live as saintly lives in the lowliest trade or calling as in the most sacred of callings. How dull, commonplace duties would be transformed! How glad we should be to do the most lowly things! Then how well we would do everything! There would be no skimping of our work, no slighting of it, no half-doing of it. No duty would seem unworthy of us, too small or too menial for us. If only we could always keep in mind that we are working in the name of Christ, we should never find any task irksome nor any duty hard.

If we really know the name of Christ as we may know it, all life would be changed for us. If we remembered Him, and saw His eyes of love looking down upon us continually, we could not let the hateful mood stay in our hearts, we could not do the mean or wicked thing, we could not say the bitter, cutting word, we could not, by our wretched jealousy, hurt the gentle heart that never had given us anything but love.

This name of Christ tests all life for us. Anything over which we cannot write this blessed Name is unfit for us to do. What we cannot do in this Name we ought not to do at all. The friendship on which we cannot put "in the name of Jesus" is not a friendship we should take into our life. The business we cannot conduct in Christ's name we would better not try to conduct at all. The gate over which this Name is not carved we should not enter.

March 15
His Example
by Thomas Guthrie (1803-1873) Scotland
Excerpted from "The Example of Christ," *The Way to Life*, published by E. B. Treat & Company, New York, New York in 1891

"Let it be so now; it is proper for us to do this to fulfill all righteousness."
Matthew 3:15 (NIV)

Now, nothing invests the ordinary means of grace with such importance, as to see our Lord, like one of ourselves, observing them. He was independent of all means, and stood in no need of such aids. Yet, able to walk without these crutches, and rise without help from such wings, He stoops to our condition, that He may teach us by His own example the devout and diligent use of all the means of grace.

First, He prayed. How much of His time did prayer occupy; how little perhaps of ours? The sun that left Him on His knees, having gone round the world, returned to find Him on the same spot, and engaged in the same employment. Jesus Christ, a whole night in prayer; alone on the mountain with God; what fact, what picture could so well illustrate the apostolic precept, Pray without ceasing!

Secondly, He punctually attended worship in the house of God. He was a living, walking, devout, divine illustration of Paul's precept: Neglect not the assembling of yourselves together. Observe the lesson: The Bible says to pray without ceasing; neglect not the assembling of yourselves together; do this in remembrance of Me; go into all the world and preach the gospel to every creature; and search the Scriptures. In all these duties Jesus leads the way.

I have no faith nor trust to put in any road to Heaven other than that which our Savior trod. Our Forerunner, He has left His footprints on the path of ordinances; and holding Him to be our Pattern as well as our Propitiation, I will venture on no path but that which He traveled. Can anything be plainer than this, that if our blessed Lord did not neglect the means of grace, much less should we, can we afford to do so?

In looking at Jesus Christ, as He moves high and apart from all of us in His perfectly spotless life, one sometimes feels as we have felt when gazing on the bright but distant glory of a star that holds on its lofty course through the far realms of space. We wish to be like Christ; we long to be like Christ; but to reach His high, and holy, and pure, and spotless character, seems to be like wishing to reach that orb so beautiful and bright and lovely. But to rise to His example, to attain to His holy and blameless life, ah! that seems as impossible as to climb the ethereal heights where that bright orb is shining. We say, Who is sufficient for these things? The one seems at times as impractical and impossible as the other. Impossible? With God all things are possible. He has never promised that we shall reach the one; but His truth and His word are pledged for it that we shall attain to the other.

If religion is not in the heart it is nowhere. It is not by fits and starts that men become holy. It is not occasional, but continuous, prolonged, and lifelong efforts that are required; to be daily at it; always at it; resting but to renew the work; falling but to rise again. It is not by a few rough, erratic blows of the hammer, that a graceful statue is brought out of the marble block, but by the labor of continuous days, and many delicate touches of the sculptor's chisel. It is not a sudden gush of water, the roaring torrent of a summer flood, but a continuous flow, that wears the rock, and a constant dropping that hollows out the stone. It is not with a rush and a spring that we are to reach Christ's character, attain to perfect saintship; but step by step, foot by foot, hand over hand, we are slowly and often painfully to mount the ladder that rests on earth, and rises to Heaven.

March 16
His Expectation
by Marvin R. Vincent (1834-1922) USA
Excerpted from "Extra Service," *God and Bread*, published by Dodd, Mead and Company, New York, New York in 1884

"When a servant comes in from plowing or taking care of sheep, does his master say, 'Come in and eat with me'? No, he says, 'Prepare my meal, put on your apron, and serve me while I eat. Then you can eat later.' And does the master thank the servant for doing what he was told to do? Of course not. In the same way, when you obey Me, you should say, 'We are unworthy servants who have simply done our duty.'"
Luke 17:7-10 (NLTSE)

In the first place, you observe that it is not unusual for our Lord to draw a disagreeable picture in order to set forth His own love and grace. What a type of hard, selfish cruelty is that unjust judge, for example: "I will hear the widow, in order to be rid of her. I will do what she asks me because she troubles me, and for fear that she may weary me to death." Is this like God? No. If the unjust judge can be moved by earnest and persistent appeal, shall not the just God be moved by the cry of His own chosen ones? Or, to take another case, is God like the irritable man who refuses to give his neighbor bread because the door is shut, and he is in bed? No, if the testy neighbor will yield to persistence, and rise, and give his friend as many loaves as he needs, will not God honor the unrelenting faith which besieges His doors, even though, to test it, He delays for a while? His delay is only the prelude to His rising, and giving like God.

We must not be repelled by a figure, therefore. But, then, there are the words, "even so you also," which compel us to recognize in this parable some features of our relation to God. The parable does not say that God deals with His servants as a master does with a slave, yet it may nevertheless express some facts and conditions of Christian service.

No Christian can shut himself up to a little routine of duty, and say, I will do so much, within such times, and no more. When a Christian stands in the field of Christian service, his heart open to God's call, his life distilling the perfume of holy love, he cannot keep his services upon one line or within certain times. Demands for ministry swarm over the lines he may have drawn; outstretched hands are thrust forth from unsuspected corners; voices arise from places given over to silence; his hands are always full. If he begins with a scheme of duties and times, the feeble hands of sickness and lack will throw his scheme into confusion, or keep him constantly enlarging it. It is a law of all work of a higher type, that it oversteps mere methodical limits. It is only work of a mechanical kind that is confined to specific times and prescribed duties.

What God may do for His servants out of His own free grace and love, what privileges He may grant His friends, is another question; but, on the hard business basis of value received, the servant of God has no case. What he does in God's service it is his duty to do. In reading the parable, put the emphasis on the word servants. We are unprofitable servants. As servants we can render no service that is not due.

In Christ's real friends, the desire for service outruns the ability. Christ's friend does not fence off from the claims of service a section of rights to rest and leisure. He would as soon think of forbidding his neighbor to enter his own house or orchard. He is not his own; his heritage is not his; his life is a practical assent to the truth which Paul so forcibly puts to the Corinthians: "You are God's tilled land: you are God's building." And therefore God's claims have the free and full range of his time and of his powers.

March 17
His Extravagance
by George H. Morrison (1866-1928) Scotland
Excerpted from "The Lavishness of Jesus," *O Christian Devotional* website

They all ate as much as they wanted, and afterward, the disciples picked up twelve baskets of leftovers.
Matthew 14:20 (NLTSE)

One of the characteristics of our Lord was a certain glorious lavishness, an uncalculating generosity that was unconcerned about the less or more. This made Him very lovable. It was one of the features of His grace. He exhibited that royal generosity which always captivates the human heart. The lavishness of Jesus struck its roots into His deepest being, and was the flower of uncalculating love. Love never asks how little can I do; love always asks how much. Love does not merely go the measured mile; love travels to the uttermost. Love never haggles, never bargains, with "nicely calculated less or more." It gives up to the point of extravagance.

We find the extravagance of Christ in every sphere, and first let us note it in His actions. "Gather up the fragments that remain, and they gathered up twelve baskets full." People find in that a lesson in economy. Christ was careful that not a crumb is lost. And it is well we should be taught that lesson — we are so apt to be careless with life's fragments. But surely a far deeper lesson, leading us to the inmost heart of Jesus, is that of His uncalculating lavishness. He took no nice and precise measurements of what that hungry multitude required. He did not think of the minimum of need; He thought of the maximum of love. He gave so generously that when every person was fed, and every little whimpering child was satisfied, there yet remained twelve baskets full. That was the manner in which Jesus gave, and in such a manner is He giving still.

The same uncalculating lavishness of love is witnessed in the teaching of His parables. I do not think there is a single parable in which that divine element is lacking. The Sower does not nicely measure things; he sows on the beaten path and on the rock. The employer of labor, at the eleventh hour, gives a full day's pay for an hour's work. The servant who was faithful with ten pounds finds himself the ruler of ten cities, no doubt to his own intense astonishment. People quarrel with the doctrine of rewards. They say we ought to do good for its own sake. Christ, knowing human nature, never hesitates to introduce rewards. But then His rewards are so amazing, so utterly unproportioned to our merit, that they entirely lose the aspect of reward, and shine as gifts of undeserved grace. When the poor prodigal came home again, a bare forgiveness would have contented him. But it evidently did not content the overflowing heart of Jesus. The best robe must be given to him; there must be a ring on his finger and shoes upon his feet; there must be music and dancing in the house.

Again, we might think a moment of the kind of thing that Jesus loved. If we are to follow Him, and take His scale of values, it is imperative that we discover that. He did not love the narrowness of Pharisees, nor had He any tenderness for lengthy prayers. He felt no sympathy with the precise exactness that tithes the mint and the anise and the cumin. But one day He saw a widow woman lavishing her little all for God, and that plucked the strings of His heart. Again, another day there came a woman with an alabaster box of precious ointment. And she broke the box and poured that precious ointment on the dear feet of Him whom she loved. And men were indignant at this gross extravagance — to what purpose is this waste? But to Jesus it was incomparably fine. It was not the squandering of madness. To Him it was the lavishness of love. It was love, despising calculation, and giving to the very uttermost.

March 18
His Fact
by William H. G. Thomas (1861-1924) England/Wales
Excerpted from "The Fact of Christ," *Christianity is Christ*, published by
Zondervan Publishing House, Grand Rapids, Michigan in 1900

Christianity is the only religion in the world which rests on the Person of its Founder. A man can be a faithful Muslim without in the least concerning himself with the person of Mohammed. So also a man can be a true and faithful Buddhist without knowing anything whatever about Buddha. It is quite different with Christianity. Christianity is so inextricably bound up with Christ that our view of the Person of Christ involves and determines our view of Christianity.

The fundamental and ultimate idea and fact of Christianity is the Person of Christ. "What do you think of Christ?" is the crucial problem today, as it has been all through the centuries. It is a test of Christianity and of humanity's relation to Christianity. For nearly nineteen centuries attention has been concentrated on the Person of Christ both by His friends and by His foes. With a sure instinct both followers and opponents have realized the supreme importance of the Person of the Founder of Christianity. On the one hand, Jesus Christ has been the center of opposition in almost every age; on the other hand, He has been the object of worship and of the heart's devotion of all Christians. We cannot get away from this central fact; it influences our thinking; it controls our action; and it tests our entire attitude to the religion of Christ.

It is no mere question of belief in this or that doctrine of the faith; nor simply an inquiry into the authenticity of this or that book of the Bible. It is the fundamental issue. Is Jesus Christ God? Christians believe and are convinced that there is no real alternative between the acceptance of this view and the removal of Jesus Christ from the supreme place which He has occupied in the Christian Church through the centuries. Either He has been given a place to which He is entitled, or else He has been so entirely overrated that His spiritual value cannot be regarded as anything more than that of an example. Jesus Christ must either be the Object of people's faith, or else merely its Model. The Christian Church has held firmly to the former belief, and is convinced that it is the only plausible position. It is not too much to say that at this point Christianity, as it has been known through the ages, stands or falls.

A special reason for giving prominence to this subject at the present time arises through the study of comparative religion. Christianity is now being compared with other religions in ways that were not possible even a few years ago, and this comparison inevitably leads up to the question of the Person of Christ. People are asking some very pointed questions: Wherein lies the uniqueness of Christianity? What was new in it? What did Christianity bring into the world that had not appeared before? The Christian answer is Christ, the Person of Christ, the uniqueness of Christ and His work.

The controversy is therefore about facts. Christianity is a historical religion, and as it claims to rest on Christ, it necessarily follows that consideration of Christ is vital to the reality and continuance of Christianity as a historical religion. For the same reason it is impossible for it to avoid criticism and comparison with other faiths, nor are Christians in the least degree afraid of any such examination. The Person and Work of Christ can and must be tried at the bar of Reason and of History, and no Christian can do other than welcome the fullest, and most searching examination of the Person of the Founder of our religion.

March 19
His Faith – 1
by James Moffatt (1870-1944) Scotland
Excerpted from "The Faith of Jesus," *Twenty Sermons by Famous Scotch Preachers*, published by George H. Doran, New York, New York in 1924

Let us run with patience the race that is set before us; looking unto Jesus, the Author and Finisher of our faith.
Hebrews 12:1-2 (KJV)

"Let us run…looking," says the writer. A strange word! "Let us run looking." But this is really the source of all movement in life. Motivating power always depends upon the direction of the mind and heart. Faith is not drifting with the tide of current practice and opinion; it is a course directed by our sense of God, and especially by our sense of the will of God for us in Jesus Christ. "Let us run, looking unto Jesus." Why? Because Jesus ran our race. He, too, had to live by faith, as we are called to do. Our English version describes Him as "the author and finisher of our faith," but the word "our" is in italics, and what the writer meant was that Jesus is "the pioneer and perfection of faith." He gives us a lead in the matter of faith, and we are to look to Him as the great Believer. He is our leader and pioneer in this kind of life, which follows the will of God, for He began the life of faith at its very beginning and carried it through to the end. He has left us a perfect pattern of what faith is and does. Part of His divine message to us lies in the fact that He too had to exercise faith in His human life, to "learn obedience by the things that He suffered," to look up to God for direction and guidance at critical moments, and to pray for aid in temptation. Jesus is the inspiration and example of faith.

If you and I are to know anything about faith, from beginning to end, we must look to Jesus who held faith in spite of appearances and worked it out triumphantly. Whenever the pace of the Church or of the individual has slackened, whenever there has been any reduction of zeal and vigor in Christianity, it has been due to the fact that for some reason or other there has been a failure to realize the faith of Jesus and to give Him the central place in our concept of religion. Now Jesus began His life on earth in the faith that He was the well-beloved Son of the Father. He had heard God assure Him of this vocation, and He ventured to hold fast to it, in spite of everything. He thought and spoke and acted by this faith in the divine word of promise. He died rather than give it up. And the same quality of tenacity is to mark our faith, whatever discouragements we have to encounter.

There is the difficulty of delay. To wait is always one of the trials of faith. Many men and women find this period of waiting extremely irritating. And it is hard, perhaps as hard as anything in the life of faith, to hope against hope, to wait bravely for the fulfilment of God's word in face of an experience that seems to mock it. No one who has had to pass through the ordeal of waiting, with desires repressed and thwarted for a time, will ever speak lightly of it. Some people really lose their faith here before it goes any further; and many more lose something of the vitality which throbs in faith. Yet, look at Jesus. Think how He was tried along this very line. From the age of about twelve to the age of about thirty, He too had to wait. During these years of which we know nothing, He was apparently left to Himself at Nazareth. No one seemed to need Him. He must have been conscious of His destiny, and yet He was assigned the humble lot of a provincial carpenter, never known beyond His little village, watching the years pass by, and hearing no voice from Heaven summoning Him to larger work and business for the Father. We often forget these eighteen years in the life of Jesus, and what they must have meant for Him. And yet it was during these dragging years that our Lord was winning His first fight of faith, against the temptations of delay.

March 20
His Faith – 2
by James Moffatt (1870-1944) Scotland
Excerpted from "The Faith of Jesus," *Twenty Sermons by Famous Scotch Preachers*, published by George H. Doran, New York, New York in 1924

Let us run with patience the race that is set before us; looking unto Jesus, the Author and Finisher of our faith.
Hebrews 12:1-2 (KJV)

Then there is the temptation of disappointment. When the openings do come, when we start to work out the life that God sets before us, it may bring acute disappointments which test the nerve of faith. Some never get the recognition to which they thought themselves legitimately entitled. Others fail to live up to the hopes of their friends. Nothing is more common then, in the lives of many people, than to find frustrated hopes producing a spirit of resentment against God, or at any rate a spirit of apathy.

Now, Jesus knew something of this temptation also. When He was at last called forward to His mission, the nation failed to answer His appeal. At first, indeed, popularity flowed to Him. It was roses, roses all the way, thousands from every part of the country thronging to Him. Apparently He had the nation in His hands. But soon His searching message proved too much for them. The early popularity faded, until He was left with a mere handful of followers. His very life was in danger; He was suspected of heresy, denounced, and opposed on all fronts. Yet He never lost His faith in God. With unwavering confidence He clung to the will of God for the world, believing to see the goodness of God in the land of the living. Jesus, in fact, resisted the temptation to be discontented, to make our personal feelings the first thing, to brood over what we have lost. Never pity yourselves. Self-pity is the most dangerous drug to take, when disappointments come. Never let yourselves dwell on lost chances or opportunities that will not return to you.

It is a fine test of life. And the best way for us to meet these temptations to grow cynical and inactive, the surest help against the pressure of the middle part of life, is to look to Jesus who Himself passed through the ordeal in front of us. Even out of these troubles and trials God can make materials for faith. He can use them to make us more thoughtful, more humble, and more sympathetic. And as we acquire these qualities, we are advancing steadily in all that faith means for a fruitful life.

Then, towards the end, there is the difficulty of death. For, however good life may have been, however full of opportunities and inspiration, still life is short. Jesus Himself encountered the same temptation. He knew the natural shrinking from death. He had to pass through the haunting recoil from bodily collapse which many of us hate and fear. Where He went we can follow, and follow safely, as we look to Him. What we have to face here He once faced.

It never can be more difficult for us than it was for Jesus our Lord. But He believed in God, and He gathers us in our fellowship to strengthen faith. When we look at things around us, there is much to discourage faith. What we see and hear in the world is often enough to take the heart out of any belief in God or in ourselves or in human nature. There is not a word that ever fell from His lips suggesting uncertainty or doubt. We see nothing in Him that does not encourage us to believe, nothing that does not make us ashamed of being apathetic or doubting God. We catch from Him the inspiration that sends us forward with new heart and hope, motivating us to believe steadily in God and goodness, to the saving of our souls. He is here to show you what faith in a living God can do for you—the faith that overcomes the world.

March 21
His Faith - 3
by Wallace MacMullen (1862-?) USA
Excerpted from "The Captain of Our Faith," *The Captain of Our Faith*, published by Jennings and Graham, Cincinnati, Ohio in 1904

Looking unto Jesus, the Author (Captain) of our faith.
Hebrews 12:2 (KJV)

He is our Captain in matters of belief. If, like skeptical Pilate, but with a better, a more earnest spirit, our question is, "What is truth?" Christ's answer is, "I am the Truth." And that description of Himself is His claim of dominion over man's intellect. He identifies Himself with the eternal reality of things. Truth is the authority to which all loyal minds do homage. Christ by His Spirit is to rule over all the movements of man's mind. Christ in His teachings has uttered the final words beyond which, in the realms in which He chose to move, man's mind cannot go. His solemn and multiple "verily" are the foundation stones on which our beliefs must rest; the cornerstones from which our creeds must take their lines. He insisted on His listeners' acceptance of His teaching. Loyalty to Him included faith in His words. He appealed to His works as evidence of the truth of His words. The objectors to His teaching had seen His miraculous works, and if His words awaken no response in their dead hearts, if His claims are not instantly endorsed, as they should be, by their own innermost lives, He will call in the evidence of their senses. "Believe Me for the very works' sake," as if to say, "The mercy of My deeds cries aloud for a recognition of the truth of My words." But not because of their mighty power—for power may be employed for evil ends—but because of their mighty love.

That's one appeal of Christ. He bids them recognize the fact that in Him "mercy and truth are met together." Then He appealed to the testimony of His own consciousness and asserted its truth.

"Though I speak of Myself, yet My testimony is true." The Pharisees objected to His testimony concerning Himself on the accepted ground that one's witness to one's self cannot be taken as reliable. But He broke away from the teaching of that low human principle—that self-estimate is worthless, a principle which is true only because and only in the measure that ignorance or falsehood holds the measuring line—and insisted that, although He bore witness to Himself, yet His witness was true; for no ignorance darkened His perfect self-knowledge, and no deceit stained His lips. He knew Himself, and spoke truly out of His perfect knowledge.

For both of these reasons, today as then, Christ's words are to command our beliefs. His works in the world, mightier than any His Judean hearers had known—works of holy ministry, works of enlightening truth; works of subduing, transforming grace; the works of the centuries, the works of today; the works in all the world; the works in our own hearts—the works are tributes to the Word. And through them the voice of Christ speaks, "Believe Me for the works' sake. They are the signs of My rank. These trophies of My power in the fields of grace establish My rights in the fields of truth. Believe Me." And we do. Some of His words need no credentials. Our souls respond to them. Our experiences establish them.

Jesus called men to trust Him, and at the same time identified Himself with God, and so fastened man's trust to its only sure Divine anchorage. And while urging trust as a necessary force in a person's life, He was not recommending a force which was absent from His own life. He, too, walked by faith. He was perfectly human. We need not fear to insist upon that. He acknowledged dependence as we must. He trusted and was delivered as we may be. At the very opening of His ministry He adopted trust as His method for life. It is the choice of the Father's plan for His life. It is the triumph of trust.

March 22
His Father - 1
by Henry Drummond (1851-1897) Scotland
Excerpted from "Going to the Father," *The Ideal Life* published by Hodder and Stoughton, London, England in 1898

"I go to My Father."
John 14:12 (KJV)

Did you ever notice Christ's favorite words? If you have, you must have been struck by two things—their simplicity and their fewness. Some half-dozen words preserve all His theology, and these are, without exception, humble, elementary, simple monosyllables. They are such words as world, life, trust, love.

But none of these was the greatest word of Christ. His great word was new to religion. There was no word there, when He came, rich enough to carry the new truth He was bringing to humanity. So He imported into religion one of the grandest words of human language, and transfigured it, and gave it back to the world illuminated and transformed, as the watchword of the new religion. That word was Father.

The world's obligation to the Lord Jesus is that He gave us that word. We should never have thought of it; if we had, we should never have dared to say it. It is a pure revelation. Surely it is the most touching sight of the world's past to see God's only-begotten Son coming down from Heaven to try to teach the ignorant inhabitants of this poor planet to say, "Our Father."

It is that word which has gathered the great family of God together; and when we come face to face with the real, the solid, and the moving in our religion, it is to find all its complexity resolvable into this simplicity, that God, whom others call King

Eternal, Infinite Jehovah, is, after all, our Father, and we are His children.

This, after all, is religion. And to live daily in this simplicity, is to live like Christ.

It takes a great deal to succeed as a Christian—such a great deal that many do not succeed. And the great reason for the lack of success is the lack of a central word. People will copy anything rather than a principle. A relationship is always harder to follow than a fact. We study the details of Christ's actions, the point of this miracle and of that, the enveloping truth of this parable and of that, but to copy details is not to copy Christ. To live greatly like Christ is not to agonize daily over details, to make anxious comparisons with what we do and what He did, but a much more simple thing. It is to re-echo Christ's word. It is to have that calm, patient, assured spirit, which reduces life simply to this—a going to the Father.

Not one person in a hundred, probably, has a central word in their Christian life; and the consequence is this, that there is probably nothing in the world so disorderly and careless as personal spiritual experience. Now the thing which steadied Christ's life was the thought that He was going to His Father. This one thing gave it unity, and harmony, and success. During His whole life He never forgot His Word for a moment. There is no sermon of His where it does not occur; there is no prayer, however brief, where it is missed. In that first memorable sentence of His, which breaks the solemn spell of history and makes one word resound through thirty silent years, the one word is this; and all through the after years of toil and travail "the Great Name" was always hovering on His lips, or bursting out of His heart. In its beginning and in its end, from the early time when He spoke of His Father's business until He finished the work that was given Him to do, His life, stripped of all circumstance, was simply this, "I go to My Father."

March 23
His Father – 2
by James A. Robertson (1803-1860) Scotland
Excerpted from "The Father of Jesus," *United Free Church Sermons*, published by Thomson & Cowan, Glasgow, Scotland in 1924

God, even the Father of our Lord Jesus Christ.
Romans 15:6 (KJV)

"The Father of Jesus—God?" we are still inclined to ask each other with an old, half-doubting, questioning look upon our faces as we hear the words again. Perhaps some of you are repeating to yourselves the answer to a question which you learned long ago at school: "There are three Persons in the Godhead, the Father, the Son, and the Holy Ghost, and these three are one God, the same in substance, equal in power and glory." And you may be musing about the old perplexity, how there can be three in one, without confusing the Persons, or dividing the substance. Yes, even though these ideas are not consciously in our minds at all, we have been unable to carry ourselves completely back to Galilee, and forget these hard and difficult notions that have somehow crept into our Christian creed out of the ancient philosophies that lie between us and Christ. But if you were to ask those questions of this fisherman disciple who has just told you in a whisper throbbing with awe that God was the Father of Jesus, he would stare at you and wonder whether or not you were insane. He would say to you, "I haven't the faintest notion what you mean. I am just a simple, uneducated man telling you in the plainest language what He has made me feel about Him. Come with me and listen to Him awhile." And you draw near and listen.

Yes, He is talking about Someone, very reverently and yet in the most intimate and familiar way. A breath blows out of the open skies and fans your cheek—a breath from the Unseen. Gentle and pure like the trembling light from a pulsing star, but convinced that he was sent; sensitive, yet all his sensitiveness transformed into divine strength—he seems to be speaking about Someone who is beside him, all about him—lending a glory to the flower at his feet; a joy to the wheeling flight of the birds overhead; a wave of life beating down through the sunshine that sweeps along the hillside; falling through the rain on the springing corn in the valley; and whispering in his heart. Someone all-great, all-knowing, without whom not a sparrow falls, who sees in secret, who can be spoken to anywhere, and best of all, alone. And listen! he calls Him the Heavenly Father, my Father—and yours. And as you listen God Himself seems to have drawn near.

But we find more than that to calm our hearts in this daring name, for God as the Father of our Lord Jesus Christ, not merely because Jesus was so intimate with Him, but because Jesus was so satisfied with Him. All the questions of your heart and mind have perhaps not been completely laid to rest by contact with that awesome intimacy. Humbly and gladly I confess that there is the last resting place for all the fiercest questioning of my heart. God—the God with whom Jesus was so intimate, the God with whom Jesus was so satisfied—He must be a Being like Jesus, related to Jesus, Father of Jesus. Nothing in all the record of the human race gleams with such splendor as this life, this holiness, this love, this death of Jesus. It is the fairest flower, the crowning glory of Creation. The great unseen Spirit that moves behind all Creation's laws—that made them, and lo! they are—cannot be less noble than His own highest achievement in this world of time. The Fountain of Life must be of essentially the same nature as the noblest and purest life that ever surged up on to the earth from its perennial spring. It would be absurd to think otherwise. I am content, with all my sin and shame and sorrow and doubt, to look upon the face of Christ, radiant with forgiving love as it shines from the cross.

March 24
His Feelings
by James Stalker (1848-1927) Scotland
Excerpted from "Christ As a Man of Feeling," *Imago Christi: The Example of Jesus Christ*, published by A. C. Armstrong & Son, New York, New York in 1890

"I always do the things that please Him."
John 8:29 (KJV)

Jesus was as refined and delicate in feeling as He was wise in speech and mighty in act; and the motives of His conduct are often incomprehensible except to those who possess in some degree the same feelings as He had. He taught humankind to feel finely, and ever since He was in the world there have been increasing numbers who have learned from Him about childhood and woman, poverty and service, and many other subjects, with sentiments totally different from those with which they were regarded before His advent.

The notices in the Gospels of the impressions made on His feelings by different situations in which He was placed are extraordinarily numerous; but a single incident — the raising of the daughter of Jairus — in which the feelings of His heart came conspicuously into view will serve as a sufficient clue. His compassion was illustrated in this incident. It was the case of a man whose only daughter was lying at the point of death; and he begged Jesus greatly for her, says Mark. The heart of Jesus could not but answer such an appeal. In a similar instance — that of a woman with an only son, the widow of Nain — it is said that when the Lord saw her following behind the body, He had compassion on her and said to her, "Weep not." He not only gave the required help in such cases, but gave it with an amount of sympathy which doubled its value. Thus He not only raised Lazarus, but wept with his sisters. All His healing work cost Him feeling.

A second feeling which Jesus showed in this incident was sensitiveness. At Jairus' request He went to the house where the dying girl was; but on the way a messenger met them, who told the poor father that all was over, and that he need not trouble the Master any further. Whereupon, without waiting to be appealed to, Jesus turned to him and said, "Do not be afraid; only believe." In this we might see a new instance of His compassion; but it also reveals something else: Jesus was extremely sensitive to the sentiments of trust or distrust with which He was regarded. If any generosity of belief was shown towards Him, His heart filled with gladness, and He acknowledged His gratification without hesitation.

A third type of feeling which He evidenced on this occasion was indignation. When He reached the house, not only was the child dead, but the place had been taken over by mourners who undertook the ghastly ceremony of mourning. Jesus burned with indignation against it all and poured His feelings out in denunciation against the parties and personalities of the time.

A fourth mode of feeling characteristic of Jesus which was illustrated on this occasion was delicacy. He took her by the hand before pronouncing the resurrection words; for He did not wish her to be startled when she woke, but to feel the support of a sympathetic presence. Many a one in an hour of agitation or when coming out of unconsciousness has felt how it steadies and strengthens to be held by a firm hand and to look into a calm face.

The last kind of feeling exhibited by our Lord on this occasion was modesty. After the miracle was performed, "He charged them strongly that no one should know it."

By taking a wider sweep we might have accumulated more illustrations. But the clue, once seized, can be easily followed in the Gospels, where the notices of how Jesus felt in the different situations in which He was placed are far more numerous than many would believe.

March 25
His Fellowship
by Paton J. Gloag (1823-1906) Scotland
"Fellowship of Christ's Sufferings," *Modern Scottish Pulpit: Sermons by Ministers of Various Denominations, First Series*, published by New York, New York in 1880

That I may know Him, and the power of His resurrection, and the fellowship of His sufferings, being made conformable unto His death.
Philippians 3:10 (KJV)

Believers are partakers with Christ in those sufferings which arise from persecution for righteousness' sake. It is evident that it is primarily to these sufferings that Paul alludes here and in other portions of his epistles. "That I may know the fellowship of His sufferings, being made conformable unto His death"; thus he expresses his readiness to endure the same persecutions which Christ endured, and, like Him, to end his life on the cross. And again, in this same epistle, he says: "Unto you it is given, on behalf of Christ, not only to believe, but also to suffer for His sake." And Peter calls on his converts to "rejoice" in persecution, inasmuch as they "are partakers of Christ's sufferings."

Paul had his wish largely gratified. He partook in full measure of the sufferings of Christ; he drank deeply of the Savior's cup. "Even unto this present hour," he writes, "we both hunger, and thirst, and are naked, and are buffeted, and have no certain dwelling place; being reviled, we bless; being persecuted, we suffer it; being defamed, we plead; we are made as the filth of the world, and are the offscourings of all things unto this day." I believe that if a man maintains a very high standard of religion; if he lives an exalted, godly life in Christ Jesus; if he condemns the world by the holiness of his conduct, he will meet with persecution in the way of petty annoyances, designed misconceptions, and coldness of affection. The world is still the same in its aversion to the children of God;

believers must still be conformed to the sufferings of Christ.

Believers are partakers with Christ in those sufferings which arise from sympathy with the distressed. These also constituted a great part of the sufferings of Christ. He felt keenly for human woe; every distress which He witnessed impressed itself, like a photographic picture, upon His soul; every cry of anguish which He heard was re-echoed from the depths of His Spirit; and perhaps, apart from His last sufferings, there is no scene of His life so affecting, and none that was the cause of such anguish unto Him as when, with weeping eyes and a breaking heart, He pronounced the doom of Jerusalem; it was infinite compassion weeping over the lost.

Believers are partakers with Christ in those sufferings which arise from grief for sin. Much of the sorrow of Christ must have been caused by His unavoidable interaction with the wicked. When infinite purity comes in contact with wickedness, feelings of sorrow and moral indignation must be the result. How distressing must it have been, then, to the pure mind of Jesus, to hear the dreadful words which were uttered, to see the wicked actions which men did, to think also on the end to which all this wickedness inevitably led—to see God dishonored and man ruined. And so it is with all true believers. The very sight of wickedness must be the cause of sorrow to them.

Believers are partakers with Christ in all those sufferings which arise from spiritual distress. Christ knew what spiritual distress was, as in the agony of Gethsemane, when He offered up strong crying and tears unto Him who was able to save Him from death; and on the cross of Calvary, when He complained of spiritual desertion. There is most certainly a mystery hanging over these sufferings of our Lord, which we cannot penetrate. Believers have a blessed consideration, knowing they have a Savior who can sympathize with them in their sorrows, that they have fellowship with Christ in these sufferings.

March 26
His Fires
by Walter Benwell Hinson (1860-1826) England/USA
Excerpted from "God the Consuming Fire," *A Grain of Wheat and Other Sermons*, published by The Bible Institute Colportage Association, Chicago, Illinois in 1922

God is a consuming fire.
Hebrews 12:29 (KJV)

The great curse of this year of our Lord is the lost sense of God. Most of us are atheists in practice all the time, and God is not in all our thoughts; many of us are atheists in practice most of the time; and all of us are atheists in practice some of the time. And there lie great stretches of time in your life and mine when consciousness of God is as foreign to us as roses to the Sahara Desert. There are great areas of our experience that are absolutely godless, so far as our recognition of the Lord is concerned.

The practice of the presence of God would revolutionize the life we are living. It would alter the very way in which we stand, if we consciously remember that we were standing in the presence of God. It would affect our conversation, and a carefulness would characterize our speech that is now absent, if we knew that God is the unseen listener to every word. And the things we do that we should leave undone, and the undone things that would be performed if we came into the realization of the Lord's continuous presence, are simply many. And we would spend our money differently, and we would use our time differently, and all our estimates of values would undergo a change, if we definitely came into the realization that we are ever in the great Taskmaster's eye.

But how our amazement would grow as we came into the understanding of the poor and the Godless way in which we do live. I need no additional proof of the truthfulness of what I assert than your strained attention at this moment. You know I am voicing your experience; I am uttering your thought; I am expressing your consciousness. If there is a prayer that comes to my tongue at this solemn moment it is the prayer of Isaiah, "Oh that You would rend the heavens, and come down," to disturb us out of our indifference, and consume the dross that has accumulated with the gold, and illumine us as to the right kind of life to live, and to consume among us the things that ought no longer to possess existence.

How that consciousness would change the life of each one of us; for if we realized that the flaming chariots and horses of God surround us, as they surrounded Elisha in the olden time when the Lord opened the eyes of the prophet's servant to see what were the real defenses of Israel, we should walk grandly, and talk like kings, and become true independents who realize that no arrow can hit until the God of covenanting grace sees fit; and we should not be talking then about being "pretty well, under the circumstances," but we should talk about being all right, because we are above the circumstances. We should come into the consciousness that our God is the God of fire that Elijah the Tishbite possessed, when he stood in the presence of a wicked king and a backslidden nation and idolatrous priests and dared make his appeal that was at the same time his challenge: "The God who answers by fire, let Him be the God." Oh, I tell you, the crying need of the times is the consuming fire of God. The lost consciousness of sin is largely to blame for this tidal wave of crime that is rolling over the whole world. We have lost our consciousness of sin. Do you know why they have no use for my Savior's cross? They have lost consciousness of the sin which alone requires it.

God's understanding of sin is that it is so colossal, only the death of His own Son can atone for it.

March 27
His Fleeing
by Arthur Brooks (1845-1895) USA
Excerpted from "Christ's Flight Into Egypt," *The Life of Christ in the World*, published by Thomas Whittaker, New York, New York in 1887

After the wise men were gone, an angel of the Lord appeared to Joseph in a dream. "Get up! Flee to Egypt with the Child and His mother," the angel said. "Stay there until I tell you to return, because Herod is going to search for the Child to kill Him."
Matthew 2:13 (NLTSE)

The flight into Egypt is not a portion of Christ's life that we mention frequently, or perhaps even think of very often. It comes as an uncomfortably dark incident just after the glories of Christmas and Epiphany, and it seems to us as if it were not necessary that the element of persecution in Christ's life should show itself so soon; but we know that there must have been a purpose in it, for nothing in that wonderful life took place by accident. It must have been hard for Joseph to hear such a message just after the adoration of the shepherds and the visit of the Magi had made him feel the greatness of the Child who was under his care and protection. But he had to obey the Lord, he had to go into Egypt; and he arose and did it without murmuring. All the past glories only convinced him more fully that it was his duty to follow God's leading, and to go down into Egypt.

He was fleeing from His own people, where He should have been joyfully welcomed as the fulfilment of the nation's hopes. A cruel king, a degraded priesthood, a nation given up to formalism, were all that He could find to receive Him. The people were religious, but their religion was narrow, intolerant, and petty. It never asked after God; it was of the earth, earthy: and there was no chance for Jesus Christ to get a foothold in such a reaction as that. It is a warning to our religious thoughts, to us who live in the light of religious privilege and knowledge. Keep religion pure, keep it high and lofty and spiritual. Never be satisfied with any other idea of it. Be ready to receive God in it, and let it be a proper place for God to dwell in. It should be a promised land, a land of rest to the weary, and of welcome to the Messiah; it should have but one idea—to make men know God. No ecclesiastical correctness, no spirit of philanthropy, no formal purity, no doctrinal rigor, can take the place of that. Christ may be driven from us, if that is all He finds; or, at best, He will be the Master only of a small band of humble followers. Strangers shall replace those who should know Him; "they shall come from the east, and from the west, and from the north, and from the south, and shall sit down in the Kingdom of God," and the children of the Kingdom be cast out. Use privileges and opportunities rightly; that is a lesson running all through the history of Christ and His relation to Israel.

After the death of Herod, Jesus returned from Egypt. But it was not to go back to Bethlehem. He turns aside to Nazareth, a place which, for some reason, was looked upon contemptuously, and which gave to Jesus His name of the Nazarene. Matthew says that this also was a fulfilment of prophecy, and was meant to signify the humility and lowliness of character which the Savior of the world was to bear. Bethlehem was the birthplace of David, and sacred memories clustered around it. Prophecy had designated it as the birthplace of the Messiah; and to be born there was, of itself, evidence in favor of one claiming to be the Christ. And yet Jesus never referred to that fact of His nativity in the city of David; He never tried to free Himself from the stain of being a Nazarene. Most willingly, through all His life, He carried that mark of humility, which was a part of the flight into Egypt. If it was humiliating to go to Egypt after all the glories of the nativity and Epiphany, it was a part of the same humiliation that He should be known all His life as coming from Nazareth, and not from Bethlehem.

March 28
His Forerunner
by Nehemiah Adams (1806-1878) USA

Excerpted from "John the Baptist," *The Friends of Christ*, published by T. R. Marvin and S. K. Whipple & Co., Boston, Massachusetts in 1853

"I tell you the truth, of all who have ever lived, none is greater than John the Baptist. Yet even the least person in the Kingdom of Heaven is greater than he is!"
Matthew 11:11 (NLTSE)

What a testimony was this for a man to receive from the Savior of the world! He is the Judge of character, himself the perfect Man. They who love and serve Him have this assurance, that He appreciates and loves everything in them which is praiseworthy. There is no such honor and happiness as to have the approval and commendation of Jesus Christ.

As we read this testimony of Christ respecting John, we naturally think of Abraham, and Moses, and Samuel, and David, and Solomon, and Elijah, and Isaiah, seven men who, in their respective classes of character and talent, have no equals in history. But of them, and of all others up to that time, the Savior says there had not risen a greater than John the Baptist. Not merely was he the greatest of prophets, as he certainly was, in being so long predicted and expected; in being the herald of Christ; and in his remarkable knowledge of the Savior, as expressed in his testimony concerning Him; but Christ elevates him above all who ever lived.

John the Baptist might not, perhaps, write such lyrics as David, or utter such strains of finished eloquence as Isaiah, or possess the quick wisdom of Solomon; but, taking him altogether, the Savior says he had never had his superior among men. For although Luke also represents Christ as speaking of John as the greatest prophet, we must believe that there were intrinsic elements in his character which made him so, in addition to the outward circumstances of his mission. As a man, not merely as a prophet, no one had been greater than he.

There, in those wilds, from the commencement of his youth until near the age of thirty, his parents, who were well advanced in years before he was born, being, in all probability, dead, he lived apart from the busy paths of people, not, perhaps, as a hermit, for there were scattered dwellings in that wilderness. He was, however, familiar with the rough face of Nature, in her tangled thickets, dark, pathless woods, overhanging cliffs, swollen streams, diversified all, with spring-tide beauty, and summer's glory, and autumn's melancholy, and winter's rage; his courage nurtured by darkness and storms, perhaps by conflicts with wild beasts, and by the solemn awe with which solitude and stillness sometimes oppresses even the bravest spirit.

Three things of great importance in his future work were secured by this solitary life. He was delivered from the superstitions and corrupting influence of the ecclesiastical rulers, and the sad degeneracy of the times. He had the best opportunities for religious improvement. His sudden appearance from the desert, with all the marks and influences of an austere life, gave him a power over the popular mind, which he could not have had if he had risen up among those who had been connected with him from childhood. John's true greatness is also seen in his unaffected superiority to the flatteries and frowns of men. The true greatness of John appeared, in a special manner, in his humility. The instruction which the character and history of John the Baptist is well suited to impart is this: It is the highest honor and privilege to be most intimately identified with the Savior of the world. This blessed friend and servant of God was prepared to die; and it was well that he was, for but a very few minutes, probably, intervened between the entrance of the executioner to his cell and the appearance of the ransomed spirit before God.

March 29
His Forgiveness
by David James Burrell (1844-1926) USA
Excerpted from "The Grace of Forgiveness," *The Evolution of a Christian*, published by American Tract Society, New York, New York in 1906

Then Peter came to Jesus and asked, "Lord, how many times shall I forgive my brother when he sins against me?"
Matthew 18:21 (NIV)

All the world loves Peter; brave, impulsive, blundering Peter; the apostle of the great heart, open hand, hot temper, and high ambition. But there were times when Peter showed himself in most unlovely ways. In some respects he was a very little man.

And at this moment it was so. He had been greatly stirred up by some things that Jesus had been saying about the proper way of dealing with unruly church members. In the Code of Discipline, as laid down by the Master, there were four steps:

- The first was, "If another believer sins against you, go privately and point out the offense. If the other person listens and confesses it, you have won that person back."
- If that failed, then, "take one or two others with you and go back again, so that everything you say may be confirmed by two or three witnesses."
- In case the offender was still unyielding, "take your case to the church" that that person may be formally cited for trial.
- And should this also prove unsuccessful, "treat that person as a pagan or a corrupt tax collector," that is, withdraw your fellowship from them.

Now, Peter had a personal interest in this matter, owing to certain grudges of his own. A self-willed, self-confident, self-opinionated person is sure to provoke animosities, and equally sure to resent criticism as a personal affront. It was, doubtlessly, this cherished sense of wrong which moved Peter to inquire, "Lord, how often should I forgive someone who sins against me? Seven times?" The teaching of the Rabbinical writings was, "If a person offends you once and asks pardon, forgive them; if twice, forgive them; if three times, forgive them; and that ends it." We may assume, therefore, that Peter, in suggesting seven times, supposed himself to be taking a most magnanimous view of the matter. But Jesus said, "Not until seven times, but until seventy times seven"; by which He meant that our spirit of forgiveness must know no limit at all.

This grace is extended to all; as it is written, "Everyone that thirsts, come to the waters; and the one who has no money, let them come and drink"; and again, "The one who comes unto Me I will not cast out." Will not? Not if they are a thief or a murderer? No, if only they "come unto Me." Heaven is full of such flagrant sinners saved by grace. Christ is able, and as willing as He is able, to save "unto the uttermost" all who come unto Him.

And the gracious pardon is complete; that is, it covers the whole record of the misspent life. The sins of the sinner are blotted out, paid, sunk into the depths of an unfathomable sea, cast behind God's back, so that He remembers them no more.

Is there no condition attached to this offer of grace? One only, the same condition which is attached to every gift; to wit, that it shall be accepted. Faith is the hand stretched forth to receive it. "The one who believes shall be saved," that is, their debts are eliminated; "and the one who believes not" is still indebted to the law; therefore "the wrath of God abides on them."

God is a great forgiver! "There's a wideness in His mercy like the wideness of the sea."

March 30
His Foundation
by Walter Benwell Hinson (1860-1826) England/USA
Excerpted from "Your Building," *A Grain of Wheat and Other Sermons*, published by The Bible Institute Colportage Association, Chicago, Illinois in 1922

For no one can lay any foundation other than the one already laid, which is Jesus Christ. If any man builds on this foundation using gold, silver, costly stones, wood, hay or straw, his work will be shown for what it is, because the Day will bring it to light. It will be revealed with fire, and the fire will test the quality of each man's work. If what he has built survives, he will receive his reward. If it is burned up,
he will suffer loss; he himself will be saved,
but only as one escaping through the flames.
1 Corinthians 3:11-15 (NIV)

The foundation is one—Jesus Christ. No preacher has to lay that in the sense of originating it. He needs only to state it. Jesus Christ is the foundation. Now I would not take Paul's word for it with half the enthusiasm that I do take it were it not that back of Paul stands Jesus. For Jesus says, "I am the foundation." Oh, I have often thought how, after He had spoken of many things in His Sermon on the Mount, He came to the close, and, in a way that must embarrass Unitarianism, He distinctly said, "Whosoever hears My words and does them, is like a man building his house on the rock, and the rain may descend, the wind blow, and the rivers rush, but that house will stand." Why? Because it is on the rock. And "Whosoever hears these sayings of Mine and does not do them, is like a man building his house on the sand, and when the rain and wind and river work their will on that house, it is gone." Why? Because it was a poor house? No, because it was built on sand!

Now, what is sand? According to Jesus, it is everything in the world except His Word. That is what He says and I never defend Jesus, I only quote Him. He says, "A house cannot fall that is built on Me." And with equal clearness He says, "A house cannot stand that is not built on Me." In what I sometimes think is the deepest thing that ever left my Lord's lips He further emphasizes this fact, that He is the foundation. For He says, "He that believes on the Son has life"—and that is consoling to those who do believe. But what about all others? "He that believes not the Son shall not see life, but the wrath of God abides on him"—a most terrific statement. Sharper than a two-edged sword it is, going into the heart and the very marrow of the bone as it distinctly asserts that the believer in Christ alone has life, and that any other, whatever his characteristics, if he does not believe in Jesus has not the life that emanates from the Son of God. John so understood Jesus, for in his epistle he said, "He that has the Son has life; and he that has not the Son shall not see life"—an echo, you see, of the utterance of Jesus Christ.

Now the last thing I shall say of that parable is this: There is an eternal difference in believers, and that is brought about by the life those believers lived after they got up on the foundation. An eternal difference, for this parable says of a man who on the good foundation has built hay, wood, and stubble—let me give you the exact words—"he shall suffer loss." Let us dare to look that in the face for a minute. He shall suffer—of course he will suffer, for there are awards or rewards, in Heaven, and they are conditioned on service rendered below. And of the saved, some shall receive an abundant entrance, and some shall be saved as by fire—merely saved. Some shall suffer loss, and some shall receive a reward; and that is absolutely righteous.

So you had better be careful, for God is soon going to let loose the fire, and as it comes moving along, the house of hay, wood, and stubble will be lost and forever gone, and the spiritual alone remains, for "The world passes away, but he that does the will of God abides forever."

March 31
His Frankness
by William Robertson Nicoll (1851-1923) Scotland
Excerpted from "The Frankness of Jesus Christ," *The Lamp of Sacrifice*, published by Eaton and Mains, New York, New York in 1906

"If it were not so, I would have told you."
John 14:2 (NIV)

If I am right, this passage expresses the perfect and lifelong frankness of Christ. He was absolutely truthful and open. He never sought to win followers by telling them that the way was broad and easy, and the triumph early and visible. From the very beginning of His ministry He warned His disciples that the way was difficult and that the gate was narrow. He urged those who thought of joining His cause to count the cost, to count it as a king counts it before he begins war, or as a builder counts it before he begins a building which may be beyond his resources. He tells them that they are not to rush hastily into the Christian life before assuring themselves how much that life means, and how fatal it is to estimate its sacrifice too cheaply. We are not to embark recklessly on a course in which, once begun, we must persevere at any cost. Not mere impetuosity, but impulse guided by reason is to move us. Nor are we to hide any peril of the way from those who seek to join us.

Let me recall a few of Christ's words, words which reveal that frankness of truth wherein we put our trust. At the very beginning of His career He said: "Blessed are you, when men shall insult you, and persecute you, and shall say all manner of evil against you falsely, for My sake." He warned one who would follow Him of the hazards he was running, "Foxes have holes, and the birds of the air have nests; but the Son of Man has nowhere to lay His head." He told the children of the bride chamber that the days of mourning would come when the bridegroom was taken away from them. He said that He came to send a sword through the closest and dearest earthly ties. His disciples saw Him pass that sword through His own relationships. "Who is My mother or My brothers and sisters? Whosoever shall do the will of God, the same is My brother, and My sister, and mother." He declared that His disciples would be hated by all people for His name's sake. He rejected, to the marvel of His disciples, those who seemed to promise best, those who might have brought to the little company worldly influence and wealth.

He told them, when the time came, that He would soon perish in Jerusalem. He was to suffer many things of the elders and chief priests and scribes, and be killed. They thought that His Kingdom was to come in a crash of splendid triumph; but it was not so. They dreamed that when that Kingdom came they would sit near Him on His throne; but He warned them that the exaltation could not be, unless they drank of His cup and were baptized with His baptism of fire. His destiny was the cross, and they also had to be cross-bearers in His procession. One by one down went tower and temple, all the earthly city of their thoughts and hopes. But the heavenly hope which was in their minds also, that survived. The new Jerusalem was no dream. If it had been, He would have told them, as He had told them in unwelcome and darkening words many a time, that their hopes were vain, that their realization could never be. Now at least and at last they were right. "In My Father's house are many mansions: I go to prepare a place for you."

It is in His love that we are to find our happiness, not in anything apart from His love. What He gives is precious as the gift of love, and we may trust Him, trust Him even when He does not speak. Do not ask for texts for everything. There are those who cannot believe the Father of the spirits of all flesh unless He is bound down by black and white. But let us have faith in the heart of things. Trust Christ in His promises, trust Him in His silences. Golden is the speech of Christ, golden also is His silence.

April 1
His Freedom
by James Boardman Hawthorne (1837-1910) USA
Excerpted from "Spiritual Freedom," *An Unshaken Trust and Other Sermons*, published by American Baptist Publication Society, Philadelphia, Pennsylvania in 1899

"Then you will know the truth, and the truth will set you free." They answered Him, "We are Abraham's descendants and have never been slaves to anyone. How can You say that we shall be set free?" Jesus replied, "I tell you the truth, everyone who sins is a slave to sin."
John 8:32-34 (NIV)

Our Lord was speaking of spiritual bondage and freedom when he said, "The truth shall make you free"; but the Jews were too carnalized to perceive His meaning. They supposed that His words had reference to political bondage, and they quickly resented the insinuation that they were then, or ever had been, politically enslaved. They said, "We are Abraham's children, and were never in bondage to any man." They were blind to the facts of their temporal condition and history.

Truth is essential to salvation. Men must have right understanding of God. Belief in an impersonal, pantheistic deity, will not lift the sinful soul out of its degradation and bondage. Men who believe that God is properly represented by that pagan image in the British Museum, which has twelve hands, and in each hand an instrument of torture, will never abhor vice and love virtue. Not until a man sees the personality, fatherhood, holiness, love, and mercy of God, revealed in the person of the Man Christ Jesus, can he have any desire to obey and honor God. But the truth of God, to be effective, must be applied to the heart and conscience by the Holy Spirit. The truth is the sword, and the Spirit is the power that wields it.

Jesus Christ said, "If I be lifted up, I will draw all men unto Me." He means not literally every man in the world, but men of every class and condition. The lifting up of Christ is our work; the drawing is the work of God's Spirit. Both are indispensable. If Christ is not lifted up by the preaching of the gospel to lost men, the Holy Spirit will not draw them, and without His drawing power the lifting up will be in vain. We cannot overestimate the quickening, subduing, and transforming power of gospel truth, when it is applied to the conscience by the Holy Spirit. When I look about me in this depraved world, I see some types of moral servitude which men call hopeless. I see the miser hugging his gold with an affection that is absolutely blind and stupid. I see the drunkard and on his bloated face all the hideous signs of vice are stamped. I see the harlot, lost to virtue and dead to shame, defying alike the scorn of men and the frown of God. I see the felon whose feet have slipped in human gore, and on whose face the darkest histories are written. Tomorrow he will ascend the scaffold and die a felon's death; and yet there is no tear in his eye, nor remorse in his heart. Do you tell me that for such there is no redemption? If you do, you limit the power of God's truth and need a better faith.

"If the Son, therefore, shall make you free, you shall be free indeed." In the light of God's truth, have you seen and felt your guilt and folly, and with true sorrow of heart lifted your eyes to Him who said, "Look unto Me, and be saved all the ends of the earth"? Do you grasp with appropriating faith, the blessed truth that "the blood of Jesus Christ His Son cleanses us from all sin"? Is there a principle of life within you which compels you in the path of obedience to God, and that empowers you to say, "Get behind Me, Satan"? With confidence and joy do you look forward to the day when death shall be swallowed up in victory, and when you shall be caught up in the air to meet your glorified Lord and Redeemer? If to these questions you can answer yes, I pronounce you free. You know the truth, and the truth has made you free. You are in God's keeping, and the gates of hell shall not prevail against you.

April 2
His Friends
by Nehemiah Adams (1806-1878) USA
Excerpted from "Mary and Martha," *The Friends of Christ*, published by
T. R. Marvin and S. K. Whipple & Co., Boston, Massachusetts in 1853

As Jesus and the disciples continued on their way to Jerusalem, they came to a certain village where a woman named Martha welcomed Him into her home. Her sister, Mary, sat at the Lord's feet, listening to what He taught.
Luke 10:38-39 (NLTSE)

The characters of these two friends of Christ have always been deeply interesting to the readers of the New Testament. They are mentioned together in three places by the writers of the Gospels. The first is in the chapter of which the text is a part.

We may infer that Martha was a woman who took great pains with everything she did, and made much of every duty, and perhaps of every trouble; being of an anxious disposition, and yet a woman of great energy, of stirring habits, thorough, and ambitious to have everything done in the best manner. Not so with Mary. It was an inestimable blessing, in her view, to have the Savior under her roof. She saw that He was neither famished nor weary; and so, instead of occupying herself with the thought of entertainment, she took that opportunity to satisfy the wants of her soul, which hungered and thirsted after righteousness. Now she had found One who could resolve all her difficulties in religion, lead her to an established hope, satisfy her desire to know more of God and spiritual things, and comfort her with the consolations of religion.

But Martha, from the time that He came into the house, was encumbered with her plans and labors to serve Him as a guest.

And Jesus answered, and said unto her, "Martha, Martha, you are careful and troubled about many things."

Here we must understand Christ as referring to her general character and disposition. The idea, suggested even by some good men, that Christ meant to say that Martha was unduly anxious to provide many things for their entertainment, and that only one article of food was really needful, is, in the language of another good man and able critic, almost "unpardonable." The Savior's concluding remark about Mary shows that He refers to the general disposition and choice. He says to Martha, twice repeating her name, for emphasis, "You are careful and troubled about many things." Everything excites in you an anxious, troubled mind. You magnify everything which you have to do, by disproportionate concern; and by being wholly absorbed in domestic cares and labors, are really losing sight of that one great thing, which alone is of real importance. The Savior then approved of Mary's disposition, as of one who had placed things in their true light, and had chosen the good part which should never be taken away from her.

The characters of these friends of Christ suggest two thoughts: There may be sin in being very busy. And religion is the only thing which we cannot lose. It is not enough for us, it will not satisfy Christ, nor be for our justification in the great day, that we were constantly at work. Do you work merely to live, or do you live for man's chief end, to glorify God and enjoy Him forever? If not, the Savior reproves you; though you were doing all this for His bodily comfort, He reproves you; and surely, then, if it is for yourselves and families, He reproves you; and sets in contrast before you the example of one who has a higher aim, a nobler spirit, an enduring portion. Thus far we see these two sisters representing two great classes, the one, losing sight of the one thing needed, by inordinate occupation with the duties and cares of life, and the other, seeking first the Kingdom of God and His righteousness.

April 3
His Friendship
by John Henry Jowett (1863-1923) England
Excerpted from "The Friends of Jesus," *Things That Matter Most*, published by Fleming H. Revell Company, New York, New York in 1913

I suppose that the greatest title ever conferred upon anyone was the one used by Jesus when He addressed His disciples as "My friends." Compared with this all other titles and nobilities are cheap and artificial. No other honor will ever come our way which for a moment can be compared with this.

Let us think a little while upon some of the characteristics of this great friendship; upon some of the distinctive signs of the friends of the Lord. First of all, then, this friendship is characterized by openness of disposition. Some lives are close and closed, and they appear to be almost incapable of friendship. You can never get beyond their doorstep. Their doors are shut, their windows are closed, their blinds are drawn. However long you know them they never let you know anything. Other lives are open to your approach, they open as a flower opens to the gentle siege of the sunshine. These are the people who are capable of friendship. One door after another opens out in the treasury of their soul. You are taken first into the realm of thought, then into the realm of desire and feeling, and then into the innermost room of prayer and praise. Concerning such a soul we say, "I know him through and through." And so it is with the friends of Christ. There is perfect openness between the soul and the Lord. There is openness on the side of the Master. He hides nothing we need to know. "I have set before you an open door." All things that I have heard of My Father I have made known unto you." "He shall take of Mine and show it unto you." And there must be a similar openness on the side of man. "If any man open the door I will come in and eat with him." There must be no reserve, no sheltered secrets, no private chamber where questionable purpose is hidden. The Lord must have the run of the house. He must know all. There must be perfect openness of disposition.

And, secondly, this friendship is distinguished by a responsive sympathy. There must not only be open doors between two friends, there must be sympathetic fellowship. It was asked by a prophet long ago concerning man and his God, "Can two walk together except they be agreed?" If two people walk together they must agree at any rate on two things: They must have a common aim, and they must have a common pace. And the friends of Christ who seek to walk with Him must share His aim, His ends, His goals. They must also keep step with Him and not move either before or behind. We mar the friendship by sudden haste, and we bruise it by destructive delay. And therefore I say that this high friendship demands a sensitive and responsive sympathy. There must be fellowship in avoidances, there must be fellowship in participations. There must be the same loves and the same hatreds. There must be the same fundamental moral tastes. We must agree on what is bitter, and we must agree on what is sweet. Friendship with the Lord aspires after that wonderful communion which the Master Himself described when He said, "I and My Father are one."

I have one bit of counsel to offer to those who are seeking to be the friends of the Lord. Keep your friendship with the Lord in good repair. There is a German proverb which says that "Friendship is a plant that we must water often." It must not be allowed to take its chance. Human friendships have to be tended, for there is no fair thing in the world which can thrive in an atmosphere of neglect. And therefore we must carefully attend to our friendship with the Lord. His friendship transforms every road. Every road unveils spiritual wonders when He walks with us, and blessings abound on every side. The very consciousness of His presence produces a peace which is itself the medium of discernment, and we are able, on the most ordinary road, to know some of "the things that God has prepared for them that love Him."

April 4
His Fulfillment
by Clarence E. Macartney (1879-1957) USA

Excerpted from "Did Christ Fulfil Prophecy?" *Twelve Great Questions About Christ*, published by Fleming H. Revell Company, New York, New York in 1923

And beginning with Moses and all the prophets, He explained to them what was said in all the Scriptures concerning Himself.
Luke 24:27 (NIV)

We are now to consider just one of the proofs of the Christian religion, the fulfilment by Jesus Christ of the ancient prophecies. This is an argument which appeals with equal power to believers and unbelievers. It is the one great evidence to which the Bible itself points. It is the argument of Christ about Himself. It is the one great argument of the apostles for the authority of Jesus Christ. This great evidence is peculiar to Christianity. No other religion risks an appeal to the fulfilment of prophecy. Christianity accepts this greatest of tests. If some centuries before Christ someone had uttered predictions of the coming of one like unto Christ, and these predictions had been fulfilled, that, in itself, would be of infinite importance. But instead of one man at one time in history uttering a prediction which has been fulfilled, we have many predictions uttered by many different men through many hundreds of years, and all at last converging in Jesus Christ. A whole people announce Him and subsist during four thousand years in order to render as a body testimony of the assurances which they have of Him, and from which they can be turned by no threats and no persecutions. "The greatest of the proofs of Jesus Christ are the prophecies. They are also what God has most provided for, for the event which has fulfilled them is a miracle which has subsisted from the birth of Christ even to the end" [Blaise Pascal, 1623-1662].

Over and over again, the Gospels, particularly the Gospel of Matthew, tells us that this or that fact in the life of Jesus was in fulfilment of prophecy, "that the Scriptures might be fulfilled," is the refrain which sounds everywhere in the New Testament. Not only did these men believe that Christ was fulfilling the prophecies, but Christ Himself believed that He was, and said that He was. "Search the Scriptures," He said, "for these are they which testify about Me"; "Moses wrote of Me"; "The Son of Man goes as it was written of Him." When He walked with the two disciples on the road to Emmaus on the day of the Resurrection, and wished to prove to them His identity, that He was really that Jesus whom they had known in the flesh, He did not work any miracle for them, nor appeal to some of His great sayings with which they might be familiar and thus confirm His personality, but He took them back into the Old Testament and said, "O fools, and slow of heart to believe all that the prophets have spoken. Ought not Christ to have suffered these things and to have entered into His glory? And beginning at Moses and all the prophets, He expounded unto them in all the scriptures the things concerning Himself." Again, when Jesus was on trial before the council of the Jews, and even by perjury and slander they could not get sufficient evidence to convict Him, the high priest put Jesus on oath and said to Him, "I beg You by the living God that You tell us whether You are the Christ, the Son of God." And Jesus answered, "I am."

No one who reads the Old Testament can doubt that all this is predicted of someone, and of some day in the future. Who is it that is thus described? We are left to one of two conclusions: Either the prophecies have not yet been fulfilled, or Christ fulfilled them. If Christ did not fulfill the prophecies, then they never will be fulfilled, for no greater proof of fulfilment could be offered than Christ has given us. The only other conclusion is that Christ fulfilled the prophecies; that to Him all the prophets bear witness; that when Christ began at Moses and all the prophets and said Moses and the prophets were speaking of Him, He was not an impostor or a deceiver, but the Christ Himself, the Son of God.

April 5
His Fullness
by Thomas Guthrie (1803-1873) Scotland
Excerpted from "The Fullness," *Christ and the Inheritance of the Saints*, published by E. B. Treat & Co., New York, New York in 1859

For God was pleased to have all His fullness dwell in Him…
Colossians 1:19 (NIV)

"All that is Mine is yours." Confining His generosity neither to kingdoms, nor continents, nor worlds, nor Heaven itself, He lays the whole universe at a poor sinner's feet. Away then with fears and cares! There is nothing we need that we shall not get, nothing we can ask that we shall not receive. It pleased the Father that in Him should all fullness dwell. Transferring divine wealth, if I may so speak, to our account in the bank of Heaven, and giving us an unlimited credit there, Jesus says, "All things, whatsoever you ask in prayer believing, you shall receive."

There is all fullness of mercy to pardon in Christ.

Had there been the smallest doubt expressed in the Bible about the fullness of pardoning mercy, had it not been made clear as noonday that the blood of Christ cleanses from all sin, from sins as well of the deepest, what a stumbling-block would that have been! I believe that it would have halted the steps of thousands now happy in Christ, or now safe in Heaven, as they went to throw themselves at His feet and cry, "Lord, save us, we perish."

There is all fullness of grace to sanctify in Christ.

"God is love." "Fury is not in Me, says the Lord." With Him is fullness of joy and pleasures for evermore. What do you wish or want? Go tell it to your Father. They that seek the Lord shall not lack any good thing. Can He who justified not sanctify? Can He who enlisted us under His holy banner not provide munitions of war enough to secure, though there may be a hard fight for it, the final victory? Can He who led the march out of Egypt not beat down our foes, and conduct our triumphant way through a thousand dangers and over a thousand difficulties on to the promised land? Oh, yes; there is all efficiency and sufficiency in Jesus Christ to crown the work of grace, and to complete what He has begun.

There is a constant supply of pardoning and sanctifying grace in Christ.

"It pleased the Father that in Him should all fullness dwell." Dwell, not come and go, like a wayfaring man who tarries but a night, who is with us today, and away tomorrow; not like the shallow, noisy, treacherous brook that fails, when most needed, in heat of summer, but like this deep-seated spring, that rising silently though richly at the mountain's foot, and having unseen communication with its exhaustless supplies, is ever flowing over its grassy boundary, equally unaffected by the long droughts that dry the wells, and the frosts that pave the neighboring lake with ice. So fail the joys of earth; so flow, supplied by the fullness that is in Christ, the pleasures and the peace of devotion. It cannot be otherwise. "If a man loves Me, says Jesus, he will keep My words; and My Father will love him, and We will come unto him, and make Our home with him."

There are times when the righteousness of God's people, always like the waves of the sea, seems like the tide at the stream, as, swelling beyond its ordinary bounds, it floats the boats and ships that lie highest, driest on the beach. But at all times and seasons, faith and prayer find fullness of mercy to pardon, and of grace to sanctify, in Jesus Christ. The supply is inexhaustible.

April 6
His Gates
by Charles H. Parkhurst (1842-1933) USA
Excerpted from "Three Gates on a Side," *Three Gates on a Side and Other Sermons*, published by Fleming H. Revell Company,
New York, New York in 1891

On the east three gates; on the north three gates; on the south three gates, and on the west three gates.
Revelation 21:13 (KJV)

Three gates on each side of the celestial quadrangle. So much as to the accessibility of the heavenly city. So that no one coming from the North need go around on to the South side in order to get in; no one approaching from the East need go around on to the West side in order to get in.

Christ is Himself gateway personified—what Scripture calls "open door." That fact is familiar; but our particular matter is that He is not simply one open door to which all of us have to come in order to enter, but that He is Himself a good many open doors, one of which is cut in the wall immediately in front of each of us to let us enter. Three gates in each wall. Christ is not only one gate—He is all the gates; and His multiplicity matches our diversity. So that each man to be saved will be saved by his own particular Christ, and enter the Kingdom through his own special, private portal.

Men have still their own special Christ. He is as various as the men are various that believe in Him. We believe in the same Christ, and yet we have not the same belief in Christ; like two men standing on the opposite side of a hill, who have a view of the same hill, but not the same view of the hill. We are in that respect like different kinds of flowers growing out in the sunshine; one flower, when it is touched by white light, will extract from the white light one particular tint, another flower will extract another particular tint from the same white light. So, while we all, in a way, believe in Christ, we each believe in our own way; and He is not the same to any two of us. If the question were to be passed around, "What do you think of Christ?" no two, except as they answered in someone else's words, would return the same answer. No one statement is quite valid for two people; just as you know that no one rainbow is quite good for two sets of eyes; each eye has its own rainbow. Each man's own study of the Gospels, each man's own personal experience, extracts from the white light of revelation his own tint. So far as there is sincerity in the matter, there will be a great deal of individuality in the matter.

This leads on to say that Christ, as you understand Him, not as I understand Him, not as your neighbor understands Him, but Christ as you understand Him, is your Christ—is your open door. You, probably, have some ideas about Him that are quite definite. Then behind those ideas are others that stretch back into the dim distance along a long line of perspective. But there is some single understanding of Him (perhaps more than one) which you have, that is defined enough so that you could think it out to yourself. You might even be able to tell it aloud. Possibly you could make a written statement of it that would look clear and read intelligibly. The particular thought you may have of Him may be that He is the Son of God; or that He is the Son of Man; or that He is the teacher of a new system of morality; or that He is the personification of the spirit of self-sacrifice; or that He is a fountain of comfort or a wellspring of strength. Some one thing or other, probably, He means to you in a unique way. There is some one point at which He touches you; some one point where His meaning as a Person is specially gathered. We dress Him in a garb woven out of our necessities. Human necessities are the cleft into which the wedge of the gospel strikes.

April 7
His Genealogy
by David James Burrell (1844-1926) USA
Excerpted from "The Genealogy of Jesus," *For Christ's Crown*, published by Wilbur B. Ketcham, New York, New York in 1896

A record of the genealogy of Jesus Christ.
Matthew 1:1 (KJV)

It is a significant fact that the genealogy of Jesus is given twice in the Gospels, by Matthew and Luke. We think it is dry reading — this catalogue of names variously spelled and not easy to pronounce; but there is a sufficient reason for it. We may learn from this genealogical table that the Christian religion centers in a personality. At this point it is differentiated from all other religions.

We learn from this genealogical table that Jesus, as the living center of Christianity, was "very Man of very man." He was of common blood and lineage with those whom He came to redeem. We shall find His divinity brought out clearly in other portions of Scripture as "very God of very God"; but at this point the distinct emphasis is put upon the fact that He took part in our human nature. And this it would appear was necessary to the accomplishment of His work.

The only-begotten Son of God entered into fellowship with us that He might retrieve the fortunes of the family name. He purposed to buy back the heritage which was ours by birth but had been squandered through sin. He took our name, He assumed our blood, in order that He might become our Redeemer, our Arbitrator. He became flesh of our flesh, bone of our bone; taking not on Him the nature of angels, but of men. He paid the ransomed price on Calvary and restored the glory of man.

There was, however, a special reason for establishing the legitimacy of Jesus. An inheritance was involved and the succession to a throne. If Jesus is to be recognized as the Messiah, three points must be distinctly shown. First, He must be in the direct line of David. The promise given to David was that the sovereignty should abide in his family until the coming of Emmanuel, in whom the ultimate hope of Israel should be fulfilled. In this genealogy it is made to appear that Jesus was the son of David. Second, it must be shown that He was descended in an unbroken line from Abraham. For the covenant with Abraham was this, "In your Seed shall all the nations of the earth be blessed." At this point also the messianic claim of Jesus is unimpeached and unimpeachable—He is the son of Abraham. Third, as He is to be a universal Savior and King of the whole human race, His lineage must be traced to Adam. This also is made clear. He vindicates His title as Son of Man.

The name of Jesus marks the end of the family line. He suffered the greatest sorrow that could befall a son of Israel in that He lived and died a childless Man. So it was prophesied; "He shall be taken from prison and from judgment: and who shall declare His generation? For He shall be cut off out of the land of the living." Had He then no posterity? No sons nor daughters?

Read on in the prophecy: "It pleased the Lord to bruise Him; He has put Him to grief: when You shall make His soul an offering for sin, He shall see His seed, He shall prolong His days, and the pleasure of the Lord shall prosper in His hand. He shall see of the travail of His soul, and shall be satisfied." Children? O yes; an innumerable multitude. The old lineage was indeed cut off; but *Anno Domini* (AD) is the divisional point in the history of the race. A new family line begins. Jesus is the re-founder of humanity, the second Adam, the firstborn among many brethren. It is our privilege—and higher privilege there cannot be—to belong to the new family line which was thus begun in Jesus the Christ.

April 8
His Gentleness
by James Russell (J. R.) Miller (1840-1912) USA
Excerpted from "The Gentleness of Christ," *The Lesson of Love*,
published by Thomas Y. Crowell & Co., New York, New York in 1903

Gentleness is not weakness. But gentleness is beautiful only when combined with strength.

Christ is gentle in dealing with sufferers. Skill in giving comfort is very rare. Many people are sure to speak the wrong word when they sit down beside those who are in pain or trouble. Job's friends were "miserable comforters." They tried to make Job believe that he had displeased God, and that this was why so much evil had come upon him. Many good people think that when they sit beside a sufferer or a mourner, they must talk about the trouble, entering into all its details, and dwelling upon all that makes it painful and hard to endure. But the truest comforter is not the one who seems to sympathize the most deeply, going down into the depths with the one who is in grief, but the one who, sympathizing with the sufferer, yet brings cheer and uplift, sets a vision of Christ before the mourning eyes, and sings of peace and hope.

Christ is very gentle with those who have sinned and are trying to begin again. He has no tolerance for sin, but is infinitely patient with the sinner. He saves by forgiving. He loves unto the uttermost. His grace is inexhaustible. However often we fail, when we come back and ask to try again, He welcomes us and gives us another chance. This is our hope—if He were not in this way gentle with us, we should never get home.

Christ is very gentle with us also in our serving Him. We sometimes hear it said, when the bareness and poverty of certain people's homes are spoken of, that "the one half do not know how the other half live." That is very true and thinking of this "other half" ought to give those who live in comfort Christly sympathy with those who live in lack and poverty. But the same distinction exists among Christians, between those who live in a happy religious environment and those who must follow Christ with almost nothing in their condition or circumstances to encourage or help them.

Those with all the refinements and inspirations of the best Christian culture about them have little understanding of the disadvantages of others who are following Christ without any of this help, in the face of most uncongenial surroundings. What kind of Christians would we be, and how beautifully would we live, if we were in their circumstances?

He is infinitely patient with all whose lot is hard. He never requires more of us than we can do. He is never unreasonable. He knows when the burdens are too heavy for us. Once He, "being wearied with His journey, sat by the well" in His exhaustion. He sympathizes with those who are weary and helps them.

There is a picture which shows a girl at her spinning wheel. The hour is late—midnight, as a clock in the bare room shows—and the spinner, exhausted by her long toil to earn enough to support her little household, has fallen asleep beside the wheel. And an angel is finishing her work. How gentle our Taskmaster is! How sweet it is to come to Him at the close of the long days and rest at His feet!

April 9
His Gift - 1
by William L. Watkinson (1838-1925) England
Excerpted from "The Greatest Gift of the Greatest Giver," *Studies in Christian Character*, published by Fleming H. Revell Company, New York, New York in 1903

Thanks be unto God for His unspeakable gift.
2 Corinthians 9:15 (KJV)

The Apostle Paul has been speaking to the Corinthians about gifts, when all at once his heart takes fire and he bursts into this thanksgiving. He glorifies God for the whole wonderful and inexpressibly blissful work of redemption. In Paul's reckoning Christ is the crowning gift of God to the race, and ecstatically he praises God for the glorious blessing. Far beyond the good and perfect gifts of the material world is the preciousness of Jesus Christ our Lord. The philosopher tells us that during the course of ages all things have evolved—the stars, the trees, the flowers, the beasts and birds; but he acknowledges that these are not the highest things: Human intelligence, conscience, love, the noble sentiments, ideals, hopes, and aspirations of the race—these are the highest products of history. It was exactly in these spiritual treasures that Christ enriched humankind, and enriched us in an infinite degree.

Christ brought truth to the highest questions of all, and taught us that truth most fully. With surpassing authority and power He vindicated and disclosed the spiritual world and the spirituality of man. He made it impossible from now on that the race should lose itself in materialism and sensuality. Christ brought peace. The Jewish world knew the severity of law—it beheld God in the terrors of Mt. Sinai; the Roman world knew the majesty and power of heaven—Jupiter sat on Olympus with the thunderbolt and eagle. But Christ spanned Mt. Sinai with the rainbow, and replaced the bird of blood with the dove of peace. He proclaimed the infinite love of God to a world of sinners.

In Christ we have in its fullness the precious doctrine of grace, forgiveness, and peace. Christ brought righteousness. He secured to us the power of purity. He inspires the strength by which the highest goodness is attainable. In the pagan legend Prometheus kindled the human soul, until then man was as heavy clay, scoffed at by the gods; but the Titan put into the weak, sluggish creature a celestial spark, and henceforth he began to gaze at the stars, to reap the fruits of the earth, to sail the sea, to understand, to govern, to prophesy. Christ kindles within us a diviner spark, and makes possible to us not merely science, philosophy, commerce, and government, but a loving heart, a gracious temper, truth in the inward parts, a holy life, sacrifice, and service. By the spark of Pentecost, out of the dull, coarse clay of carnal man He created immortal apostles and saints. Cried David in his lamentation over Saul and Jonathan, "You daughters of Israel, weep over Saul, who clothed you in scarlet, with other delights, who put on ornaments of gold upon your apparel." But Christ has done infinitely more for men and women than clothing them in scarlet; He has clothed them in white and put upon them ornaments of grace rarer than jewels of gold. Christ brought us hope. He came into the world in an age of weariness and despair, and He made everything to live by putting into the heart of the race a sure and splendid hope. He brought life and immortality to light. He caused men to forget hardship and suffering when He opened the Kingdom of Heaven to all believers.

The advent of Jesus mightily enriched the race in incorruptible treasure—in knowledge, kindness, purity, and hope. How much it enriched us none may tell. The gift is "unspeakable." It is infinite; it passes knowledge. It is little use attempting to describe the indescribable, little use attempting to utter the unutterable. Nothing is left except to wonder; nothing is left to say except Hallelujah!

April 10
His Gift - 2
by John J. Black (1818-1882) Scotland/USA/Canada
Excerpted from "What Is the 'Gift of God?'" *Modern Scottish Pulpit Sermons by Ministers of Various Denominations*, published by Robert Carter & Brothers, New York, New York in 1880

Jesus answered her, "If you knew the gift of God and who it is that asks you for a drink, you would have asked Him and He would have given you living water."
John 4:10 (NIV)

Two things must be noticed regarding this story, before we come to consider the words we have selected. The first point is—the value our Master puts upon a single soul. "He must needs go through Samaria," the "needs" being, that there, in Sychar, dwelt a sinner on whom He had set His love. So we find Him going far to the northwest, to put Himself in the way of the Syrophoenician; and, once again, He crossed the Sea of Galilee, that He might still the storm in a maniac's breast, as He had hushed another storm "immediately" before upon the lake. Easily-wearied workers, take shame to yourselves for your excuses when you also mark that it was the wearied Jesus who, in each of these cases, won the poor sinner to His feet. "Being wearied"—"asleep on a pillow." Blessed words are these for the suffering and the seeking, but words having a sting in them for us who merely profess to follow His example.

But the second matter we would bring before your notice is the plan that our Lord adopts in bringing the Samaritan to Himself. She is a stranger, and separated from Him by the wide breach of political hate. This difficulty must be overcome, but not by making light of it, or fighting over it, as we often do. Our Lord stood loyally to His country's colors and His Church's principles. With no uncertain sound He rang out the rally call of the South,

"Salvation is of the Jews." But He declined to argue that question. That was not His business there. Her soul was dearer to Him than His nationality. Everything must be put aside until the work is done which His Father had given Him to do here. "To seek and to save that which was lost," was the burden laid upon Him. He had sought her, and now He must save. For this, He first attracts her attention, "Give Me a drink." He then excites her wonder, "If you knew the gift of God, and who it is that asks you for a drink, you would have asked Him, and He would have given you living water." From wonder, He goes on to conviction, "Go, call your husband, and come here." Having brought her to the dust, He there can reveal Himself to her, and bid her to become a worshipper. Thus her Samaritan belief became strangely true. At Gerizim's foot she worshipped—now, to her joy however, knowing "what" she worshipped. The worshipper is soon a worker, and the chief, perhaps, of Sychar's sinners is gone away to tell what a Savior she had found. Thus it was that the Master enlisted and educated His first Samaritan missionary.

The fulness of the word, "The gift of God," appears again when we consider how it is pressed upon our acceptance. We are not told of it, and then left to seek it out, but, as Paul quotes in the tenth chapter of Romans, "The word is near you." The gift is brought to our very door, and we are pressed, even begged, to make it ours. The picture before us presents this very truth. Christ is here the Seeker. He had traveled from Judea, that He might place the gift within her reach. So He weariedly journeyed from town to town, and patiently pleaded, and waited, and wept. So He commissioned His disciples to do when He was gone, and so He still stands at the door and knocks. "If any man hear My voice, and open the door, I will come in to him, and eat with him, and he with Me." Nothing seems to us to make the gift more precious than this, that the Lord still holds the right of presentation in His own hand, and claims the pleasure of bestowing it on "whom He will."

April 11
His Giving
by John Clopton Reynolds (1825-1906) USA
Excerpted from "Christian Giving," *The Moberly Pulpit,* published by
Christian Publishing Company, St. Louis, Missouri in 1881

"It is more blessed to give than to receive."
Acts 20:35 (NIV)

Your candid and serious attention is asked at this time to one of the most important themes pertaining to the Christian life. It is Christian giving. It is eminently practical. It permeates the entire Christian dispensation. Christianity itself is a gift. Our salvation is a gift. Christ our Lord and Master is a gift. His shed blood that takes away our sins is a free gift. We cannot pay for it and can only receive it as a gift bestowed upon us by divine love. God Himself is the first and greatest and best giver. He has given us countless blessings. His noblest gift is His Son whom He has given to take away our sins, to redeem us from the grave and to open to us the gates of the golden city. He has become our King, and His Word is our law. Let us now honestly direct our attention to His Word and see what He requires of us. In the Sermon on the Mount He said to His disciples: "Give to him that asks you: and from him that would borrow from you, turn not away."

These words are addressed to His disciples. If we, today, are His disciples, these words are applicable to us. The duties here enforced are our duties. On us they are binding. With all the authority of the King's command we are required to give. If any one of us is not a giver, he is in rebellion against the law of the Lord and living in sin. There is no specification here as to what we shall give, or to whom we shall give, or how much we shall give, only that we must give "to him that asks." The Savior in this discourse deals with general principles. He simply lays down the law of His Kingdom that all His subjects must be givers, must be generous, must be liberal, must not be grasping and stingy. The specifications as to when, to whom, how much, and for what purpose we should give, we are not told. These are to be learned from the Savior's subsequent teachings, and from the words of the apostles and the example of the early Christians when they acted under the personal supervision of the apostles. But the law of Christ is here clearly laid down that Christians must be givers. To be a Christian, a man must give. The man who does not give is not a true follower of Christ, however deeply and completely he may have been immersed, and however plainly his name may be written on a church roll. To be a practical, real Christian, he must imitate the character of God and follow the example of the Savior. He cannot imitate the character of God without being a giver, a liberal giver. To give sparingly, or grudgingly, or not according to ability, is no imitation of God's character. To give simply to be seen of men does not at all imitate the divine character. He who does not give does not follow Jesus. While on earth Christ went about doing good. He was a giver on the grandest scale. He was able to give to each suffering one just the blessing that he needed. If the sufferer were sick He healed him, blind He opened his eyes, deaf He unstopped his ears, lame He made him rise up and walk, insane He clothed him in his right mind, if heart-broken He soothed his troubled soul with words of cheer and hope. To do all these things Jesus possessed unlimited power. To do them, our power is limited. We cannot go beyond our ability.

Brethren and sisters, we need to have broader, deeper, higher, grander and more Christlike understanding of Christian generosity. Let us all become givers! While there is some liberal giving, it is largely done by the few, while the many have not been doing much.

That we may all be stirred up to more zeal, to more love, to more prayer and to more Christian giving in this life, and that we may so live, and so work, that we may be crowned with glory in the everlasting Kingdom, is my prayer for Christ's sake.

April 12
His Glory - 1
by Amzee Clarence Dixon (1854-1925) USA
Excerpted from "Christ's Earthly Glory," *Milk and Meat*, published by
The Baker & Taylor Co., New York, New York in 1893

*This, the first of His signs, Jesus did at Cana in Galilee,
and manifested His glory.*
John 2:11 (ESV)

A study of this miracle will give us a glimpse of the true glory of our Lord while upon earth.

We see the glory of His social nature. While bearing the sorrows of the community, He shared equally their joys. He broke up several funerals, but never a feast. He promoted the right kind of festivity. He came to increase our joys and diminish our sorrows, and He knows as no other does how to make our very sorrows channels of joy. The social life of every Christian should show forth the glory of Christ.

We see the glory of His power. It was quietly displayed; no outward show. He simply willed, and it was done. It displays itself not in the tempest, the earthquake, or the fire, but in the still small voice. The great powers of nature are invisible and inaudible. The quiet working of nature that lifts the clouds and distils the rain, giving life and beauty to meadow, field, and plain, displays the true glory of God. The heavens declare His glory by quietly shining, and the firmament show His handiwork without making much about it.

We see the glory of His sympathy. Sympathy with the embarrassed and perplexed. Here was a family with more guests than they expected, and their supplies ran short. The Lord comes just in time to relieve their embarrassment. It suggests to us that

Christ is ever sympathetic with the little worries and perplexities of life. It is easier to bear a great calamity than these little irritations. Henry Morton Stanley [Welsh-American journalist/explorer, 1841-1904] says that he did not fear the lions and elephants of the African forest as much as the mites and the ants. They killed more people than the savages.

We have read of a battle against cannibals gained by the use of tacks. They had taken possession of a whaling vessel and bound the man who was left in care of it. The crew, on returning, saw the situation, and scattered upon the deck of the vessel the tacks, which penetrated the bare feet of the savages, and sent them howling into the sea. They were ready to meet lance and sword, but they could not overcome the tacks on the floor. We brace ourselves up against great calamities. The little tacks of life, scattered along our way, piercing our feet and giving us pain, are hard to bear.

We see the glory of His method. The world's method is to give the best wine first and keep the worst for the last. There may come into our lives sickness and death. We may have truly a hard time of it; but, depend upon it, the good time will come to the Christian, and these severe experiences will make the coming glory all the brighter. "I have fought a good fight, I have finished my course, I have kept the faith: henceforth there is laid up for me a crown of righteousness." The "henceforth" is the Christian's good wine. His life may be a battle to fight, a race to run, a charge to keep; but victory will crown the battle. The prize is at the end of the race, and the "Well done" from the Master's lips will make us glad that we kept the charge He committed to us.

April 13
His Glory - 2
by David James Burrell (1844-1926) USA
Excerpted from "We Beheld His Glory," *The Morning Cometh: Talks for the Times*, published by American Tract Society, New York, New York in 1893

And we beheld His glory, the glory as of the only-begotten of the Father, full of grace and truth.
John 1:14 (KJV)

John was the apostle of the glory of Christ. He saw it more clearly than others, doubtless because as the beloved disciple he entered into the secret place of his Lord's confidence.

We beheld His glory as of the only-begotten of the Father. He had nothing less than the glory of Godhood. He was the only-begotten of the Father. His glory was like that of the Shekinah, at once the shining forth and the suggestion of deity. He was God manifest in flesh. To attribute to Jesus all the foregoing tokens of greatness while denying Him this divineness, this glory as of the only-begotten of the Father, is to fall infinitely short of the truth.

He claimed to be very God of very God. His claim was verified at His birth by the singing of the angels; at His baptism by the voice from Heaven; at His transfiguration by the enfolding cloud which was again the Shekinah, the excellent glory, and the voice saying, "This is My beloved Son"; at His death by the shrouding of the heavens and the rocking of the earth; at His resurrection by the breaking of the bands of death when He took captivity captive; at His ascension when He arose with uplifted hands and vanished from sight leaving His blessing upon the world; at Pentecost when there came a baptism of fire and of power because Jesus had breathed upon His disciples; and all along history by innumerable miracles of grace, for He still walks up and down our thoroughfares opening blind eyes, wiping away the scales of leprosy, dispossessing those who have been demented by unclean spirits, and raising the dead. This is the glory of Jesus of Nazareth, the glory as of the only-begotten of the Father.

His coming to the earth was to show the grace of God toward us. He brought the message, "God so loved the world that He gave His only-begotten Son, that whosoever believes in Him should not perish, but have everlasting life." As the Shekinah led the children of Israel out of the land of Egypt, out of the house of their bondage, so did this living anti-type of the Shekinah, the only-begotten of the Father, come to deliver our ruined race from the bondage of spiritual and eternal death. The word truth, here, characterizes our Lord's devotion to this work. *Aletheia* is a large word; it means more than authenticity. It means loyalty to a noble purpose. It means an unswerving devotion to a supreme objective in life. Jesus was true to His errand of grace. He never forgot it, He never swerved from it. He set His face steadfastly towards the cross. He never flinched. As He set forth He caught up the handwriting of ordinances which was against us, the decree, "The soul that sins it shall die." It was His purpose to erase that decree with blood and nail it to His cross. For thirty weary years He was ever mindful of His mission. With that grim death sentence in His hand He ran the gauntlet of men and devils. They reviled Him and spit upon Him—on He ran; they scourged Him, they loaded Him with shame and defamation—on He ran, until He reached the hilltop outside the walls of the Holy City, and there, while they nailed Him to the cross, He delivered His message of grace; while His enemies seemed to be nailing Him to the accursed tree He was blotting out the handwriting of ordinances which was against us with His own precious blood and nailing it to His cross (Colossians 2:14).

His work was done, His glory—the glory of the only-begotten of the Father—was perfected in this message of grace.

April 14
His Grace
by William H. G. Thomas (1861-1924) England/Wales

Excerpted from "Grace," *Grace and Power*, published by Fleming H. Revell Company, New York, New York in 1916

Our Lord came that there might be a gospel to preach. Then He sent His Apostles to preach it. The gospel that He was in His Person, and that He provided by His Word, and the gospel that they received and proclaimed, is best stated in the one word, Grace: "The Gospel of the Grace of God"; "the Grace of our Lord Jesus Christ"; "the Word of His Grace."

What do we mean by "Grace"? It is a large word, a great word, an all-inclusive word, perhaps the greatest word in the Bible, because it is the word most truly expressive of God's character and attitude in relation to man. It comes from two or three roots in the Hebrew and Greek. In the Greek we find words and derivatives meaning "grace," "gift," to "give freely," to "forgive," to "bestow graciously," "joy," to "rejoice," "thanksgiving," to "give thanks," "thankful." In English (derived from the Latin) we have "grace," "gratis," "gratitude," "grateful," "gracious," "gratuity," "graceful," and such opposites as "ungrateful," "ungracious," "disgraceful." The subject is large, and has many aspects; the passages, too, are numerous and well worthy of the closest study.

What does the word mean? The root seems to mean "to give pleasure," and then it branches out comprehensively in two directions—one in relation to the Giver; the other in relation to the receiver of the pleasure. Grace is first, a quality of graciousness in the Giver, and then a quality of gratitude in the recipient, which in turn makes him gracious to those around.

But the idea has two distinct yet connected aspects even when applied only to God the Giver.

It expresses the Divine attitude to man as guilty and condemned. Grace means God's favor and goodwill towards us (Luke 1:30). So the mother of our Lord is described as "permanently favored" ("graced," Luke 1:28). This favor is manifested without any regard to merit; indeed, grace and merit are entire opposites. Grace is thus spontaneous (not prompted from outside); free (no conditions are required); generous (no stinginess is shown); and abiding (no stopping is experienced). It is also (as favor) opposed to "wrath" which means judicial displeasure against sin. Further, it must be distinguished from mercy even though mercy is one of its methods of expression. Mercy is related to misery and to the (negatively) non-deserving. Grace is related to redemption and to the (positively) undeserving.

It then expresses the Divine action to people as needy and helpless. Grace means not merely favor but also help; not only kindness but also support; not simply feeling but also force; not solely goodwill but also good work. It is Divine favor expressed in and proved by His gift; attitude shown by action. Thus from grace comes gift, which invariably implies a gift of or by grace (Romans 5:15; 1 Corinthians 4:6; Romans 12:6).

These two ideas are thus connected and united as Cause and Effect. They tell of God's Heart and God's Hand. Etymologically, therefore, Grace is a term that refers to the beautiful which gives delight. Theologically, it means God's favor as seen in His gift. Practically, it implies God's presence and redemptive power in human life. It includes the two ideas of God's attitude and God's action; His graciousness and His gift; His pleasure and His provision; His blessing and His support. In a sentence, we may define God's grace as His favor to the sinner, that favor being shown and proved by His gift.

April 15
His Growing - 1
by Hannah Whitall Smith (1832-1911) USA/England
Excerpted from "Growth," *The Christian's Secret of a Happy Life*,
published by Willard Tract Repository, Boston, Massachusetts in 1885

When the believer has been brought to the point of entire surrender and perfect trust, and finds himself dwelling and walking in a life of happy communion and perfect peace, the question naturally arises, "Is this the end?" I answer emphatically, "No, it is only the beginning."

And yet this is so little understood, that one of the greatest objections made against the advocates of this life of faith is that they do not believe in growth in grace. They are supposed to teach that the soul arrives at a state of perfection beyond which there is no advance, and that all the exhortations in the Scripture which point towards growth and development are rendered void by this teaching.

Exactly the opposite of this is true. I have thought it important next to consider this subject carefully, that I may, if possible, fully answer such objections, and may also show what is the scriptural place to grow in, and how the soul is to grow.

The text which is most frequently quoted is 2 Peter 3:18, "But grow in grace, and in the knowledge of our Lord and Savior Jesus Christ." Now this text exactly expresses what we believe to be God's will for us, and what also we believe He has made it possible for us to experience. We accept, in their very fullest meaning, all the commands and promises concerning our being no more children, and our growing up into Christ in all things, until we come unto a perfect man, unto the measure of the stature of the fulness of Christ. We rejoice that we need not continue always to be babes, needing milk; by that we may, by reason of use and development become such as have need of strong meat, skillful in the word of righteousness, and able to discern both good and evil. And none would grieve more than we at the thought of any finality in the Christian life beyond which there could be no advance.

But then we believe in a growing that does really produce maturity, and in a development that, as a fact, does bring forth ripe fruit. We expect to reach the aim set before us, and if we do not, we feel sure there must be some fault in our growing. No parent would be satisfied with the growth of his child, if, day after day, and year after year, it remained the same helpless babe it was in the first months of its life; and no farmer would feel comfortable under such growing of his grain as should stop short at the blade, and never produce the ear, nor the full corn in the ear. Growth, to be real, must be progressive, and the days and weeks and months must see a development and increase of maturity in the thing growing. But is this the case with a large part of that which is called growth in grace?

I was once urging upon a company of Christians the privileges and rest of an immediate and definite step into the land of promise, when a lady of great intelligence interrupted me, with what she evidently felt to be a complete rebuttal of all I had been saying, exclaiming, "Ah! but, my dear friend, I believe in growing in grace." "How long have you been growing?" I asked. "About twenty-five years," was her answer. "And how much more unworldly and devoted to the Lord are you now than when you began your Christian life?" I continued. "Alas!" was the answer, "I fear I am not nearly so much so"; and with this answer her eyes were opened to see that at all events her way of growing had not been successful, but quite the reverse. They are trying to grow *into* grace, instead of *in* grace.

April 16
His Growing - 2
by Hannah Whitall Smith (1832-1911) USA/England
Excerpted from "Growth," *The Christian's Secret of a Happy Life*,
published by Willard Tract Repository, Boston, Massachusetts in 1885

What is meant by growing in grace? It is difficult to answer this question, because so few people have any understanding of what the grace of God really is. To say that it is free, unmerited favor, only expresses a little of its meaning. It is the wondrous, boundless love of God, poured out upon us without measure, not according to our deserving, but according to His infinite heart of love, which passes knowledge, so unfathomable are its heights and depths. I sometimes think we give a totally different meaning to the word "love" when it is associated with God, from that we so well understand in its human application. But if ever human love was tender and self-sacrificing and devoted; if ever it could bear and forbear; if ever it could suffer gladly for its loved ones; if ever it was willing to pour itself out in a lavish abandonment for the comfort or pleasure of its objects—then infinitely more is Divine love tender and self-sacrificing and devoted, and glad to bear and forbear, and to suffer, and to lavish its best of gifts and blessings upon the objects of its love.

Put together all the tenderest love you know of, dear reader, the deepest you have ever felt, and the strongest that has ever been poured out upon you, and heap upon it all the love of all the loving human hearts in the world, and then multiply it by infinity, and you will begin perhaps to have some faint glimpses of what the love of God in Christ Jesus is. And this is grace. And to be planted in grace is to live in the very heart of this love, to be enveloped by it, to be steeped in it, to revel in it, to know nothing else but love only and love always, to grow day by day in the knowledge of it, and in faith in it, to entrust everything to its care, and to have no shadow of a doubt but that it will surely order all things well.

To grow in grace is opposed to all self-dependence, to all self-effort, to all legality of every kind. It is to put our growing, as well as everything else, into the hands of the Lord, and leave it with Him. It is to be so satisfied with our Husbandman, and with His skill and wisdom, that not a question will cross our minds as to His modes of treatment or His plan of cultivation. It is to grow as the lilies grow, or as the babes grow, without a care and without anxiety; to grow by the power of an inward life principle that cannot help but grow; to grow because we live and therefore must grow; to grow because He who has planted us has planted a growing thing, and has made us to grow.

Surely this is what our Lord meant when He said, "Consider the lilies, how they grow; they toil not, neither do they spin: and yet I say unto you, that even Solomon in all his glory was not arrayed like one of these." Or, when He says again, "Which of you by taking thought can add one cubit unto his stature?" There is no effort in the growing of a child or of a lily. They do not toil nor spin, they do not stretch nor strain, they do not make any effort of any kind to grow; they are not conscious even that they are growing; but by an inward life principle, and through the nurturing care of God's providence, and the fostering of caretaker or gardener, by the heat of the sun and the falling of the rain, they grow and grow.

If I could only make each one of my readers realize how utterly helpless we are in this matter of growing, I am convinced a large part of the strain would be taken out of many lives at once. Grow, dear friends, grow, I beg you, in God's way, which is the only effective way. See to it that you are planted in grace, and then let the Divine Husbandman cultivate you in His own way and by His own means.

April 17
His Guidance
by Reuben Archer (R. A.) Torrey (1856-1928) USA

Excerpted from "How God Guides," *The Voice of God in the Present Hour*, published by Fleming H. Revell Company, New York, New York in 1917

Yet I am always with You; You hold me by my right hand. You guide me with Your counsel, and afterward You will take me into glory.
Psalm 73:23-24 (NIV)

There are no promises of God's Word more precious to the person who wishes to do His will, and who realizes the goodness of His will, than the promises of His guidance. What a cheering, gladdening, inspiring thought that is contained in the text, that we may have the guidance of infinite wisdom and love at every turn of life, and that we have it to the end of our earthly pilgrimage. There are few more precious words in the whole book of Psalms, which is one of the most precious of all the books of the Bible, than these: "Yet I am always with You; You hold me by my right hand. You guide me with Your counsel, and afterward You will take me into glory." How the thoughtful and believing and obedient heart burns as it reads these wonderful words of the text.

First of all God guides by His Word. We read in Psalm 119:105, "Your word is a lamp unto my feet, and a light unto my path," and in the 130th verse of this same Psalm we read, "The entrance of Your words gives light; it gives understanding unto the simple." God's own written Word is the chief instrument that God uses in our guidance.

God also leads us by His Spirit, i.e., by the direct leading of the Holy Spirit in the individual heart. Beyond a question there is such a thing as an "inner light." We read in Acts 8:29, "And the Spirit said unto Philip, Go near and join yourself to this chariot." In a similar way we read in Acts 16:6-7, of the Apostle Paul and his companions: "And they went through the region of Phrygia and the region of Galatia, having been forbidden by the Holy Spirit to speak the word in Asia; and when they were come over against Mysia they evaluated going into Bithynia; and the Spirit of Jesus did not allow them to go there." In one of these passages we see the Spirit of God by His Holy Spirit giving direct personal guidance to Philip as to what he should do, and in the other passage we see the Spirit restraining Paul and his companions from doing something they would otherwise have done. There is no reason why God should not lead us as directly as he led Philip and Paul in their day, and those who walk near God can testify that He does so lead. Furthermore, let me repeat again that we should bear in mind about the Spirit's guidance, that He will not lead us to do anything that is contrary to the Word of God. The Word of God is the Holy Spirit's book, and He never contradicts His own teaching. Many people do things that are strictly forbidden in the Word of God, and justify themselves in so doing by saying the Spirit of God guides them to do it, but any spirit that guides us to do something that is contrary to the Holy Spirit's own book cannot by any possibility be the Holy Spirit.

In the third place God guides us by enlightening our judgment. We see an illustration of this in the case of the Apostle Paul in Acts 16:10. God had been guiding Paul by a direct impression produced in his heart by the Holy Spirit, keeping him from going to certain places where he would otherwise have gone. Then God gives to Paul in the night a vision, and, having received the vision, Paul, by his own enlightened judgment, concludes from it what God has called him to do. This is God's ordinary method of guidance when His Word does not specifically tell us what to do. We go to God for wisdom, we make sure that our wills are completely surrendered to Him, and that we realize our dependence upon Him for guidance, then God clears up our judgment and makes it clear to us what we should do.

April 18
His Habit
by James Rankin (1832-1911) Scotland
Excerpted from "Habit and Holiness," *Modern Scottish Pulpit: Sermons by Ministers of Various Denominations, First Series*, published by Robert Carter & Brothers, New York, New York in 1880

And He came to Nazareth, where He had been brought up: and, as His custom was, He went into the synagogue on the Sabbath day, and stood up to read.
Luke 4:16 (KJV)

Here, in our text, is one case of Jesus conforming to a good common custom—perhaps not only following the custom, but getting help from it to promote His own spiritual life. From this one well-authenticated custom of Jesus in regard to Sabbath observance, I purpose, in connection with the text, to set before you the value and use of habit, as an aid to holy life and character, placed by God's providence within our reach, and which we are bound to develop. The capacity of forming habits is a very valuable part of human nature, as originally framed by God. By doing a thing often, we come to do it easily, and even to gain a liking and craving to do it.

The instance in the text applicable to Jesus is the custom of being present at public worship every Sabbath. How great an aid is this to everything that is good! It puts us in the way of the chief means of grace; it puts us in the way of the best human companionship. God Himself, in His wisdom and goodness, has provided for this fundamental good habit in the ordinance of the Sabbath day, which returns at measured intervals, to call us away from worldly toil and care, to rest for body and soul, refreshing fellowship with God. If we neglect God's ordinance, or devote it to mere idleness and mirth, we put ourselves recklessly in the way of evil, and out of the way of good. Wherever we are, whether at home, or visiting friends, or traveling abroad, let us be careful to keep the good custom of going to church every Sunday. It is a primary condition of all true blessing here on earth.

A habit of prayer. The prayer to which I refer specially at present is family and personal prayer. Public or common prayer is implied in Sunday observance and going to church. If there is no habit of family prayer, the prayer is not likely to be made at all. All the details of family worship imply arrangement—a certain hour—a fixed place—books at hand—a person responsible for conducting the service. Family worship thus becomes one of the most beautiful features of domestic order in every house where it is duly attended to.

Labor may be the subject of another of those good habits, in a religious point of view. One of the fundamental conditions of a happy earthly life is to have plenty of work to do, and to do it with a will. Absolute idleness is an idiotic and unchristian state.

A habit of learning may well form the sequel to a habit of labor. Work, done in a right spirit and method, leads to experience and intelligence in the line of the work so prosecuted. But the learning ought to be wider than a person's own work, and especially should have more of a religious direction than the average of ordinary work.

Charity, to which we now come, can, of course, be commended only to those who are themselves above immediate need. To expect charity from persons in debt, or those who are living beyond their income, or are themselves receiving charitable help, would be folly and sin. Self-denial, however, is the main fountain of charity. We all have need of the habit of charity. Even a little of it would produce a mighty improvement both in the world and the Church.

April 19
His Headship
by Albert Benjamin (A. B.) Simpson (1843-1919) Canada
Excerpted from "Christ Our Head," *The Names of Jesus*, published by The Christian Alliance Publishing Company, New York, New York in 1892

And He is the head of the body, the Church. He is the beginning, the firstborn from the dead, that in everything He might be preeminent. For in Him all the fullness of God was pleased to dwell...
Colossians 1:18-19 (ESV)

It is perfectly natural to follow the wishes of the head, so the Lord Jesus Christ, our living Head, is the true Lord and sovereign of His people's lives, and it is the place of their bodies to be instinctively obedient to His every wish. If He is indeed our Head, it will be our second nature to do His bidding. Indeed, no other part of the body has any power to will, and none of Christ's children should have any will apart from their Master's. There is a great difference between being guided by your own head or somebody else's. If Christ is not your living Head you will not want His authority and government. Before, therefore, we can truly obey Him we must fully receive Him and be so united with Him that His interests are ours, and His will is just the expression of our inmost being. Beloved, is Christ our recognized and honored Head, and is our life a glad and constant obedience to His every wish and prompting?

In the human body the head is the source and seat of life, and so the Lord Jesus is the source of His people's life. There is no life apart from the head, and we have none apart from Him. Our regeneration comes through the quickening power of His life, our sanctification is His indwelling in us. Our physical life may be made manifest in the flesh. We are dependent upon Him for our fruit, for our joy, for our love, for all our spiritual grace and experiences, and He loves to impart His life to us and fill us more abundantly if we will but receive it. We are not held responsible for our own life. We are not expected to manufacture either faith or love, but to receive from Him life and love, and the grace that He is ever longing to impart. Every sorrow and pain we feel is instinctively telegraphed to Him, and touches His living heart to the quick, "For we have not a high priest who is not able to be touched with the feeling of our infirmities."

When the pressure seems intolerable, when sorrow gnaws the heart, and Satan hurls his arrows of flame into our quivering spirit, when the world opposes us as it once did Him, and flesh and heart are ready to faint and fail, it is just Christ in one of His members suffering there, and the living Head will not fail nor forget to help the suffering member, and will also help us in the matter of religious feeling. All sensation must come from the brain, and so all spiritual feeling must come from Christ. Let us not, therefore, try to work up our feelings, but keep close to Him, and the tides of His love will flow into our consciousness and spiritual sensibilities. The secret of joy and love simply lie in nearness to Jesus, and His joy and love will spring within us from the Head. The most effortless and spontaneous life will ever be the best. Oftentimes He may wish us to be inactive. Let us be submissive in this, and when He rests in His love, let us rest with Him, and when He rejoices over us with singing, let us swell the chorus in glad response, our hearts keeping time to His, as the sand upon the ocean shore is wet or dry as the ocean tide rises and falls in the sea below.

The head is the seat of thought, intelligence, judgment, direction, knowledge. So Christ is our wisdom, our guide, our mind. We need not think so much, or rather He will think in us His thoughts, if we suspend our judgment, and draw upon His glorious mind for our knowledge, our light, our views, our opinions and plans.

April 20
His Healing
by Andrew Murray (1828-1917) Scotland/South Africa
Excerpted from "Jesus Heals the Sick," *Divine Healing*, originally published in 1900

He healed all that were sick, that it might be fulfilled which was spoken by Isaiah the prophet, saying: "Himself took our infirmities and bore our sicknesses."
Matthew 8:16-17 (KJV)

It was because Jesus had taken on Him our sicknesses that He could, that He ought to heal them. If He had not done so, one part of His work of redemption would have remained powerless and fruitless. This text of the Word of God is not generally understood in this way. It is the generally accepted view that the miraculous healings done by the Lord Jesus are to be looked upon only as the proof of His mercy, or as being the symbol of spiritual graces. They are not seen to be a necessary consequence of redemption, although that is what the Bible declares. The body and the soul have been created to serve together as a habitation of God; the sickly condition of the body is, as well as that of the soul, a consequence of sin, and that is what Jesus came to bear, to atone and to conquer. When the Lord Jesus was on earth, it was not in the character of the Son of God that He cured the sick, but as the Mediator who had taken upon Him and borne sickness, and this enables us to understand why Jesus gave so much time to His healing work, and why also the writers of the Gospels speak of it in a manner so detailed. Read for example what Matthew says about it: "Jesus went about all Galilee, teaching in their synagogues, and preaching the good tidings of the Kingdom, and healing all manner of sickness, and all manner of disease among the people. And His fame went throughout all Syria; and they brought unto Him all sick people that were taken with various diseases and torments, and those that were possessed with devils, and those which were lunatic, and those that had the palsy; and He healed them" (Matthew 4:23-24). "And Jesus went about all the cities and villages, teaching in their synagogues and preaching the gospel of the Kingdom and healing every sickness and every disease among the people" (Matthew 9:35). When the disciples of John the Baptist came to ask Jesus if He were the Messiah, that He might prove it to them, He replied: "The blind receive their sight, and the lame walk, the lepers are cleansed, and the deaf hear, the dead are raised up, and the poor have the gospel preached to them" (11:5). After the cure of the withered hand, and the opposition of the Pharisees who sought to destroy Him, we read that "great multitudes followed Him, and He healed them all" (12:15). When later, the multitude had followed Him into a desert place, it is said, "And Jesus went forth and saw a great multitude, and was moved with compassion toward them, and He healed their sick" (14:14). Farther on: "They sent out into all that country round about and brought unto Him all that were diseased; and begged Him that they might only touch the hem of His garment; and as many as touched were made perfectly whole" (14:35-36).

Let us add to these many texts those which give us in detail the account of healings accomplished by Jesus, and let us ask ourselves if these healings afford us only the proof of His power during His life here on earth, or if they are not much rather the undoubted and continual result of His work of mercy and of love, the manifestation of His power of redemption which delivers the soul and body from the dominion of sin? Yes, that was in very deed the purpose of God. If then, Jesus bore our sicknesses as an integral part of the redemption, if He has healed the sick "that it might be fulfilled which was spoken by Isaiah," and if His Savior-heart is always full of mercy and of love, we can believe with certainty that to this very day it is the will of Jesus to heal the sick in answer to the prayer of faith.

April 21
His Hearing
by George Müller (1805-1898) Germany/England
Excerpted from "The Prayer-Hearing God," found on various websites about George Müller

"Ask, and it shall be given you; seek, and you shall find; knock, and it shall be opened unto you; for every one that asks receives; and he that seeks finds, and to him that knocks it shall be opened."
Matthew 7:7-8 (KJV)

Here is the first point specially to be noticed regarding prayer: "If we ask anything according to His will He hears us, and if we know that He hears us, whatsoever we ask we know that we have the petitions that we desired of Him." If, therefore, we pray, and desire to have our petitions granted, it motivates us first to see to it that we ask for things according to His mind and will; for our blessing and happiness are intimately connected with the holiness of God.

The second point we should notice is that we do not ask on account of our own goodness or merit, but, as the Scripture expresses it, "In the name of the Lord Jesus Christ." I refer you to John 14:13-14, "And whatsoever you shall ask in My name, that will I do, that the Father may be glorified in the Son. If you shall ask anything in My name, I will do it." The statement is given twice, in order to show the great importance of this truth.

A third condition is that we exercise faith in the power and willingness of God to answer our prayers. This is deeply important. In Mark 11:24, we read, "What things soever you desire, when you pray, believe that you receive them, and you shall have them." "What things soever you desire"—of whatever kind—"believe that you receive them and you shall have them." We must believe that God is able and willing. To see that He is able, you have only to look at the resurrection of the Lord Jesus Christ; for having raised Him from the dead, He must have almighty power. As to the love of God, you have only to look to the cross of Christ, and see His love in not sparing His Son, in not withholding His only-begotten Son from death. With these proofs of the power and love of God, assuredly, if we believe, we shall receive—we shall obtain.

Suppose now we ask, firstly, for such things as are according to the mind of God, and only such things can be good for us. Secondly, that we expect answers on the ground of the merit and righteousness of the Lord Jesus Christ, asking in His name. And thirdly, that we exercise faith in the power and willingness of our Heavenly Father to grant our requests. Then fourthly, we have to continue patiently waiting on God until the blessing we seek is granted. For observe, nothing is said in the text as to the time in which, or the circumstances under which, the prayer is to be answered. "Ask, and it shall be given to you." There is a positive promise, but nothing as to the time.

Moreover, we are never to lose sight of the fact that there may be particular reasons why prayer may not at once be answered. One reason may be the need for the exercise of our faith, for by exercise faith is strengthened. Another reason may be that we may glorify God by the manifestation of patience. This is a grace by which God is greatly magnified. Our manifestation of patience glorifies God. There may be another reason. Our heart may not yet be prepared for the answer to our prayer. Now all have sometimes long to wait for answers to prayer.

I have found it a great blessing to treasure up in the memory the answers God graciously gives me. I have always kept a record to strengthen the memory. I advise the keeping of a little memorandum book.

April 22
His Heart - 1
by James Russell (J. R.) Miller (1840-1912) USA
Excerpted from "Near the Heart of Christ," *The Hidden Life*, published by Thomas Y. Crowell & Company, New York, New York in 1895

"Continue in My love," was Jesus' exhortation. That is more than coming now and then, for an hour, into the warmth of His love. Perhaps most Christians do little more than this. They try to get into the love of Christ for a few moments in the morning, before they go out into the world's chill air. In the evening, too, when the day's toils, tasks, and struggles are over, they creep back into the love of Christ for a blessing, as they confess faults, failures, and sins, and ask for forgiveness. They like to be folded near the heart of Christ during the night. It is a safe place to be through the dark hours.

Then they try to come into the love of Christ on Sundays, when they meet with God's people for prayer. Especially at the Lord's Table [Communion] do they feel that they are in the warmth and tenderness of the love of Christ, when they receive the emblems of the supreme act of that love. These moments and hours of resting near the heart of Jesus are very precious. They are full of blessing. They exalt these lives of ours, and give us visions of heavenly glory.

But there is something better than this possible to the believer in Christ. To continue in the love of Christ is to dwell all the while, without break, without interruption, in this love. In the Revised Version of the Bible, the word is "abide" — "Abide in My love." To abide is to make one's home in the place; we are to make our home in the love of Christ. Not only in the morning hour of prayer, when we are seeking blessing for the day, are we to linger in this warmth, but just as really are we to stay in it when we go out into the midst of the world's strifes and duties.

Work is not incompatible with communion with Christ. Duty does not disturb the glow of true religion. If only our heart is right and our life sincere, we may abide in the love of Christ just as really when we are busy with our common tasks and toils as when we are bending over our Bible, or kneeling in prayer, or receiving the Lord's Supper.

Jesus said, "If you keep My commandments, you shall abide in My love; even as I have kept My Father's commandments, and abide in His love." It is a wonderful measure of nearness that is thus made possible to us—we shall abide in Christ's love, even as He abides in His Father's love. It seems almost incredible that such intimacy, such closeness, as that which existed between Christ and His Father, should be possible for us. Yet it is nothing less than this that is promised.

The way we can attain this unbroken abiding is also made very plain: "If you keep My commandments, you shall abide in My love." Meeting temptation, carrying burdens, facing dangers, mingling with people and ministering to them—none of these experiences or duties will interfere with true closeness to Christ, if meanwhile we are living obediently. Nothing will interrupt this communion and hide the light of the love of Christ, but sin. Sin is the only undivine thing in this world, and only sin can hinder our living near the heart of Christ.

There is no other spiritual culture like that which comes from such abiding in the love of Christ. Not all Christians are staying near to that infinite source of all spiritual life and power. Some are living far off; the multitude seek no special closeness to the Master, are satisfied with a very ordinary fellowship; only the few long for that abiding in which John was so wondrously blessed. If we keep ourselves in the love of Christ continually, we shall be led into closer and ever closer fellowship with Him; and then what our friends call the end, when they stand by us at the last, will be but passing through the veil into the perfect communion.

April 23
His Heart – 2
by Charles H. Parkhurst (1842-1933) USA
Excerpted from "Love Considered as a Dynamic," *The Pulpit and the Pew*, published by Yale University Press, New Haven, Connecticut in 1913

The gospel is not an idea but a passion, the outflow upon the world of an Infinite Affection.

"Heart" is a word that is constantly recurring in Scripture. "Brain" is, I believe, a term that is not once found there. Heart, in the sense in which it is currently understood, suggests the warm center of life. When we say of a man that he has a good deal of heart we mean that he is pleasant and warm; he may be brilliant or he may not; but he is such a person that snuggling up to him away from the chilly exposure, that there is so much of, is like getting around upon the south side of the house in midwinter, and letting the sunshine permeate us, and watching the snow slide off the twigs, and the water drops form on the points of the hanging icicles.

We are not trying to be precise. Precision is fatal. But there is what we may call the tropical side of a man. There is that which is called the heart of civilization and the heart of religion, as opposed to its brain and gristle. And there is what, without anything like fancifulness, could be designated the tropical area of the Bible, as distinguished from other portions that show a lower temperature and lie nearer the poles.

The emphasis of current thought lies on light, rather than on heat. A bright man is held in higher esteem than a man with fiery impulses. Brain counts for a good deal more today than heart does. It will win more applause and draw a larger salary. Emotion we are a little afraid of. We are cautioned not to let our feelings run away with us. We want to know that a conclusion has been reached in cold blood before we are disposed to submit our judgment to it. Exuberance is in bad taste.

It is something to reflect upon — the amount of mental energy that a man can expend upon matters of Christian truth, for example, upon the verbal forms of Christian truth and the relation of those forms to each other, without being touched, still less being quickened, by the realities that those forms were intended to represent. When a speaker is handling a truth, it may be of religion or philosophy, or whatever else, if he does it with dexterity, and if in the process his own mind is quickened into unusual activity, his activity communicates itself to the minds of his hearers, as the movement of one wheel communicates itself to the companion wheel into which it meshes. Mere intellectual activity upon religious themes is not religion any more than working a flying trapeze in a church is what the Bible means by "Godly exercise." An ox can devour the painting accidentally left upon the easel in the pasture where he is grazing, without becoming himself artistic.

Christianity is an energy. It is not an idea. It is not a picture, nor a philosophy, nor a theology, nor a memory. It is a producer, it is spiritual dynamic, and of course, then, like everything else that does things, begins in a passion; not brain, although like all passion, agreeable to brain; like all fire, to be restrained from becoming mere inferno. It is a passion; first of all, it is the passion of Him who "so loved the world that He gave His only-begotten Son, that whosoever believes in Him should not perish, but have everlasting life." Redemption is not the outcome of God's intellect. It is love, not thought, warmth, not light. Divine love has been disclosed in intelligent ways, but it is the love itself that makes out the genius of the matter and that does the work. Argumentation is not an energy. Love is.

April 24
His Hopefulness
by James Russell (J. R.) Miller (1840-1912) USA
Excerpted from "The Hopefulness of Jesus," *The Hidden Life*, published by Thomas Y. Crowell & Company, New York, New York in 1898

It is cheering to know that our Leader never faltered, never lost heart, for one moment. The story of Jesus, from the moment of His birth until the day when He was taken up, is one of magnificent hopefulness. There was an old prophecy concerning Him which said, "He shall not fail nor be discouraged, until He has set judgment in the earth." And He never was discouraged. Life was not easy for Him: It was always hard; but hope never languished in His heart.

His beginning was lowly and feeble in human eyes. He was born of a peasant mother. Though angels sang of His coming into the world, the shepherds found the wonderful Babe wrapped in swaddling clothes, lying in a manger. His early years were spent in poverty. He learned a trade—He whose hand had made the heavens worked at a common carpenter's bench. Yet the lowliness of His circumstances did not embitter His spirit. He never complained that His earthly life was not in keeping with the glory of His person or the dignity of His mission. He never said that He could make nothing of His life because of the narrowness and weakness of His environment. Indeed, out of His very poverty and toil, and out of the very limitations of His condition, came some of the finest things in His character.

Nor did the hopefulness of Jesus fail Him in the days of His poverty and trial, or in the midst of His difficult circumstances. He lived a life of sweet contentment, and learned the lessons that were set for Him. He never lost His joy. One secret was that He was ever doing His Father's will; and this gave Him gladness, even in the hour of bitterest pain. Another secret was His confidence in the final outcome of the work He was doing at such tremendous cost. He knew His mission could not fail.

The danger of narrow circumstances is that the heart may lose its sweetness and grow bitter. But Jesus went through His years of poverty, lack, hardship, and toil with small earnings, and all the petty annoyances and frets of Galilean peasant life, with a heart as quiet, peaceful, and loving as if He had been living yet in Heaven. He was never fretted or worried. He was never afraid to see the last farthing go, or the last loaf eaten. He lived Himself His own lesson against anxiety before He gave it to His disciples. Few men have ever worked in this world whose lives seemed more utter failures at the end than did the life of Jesus. There seemed no room for Him in this world. He found no welcome when He first came. During the wonderful years of His public ministry, though crowds followed Him, He was not loved, except by a very few. Most of those who followed Him, followed Him only for His miracles, through curiosity, or for the help they might get from Him. At the last all men forsook Him. Then all ended on a cross.

Yet in this long experience of unwelcome, rejection, and ingratitude, He was never discouraged. He foresaw the end, but He came toward the dark tragedy like a conqueror. Hope shone in His face, and burned in His words, like a flame of glory. In the same sentence in which He said He must be killed, He said also that He would be raised again the third day. Instead of speaking of His work as a failure, He spoke of the Kingdom He was to establish as one that would fill the world. He went on making plans for the future, beyond His death, as if death would be only an incident in His great mission. What was the secret of this magnificent hopefulness of Jesus? He knew that His work was only beginning. He was a Sower, not a reaper. Ages to come would witness the harvest from His life, His teachings, His tears, His blood. He would rise again, and His name and glory and His saving health would fill all the earth. He would see of the travail of His soul, and would be satisfied.

April 25
His Humanity
by Samuel Dickey (S. D.) Gordon (1859-1936) USA
Excerpted from "The Human Jesus," *Quiet Talks About Jesus*, published by A. C. Armstrong & Son, New York, New York in 1906

Now, Jesus was human; truly naturally human, God's human, and then more because of the conditions He found. The love act of creation brought with it self-imposed limitations to God. And now the love act of saving brings still more. God made man in His own image. In His humanity Jesus was in the image of God, even as we are. Adam was an unfallen man. Jesus was that and more, a tested and now matured unfallen man, and by the law of growth ever growing more. Adam was an innocent, unfallen man up to the temptation. Jesus was a virtuous unfallen man. The test with Him changed innocence to virtue.

In His experiences, His works. His temptations, His struggles, His victories, Jesus was clearly human. In His ability to read people's thoughts and know their lives without finding out by ordinary means, His knowledge ahead of coming events, His knowledge of and control over nature, He clearly was more than the human we know. Yet until we know more than we seem to know now of the proper powers of an unfallen man matured and growing in the use and control of those powers, we cannot draw here any line between human and divine. But the whole presumption is in favor of believing that in all of this Jesus was simply exercising the proper human powers which with Him were not hurt by sin but ever increasing in use.

Jesus insisted on living a simple true human life, dependent upon God and upon others. He struck the keynote of this at the start in the wilderness. Everything He taught He put through the test of use. He was what He taught. As a man He has gone through all He calls us to. He blazed the way into every thicket and woods, and then stands ahead, softly, clearly calling, "Come along after Me."

He experienced all the proper limitations of human life. He needed food and sleep and rest and needed to give His body proper thought and care. He was under the human limitations regarding space and material construction. He got from one place to another by the slow process of using His strength or joining it with nature or that of a beast. He entered a building through an opening as we do. Both of these are in sharp contrast with the conditions after the resurrection. His stock of knowledge came by the law of increase, the natural way; some, and then more, and the more gaining more yet. He was hungry sometimes without food at hand to satisfy His hunger. Jesus got tired. Could there be a closer touch! He fell asleep on a pillow in the stern of the boat one day crossing the lake. And the sleep was like that of a very tired man, so sound that the wild storm did not wake Him up. Jesus knew the pinch of poverty. He was the eldest in a large family, with the father probably dead, and so likely was the chief breadwinner, earning for Himself and for the others a living by His trade. Jesus was a homeless man. Forced from the home village by His fellow townsmen, for those busy years he had no quiet home spot of His own to rest in. And He felt it.

And Jesus knew the sharp discipline of waiting. He knew what it meant to be going a commonplace, humdrum, treadmill round while the fires are burning within for something else. He knew, and forever cast a sweet soft halo over all such labor as people call drudgery, which never was such to Him because of the fine spirit breathed into it. Drudgery, commonplaceness is in the spirit, not the work. Nothing could be commonplace or humdrum when done by One with such an uncommon spirit. Today up yonder on the throne there's a Man—related to us, bone of our bone, heart of our heart, toil of our toil. He—knows.

April 26
His Humility

by Andrew Murray (1828-1917) Scotland/South Africa
Excerpted from "His Humility," *Humility: The Beauty of Holiness*, published by Fleming H. Revell Company, London, England in 1910

"But I am among you as the one who serves."
Luke 22:27 (ESV)

In the Gospel of John we have the inner life of our Lord laid open to us. Jesus speaks frequently of His relation to the Father, of the motives by which He is guided, of His consciousness of the power and spirit in which He acts. He took the place of entire subordination, and gave God the honor and glory which is due to Him. And what He taught so often was made true to Himself: "He that humbles himself shall be exalted." As it is written, "He humbled Himself, therefore God highly exalted Him."

He was nothing, that God might be all. He resigned Himself with His will and His powers entirely for the Father to work in Him. Of His own power, His own will, and His own glory, of His whole mission with all His works and His teaching—of all this He said, It is not I; I am nothing; I have given Myself to the Father to work; I am nothing, the Father is all.

This life of entire self-denial, of absolute submission and dependence upon the Father's will, Christ found to be one of perfect peace and joy. He lost nothing by giving all to God. God honored His trust, and did all for Him, and then exalted Him to His own right hand in glory. And because Christ had thus humbled Himself before God, and God was ever before Him, He found it possible to humble Himself before men too, and to be the Servant of all. His humility was simply the surrender of self to God, to allow Him to do in Him what He pleased, whatever men around might say of Him, or do to Him.

It is in this state of mind, in this spirit and disposition, that the redemption of Christ has its virtue and effectiveness. It is to bring us to this disposition that we are made partakers of Christ. This is the true self-denial to which our Savior calls us, the acknowledgment that self has nothing good in it, except as an empty vessel which God must fill, and that its claim to be or do anything may not for a moment be allowed. It is in this, above and before everything, in which the conformity to Jesus consists, the being and doing nothing of ourselves, that God may be all.

It was because this humility was not only a temporary sentiment, awakened and brought into exercise when He thought of God, but the very spirit of His whole life, that Jesus was just as humble in His interaction with men as with God. He felt Himself the Servant of God for the men whom God made and loved, as a natural consequence. He counted Himself the Servant of men, that through Him God might do His work of love. He never for a moment thought of seeking His honor, or asserting His power to vindicate Himself. His whole spirit was that of a life yielded to God to work in. It is not until Christians study the humility of Jesus as the very essence of His redemption, as the very blessedness of the life of the Son of God, as the only true relation to the Father, and therefore as that which Jesus must give us if we are to have any part with Him, that the terrible lack of actual, heavenly, evident humility will become a burden and a sorrow, and our ordinary religion be set aside to secure this, the first and the chief of the marks of Christ within us.

Brothers and sisters, are you clothed with humility? Ask your daily life. Ask Jesus. Ask your friends. Ask the world. And begin to praise God that there is opened up to you in Jesus a heavenly humility of which you have hardly known, and through which a heavenly blessedness you possibly have never yet tasted can come in to you.

April 27
His Hurt
by Robert Murray McCheyne (1813-1843) Scotland
Excerpted from "'Will You Also Go Away?'" *The Works of the Late Robert Murray McCheyne, Vol. II*, published by Robert Carter, New York, New York in 1847

After this many of His disciples turned back and no longer walked with Him. So Jesus said to the twelve, "Do you want to go away as well?" Simon Peter answered Him, "Lord, to whom shall we go? You have the words of eternal life."
John 6:66-68 (ESV)

Many who seem to be disciples of Christ, go back, and walk no more with Jesus.

So here the multitude that followed Christ were pleased with a great many things in Him. When He fed them with the five barley loaves and the two fishes, they said: "Lord, it is good for us to be here" — "This is in truth that prophet that should come into the world." And, again, when Jesus told them of bread from Heaven that would give life, they said most devoutly: "Lord, evermore give us this bread." But when Christ said: "He that eats My flesh, and drinks My blood, dwells in Me, and I in him," by and by they were offended. When He told them that He would be their life, and would dwell in them, they said: "It is a hard saying, who can bear it?" They did not believe; they went back, and walked no more with Jesus.

First Warning: Many go so far with Christ, who do not go the whole way. Many hear Christ's words for a time with joy and eagerness, who yet are offended by them at last. This is a solemn warning. Do not think you are a Christian because you sit and listen to the words of Christ. Do not think you are a Christian because you have some pleasure in the words of Christ. Many are called; few are chosen. Many went back, and only twelve remained. So doubtless it will be found among you. Those only are Christians who feed upon Christ, and live by Him.

Second Warning: Those that go back, generally walk no more with Jesus. Perhaps they did not intend to bid an eternal farewell to the Savior. Perhaps they said, as they retired, I will go home and think about it; I will hear Him again concerning this matter. At a more convenient season I will follow Him. But, alas! that season never came; they walked no more with Jesus. Take warning, dear friends, you that are anxious about your souls. Oh! do not be easily offended. Do not lose a sense of your lost condition. Oh! do not grow careless of your Bible and the means of grace. Oh! do not go back to the company of sinners. These are all marks of one who is going away from Jesus. Wait patiently for the Lord, until He inclines His ear and hears your cry. Still press to hear the words of Jesus. Still cry for the teaching Spirit. "If any man draws back, My soul shall have no pleasure in him"; "No man having put his hand to the plow, and looking back, is fit for the Kingdom of God."

"Then said Jesus to the twelve, Will you also go away?" I have no doubt the heart of Jesus was grieved when the multitude went away, and walked no more with Him. That good Shepherd never yet saw a lost sheep running on to destruction, but his heart bled for it. He could see all the future history of these men; how they would lose all their impressions; how they would harden in their sins; how, like a rolling snowball, they would gather more and more wrath around them, and, I do not doubt, He wept in secret over them, and said: "If you had known, even you; but now they are hidden from your eyes." He traced their history up to that hour when He would say, "Depart from Me." But however much Christ grieved over their departure, this only fanned the flame of His love to His own, so that He turned round and said, "Will you also go away?"

April 28
His Identification
by George H. Morrison (1866-1928) Scotland
Excerpted from "Son of Man," *O Christian Devotionals* website

"Who do people say the Son of Man is?"
Matthew 16:13 (NIV)

There are two names which our Lord was inclined to use when He spoke about His person or His work. The one was the Son of God, and the other was the Son of Man. It was not often that He used the former title, if we may judge by the Synoptic Gospels [Matthew, Mark, Luke], and when He used it, it was always in some moment of unusual importance and seriousness. But it is different with the latter, "the Son of Man." This was constantly upon the lips of Christ. It seems to have been His most familiar word when He referred to His person or His work. And so deeply engraved is this upon our hearts, and kneaded into the thought of Christendom, that whenever we hear the expression "Son of Man" we at once revert to the figure of our Savior. Under this name, then, our Lord described Himself. By this He conveyed His thought about Himself. It was a name He loved with deep affection, and which welled to His lips in the most diverse circumstances. Nor should it be forgotten that in the whole New Testament, where the title "Son of Man" occurs so often, only on two occasions is it used by anyone other than the Lord Himself.

Now it is notable that in all His use of it our Lord never pauses to define the name. He does not explain what it conveyed to Him, nor what He meant it should convey to others. When our Lord gave Simon his new name of Peter, He was careful to interpret its significance. "You are Peter," He said, so that all could hear, "and on this rock I shall build My Church." But when He laid aside His own name Jesus, and began to speak of Himself as Son of Man, He offered no explanation of the name, and never declared the reason for His choice. Equally noticeable too is this, that no one ever asked Him to define it. It seems to have been accepted without comment, and at least in a measure to have been understood. For people were not slow to interrogate the Savior, and to ask Him what He meant by this or that, but we never find anyone enquiring of Him what was the meaning of this "Son of Man."

Now the reason for that absence of all questioning will suggest itself to every reader at once. This was no new name, coined at a moment's need, it was a name that was wreathed with old association. There was not a Jew who heard the Master use it but would find it encircled with familiar thoughts. It was a name they had been accustomed to since childhood in their reading or hearing of the ancient Scriptures. And it came to them, not as a word of novelty, nor with the captivating touch of the unknown, but as a word that was a heritage of Israel from the far-off day of prophets and psalmists. In other words, this was a borrowed name, and it was borrowed from the roll of the Old Testament. It was not a title coined for the occasion; it was fragrant with happy and with holy memories. And what Christ did was to take the sacred name, and to breathe upon it with the breath of life, so that it glowed into a new significance and expanded into undreamed-of fullness.

It is the perfect Man who is to reign, in the golden age to which the Jew was looking. And yet this Man is something more than man, for He stands in the heavens encircled by its clouds, and the passing of ages leaves no trace upon Him, and the Ancient of Days receives Him as His fellow. It was such thoughts the Jews associated with the name "Son of Man." It is not a matter of debate if such thoughts were in the mind of Jesus. There can be no question in the matter, for we have the testimony of Christ Himself. He would never have used it had He not wished to intimate that He was the promised Messiah of the Jews. And so it tells us that here is Christ, the Man in whom all humanity is centered, yet the Man who knew that He was more than man, the Fellow of the everlasting God.

April 29
His Illumination
by James W. Alexander (1804-1859) USA
Excerpted from "Spiritual Illumination," *Faith: Treated in a Series of Discourses*, published by Charles Scribner, New York, New York in 1862

For God, who commanded the light to shine out of darkness, has shined in our hearts, to give the light of the knowledge of the glory of God in the face of Jesus Christ.
2 Corinthians 4:6 (KJV)

The objects which the unrenewed eye cannot take in are spiritual objects. For "the natural man receives not the things of the Spirit of God, for they are foolishness unto him: neither can he know them, because they are spiritually discerned." The objects themselves are luminous and lovely; they are presented in clearness of revelation; but they are presented to the blind. Men of enlightened and cultivated powers as to every other field, wander in this, without attention, interest, or distinct knowledge. This is the history of the gospel in every age: "If our gospel is hidden, it is hidden to them that are lost; in whom the god of this world has blinded the minds of them which believe not lest the light of the glorious gospel should shine unto them" (2 Corinthians 4:4).

These are strong words, but they are those of the Holy Ghost; and no words are too strong to represent the absence of all spiritual light in most of those who live amidst the clear shining of Christian day. It is an incantation, and the illusory process is ascribed to the evil one. Part of the malady, and its most fearful symptom, is that the blind man does not know that he is blind. "Are we blind also?" asked the indignant Pharisees (John 9:40), when Jesus pointed out this dazzling consequence of His light on proud minds. Sinners may be addressed as was Laodicea in Revelation 3:17, "and do you not know that you are wretched, and miserable, and poor, and blind." Complete experience is on the part of those only who have been in both conditions, and who, with eyes newly opened, look back to the day when they were without sight. And they marvel how they could remain so long without impression from the truth.

The darkness, while it remains, is an effective preventive of all right views, feelings, and determinations. To remove this, and to communicate to the soul correct understanding of divine realities, God is pleased to intervene in the case of His people by a direct and instantaneous act terminating on the mind itself, and empowering it to see. This act is previous to all saving exercises, and is of God's sovereignty. Though known only by its effects, it gives life, and in giving life, gives the power of spiritual vision. It is variously represented as giving sight to the blind, and as giving light to an eye in darkness.

This spiritual illumination takes place at the new birth. The instrument employed by the sovereign Spirit in all the acts, believing, feelings, and decisions of the soul so regenerated, is Truth. The renewed mind beholds divine objects in a new and indescribable manner, in their self-evidencing brightness, in their beauty, loveliness, and glory, so as to appreciate, taste, and relish them, and in a certain as yet imperfect degree discern them as they are. This new and spiritual understanding, which cannot be represented to such as possess no experience, comprises all the circle of revealed truth, and all the objects of the spiritual interest; but in its first actions it more especially fixes on and takes in the glory of grace in the face of Jesus Christ, which object it now, for the first time, understands. Under the enlightening of the Holy Ghost the mind most particularly views with perception and interest the truth that God is reconciled to it through this Redeemer. And all this understanding of the new creature is preparatory to saving faith, from which, when both are in high measure, it cannot be distinguished.

April 30
His Immutability - 1
by Henry Ward Beecher (1813-1887) USA
Excerpted from "The Immutability of God Interpreted and Applied,"
Forty-Six Sermons, published by R. D. Dickinson, London, England in 1885

Jesus Christ the same yesterday, and today, and forever.
Hebrews 13:8 (KJV)

As far as the Word of God passed into the hands of men, it became a fundamental part of their idea of God that He was immutable [unchanging]. That being the philosophy, taught and received in all its phases, there sprang out of it, in the course of time, troublesome tendencies, which need to be corrected on the other side. The indiscriminate teaching of this doctrine of God's immutableness has led to a notion of Divine serenity and eternal calm as a part of the nature of God, and indispensable to right understanding of Him. It has been supposed that variation of feeling was inconsistent with unchangeableness; that God is unchangeable in the sense that His feelings flow forever in the same key; that God would be less than perfect if He suffered Himself to be changed in feeling by external influences; and that, from considerations of His own interior consciousness, He determines how much and how little He shall feel if He ever changes the volume of His feeling. Thus it has come with many to be supposed that the immutableness of God implies one kind of feeling, eternally flowing in one volume, and with an even current to the end.

This supposition has been enhanced by the idea that God, knowing all things, could not be subject to those causes of change which act upon us. It has been said that we fluctuate because we are surprised; that we are surprised because we have not the power of foreseeing and knowing all things; that our emotions come and go according to the ever-changing moods and interpretations of our understanding, which understanding, beginning with imperfect hypotheses, comes to imperfect conclusions, and puts us in a condition of changeableness; and that such cannot be the case with God, who, seeing the end from the beginning, never learns anything. It is said that God's feeling cannot change, because He is exempt from those illusions, partial views, and imaginations which in us cause incessant fluctuation. Hence it has been supposed that God neither kindles with joy nor is saddened with grief; that He is moved neither with ecstasy nor sorrow; that in serenity and calm He holds Himself aloof from the fluctuations of emotion and feeling for evermore. And there are some dispositions to whom this view of God seems attractive.

Now, in the first place, this is wholly opposed to the representations both in the Old and in the New Testament. There is the general principle laid down that God is unchangeable; but that has respect to His moral disposition, and to the comprehensive method by which He administers, rather than to the specific flow of His feeling. There can be conceived no greater range of variation than that which is ascribed to the feelings of Jehovah—of gladness and sorrow; of delight and sadness; of esteem and of wrath. He is represented as experiencing moral emotions in all their shades or degrees of intensity. Let a man read the Old Testament and be asked, "Is God a being subject to rise and fall of feeling?" and he would be surprised that such a question should be addressed to him. There is no word in the English tongue that is not employed to signify the gradations of feeling attributed to God—that is, gradations of feeling in right attributes. There is no fluctuation of feeling in God as between good and bad. He is always good, always high, always holy, always loving, always boundless in mercy, though He is just and severe in penalty, and not without indignation. But it is taught throughout the Scriptures that God's feelings are graded according to the circumstances which are brought before Him in the Divine administration.

May 1
His Immutability - 2
by Henry Ward Beecher (1813-1887) USA
Excerpted from "The Immutability of God Interpreted and Applied," *Forty-Six Sermons*, published by R. D. Dickinson, London, England in 1885

Jesus Christ the same yesterday, and today, and forever.
Hebrews 13:8 (KJV)

A God whose feelings never move; a God that never has a new suggestion or a new emotion; a God that is in a state of quietness — such a God the human mind cannot approach. It is utterly impossible to bring the heart to love an impassive God. No man can creep up on such a smooth and glassy surface, and hold on to it, and experience toward it feelings of adoration, and sympathy, and yearning, and love, and desire. A crystal set in the center of the earth would answer the purpose of a divinity as well as a God that had no change of thought or emotion. It is impossible for men to be drawn toward a being so entirely different from that which the human soul was constituted to cherish and to love.

It may seem as though this was a matter of mere unimportant speculation; but it is much more important than many imagine. For there are those who teach that God cannot suffer, and that suffering is incompatible with perfection. They hold to the view that God dwells in an eternal calm of joy which makes it impossible for Him to suffer. So universal had this idea become that, when the doctrine of Christ as God was believed and advocated, men said, "What! do you teach that God died?" Why, within my remembrance, the New England hymn books were changed to get rid of the idea that God died in Christ. The incompatibility of suffering with perfection was one of the arguments employed by controversial writers to show the preposterousness of the dogma that God, in the person of the Savior, suffered for the world. The orthodox mind even began to be pained at the mention of such a thing. It was declared to be blasphemous to attribute suffering, and much more blasphemous to attribute death, to God. To teach me that God cannot suffer is to take away from my mind the most fundamental understanding of what it is to be God. I cannot conceive of a being worthy of universal sympathy, and honor, and glory, that cannot suffer. Nor does the fact that God knows all things and foresees all things change that indispensable quality of mind which makes it necessary that love should fluctuate. Can I look upon my child and see all the things that are happening to him, and not have my feelings moved, though I know that in the end he will overcome the troubles by which he is beset? My sympathy for him leads me to follow him with my moods, and I go up and down the ways through which he is called to pass. And is it to be taught that God, sitting in Heaven, and beholding the sufferings of the world, is unmoved? To bear humankind in His bosom; to bow down His majesty and become a Man, that He might put Himself underneath the human race and lift them up—is that the conduct of a God that does not know how to suffer? Is there in such conduct no token of variability, of everlasting changeableness of feeling—not in kind, but in enlargement, in diminishment, in adaptation?

And can you conceive of a human soul attempting to love a being that is so perfectly untroubled, so entirely undisturbed, that in a period of six thousand years there was not a single ripple on His soul? But if there is, in the boundlessness of the Divine mind, such exquisite susceptibility, that a child speaking, can produce an impression, in its measure, upon the Divine feeling, and that a patriarch, praying, can produce upon it, in his measure, a mightier impression; that in such feelings, joy and sorrow, with endless iterations and fluctuations, come and go, keeping evermore within the bounds of righteousness, then is not the nature of God one toward which your soul should aspire, and one which should draw out your sympathy and command your love? It was such susceptibility that the disciples found in the Savior.

May 2
His Immutability - 3
by Henry Ward Beecher (1813-1887) USA
Excerpted from "The Immutability of God Interpreted and Applied," *Forty-Six Sermons*, published by R. D. Dickinson, London, England in 1885

Jesus Christ the same yesterday, and today, and forever.
Hebrews 13:8 (KJV)

It is important to show that God is not immutable in another sense. It is sometimes urged by critics in this matter that He never changes His mind nor His purpose. There has been perplexity on account of the representations of Scripture in reference to God's repenting. In one place we read, "The Strength of Israel will not repent; for He is not a man that He should repent." And yet in other places it is recorded that God repented that He had made man, and repented that He had established kingdoms. Again and again you will find in the Bible declarations of God's having repented. It is supposed that He could not repent, and yet it is said repeatedly that He did repent. Repentance has two meanings. Its original meaning was simply changing one's course without any intimation respecting the nature of the change as good or bad. But it has come to have a technical meaning, signifying change on account of profound self-consciousness of wrong. Repentance now means conviction of having done wrong, and a change in consequence of that conviction.

God never does repent as man does, who is imperfect, and who turns back on his path because he has gone wrong. God never goes wrong, and He never has occasion to repent in the sense of changing from a wrong to a right course; but He may and does repent in the original sense. If you are about to punish a child that has done wrong, and he bursts into tears and says, "I have done wrong: punish me! punish me! only help me!" you relent, and your hand goes down, and you say to yourself, "I meant to punish him, but this repentance disarms me," and, turning to the child, you say, "Go free, and sin no more."

The Scriptures teach that God adapts His feelings to the facts that arise in the administration of His moral government. There is a difference between the Bible and the systems that are based upon nature. All theologies outside of the Bible make God to be a fate. Inflexible, intense, and certain fate is part and parcel of every system that is founded upon mere naturalism. In the Bible, however, God is represented as turning with all the facility of change that belongs to the parental mind. Prayer, repentance, and the hope of salvation are based upon the truth that God, although immutable in some respects, is in other respects subject to endless variations and flexibilities. God is forever young and forever old. He is not, as men are, changed by time. It is blessed to think of being eternally young; but the thought that, while men are wrinkled, and bent, and scarred by disease, and toil, and suffering, and are subject to all manner of infirmities, there is One that is unchanged by time, and is forever in the bloom of youth—this thought comes home with sweetness and comfort to every heart.

There is no change in the great moral attributes which form the basis of the Divine character—justice, and truth, and love. That which was love in the beginning, is love now, and will be love for evermore. Truth and justice are the same now that they were in the beginning, and that they ever will be. Nor is there any change in the essential purposes of God's moral government. It is not to be supposed that He came to the head of the affairs of the universe without a plan. It is not to be supposed that He made one thing, and then determined what next He would make. It is to be supposed (and nature as well as Scripture bears witness to it) that God saw the end from the beginning, that He follows a plan eternally ordained, and that the whole vast administration of creation is carried on in pursuance of certain great fixed ideas.

May 3
His Impartiality
by Charles Bayard Mitchell (1857-1942) USA
Excerpted from "The Impartial God," *The Noble Quest and Other Sermons*, published by Jennings and Graham, Cincinnati, Ohio in 1905

"God is no respecter of persons."
Acts 10:34 (KJV)

See Jesus in search of the rich wicked. He was entering Jericho, and the richest man in town had been ostracized by the orthodox folk of the place. The little man [Zaccheus] had climbed a tree to catch a view of the passing Savior. He was the last man whom they would have selected as a convert to the new faith; but Jesus saw in him the possibilities of true holiness and spoke to him, and invited Himself to dine with him, and won him to His heart forever.

Look at that rich young Jew seated at the receipt of customs, taxing his fellow Jews and hated by them all. He would not have been selected by any orthodox Jew for any place of trust and responsibility; for he had made himself a partner to the despised Roman Empire, and was collecting money to help run the Roman government; but Jesus saw in him a future disciple, and called him to follow Him, which he did, and became one of His able and potent powers for good for all time. God can love even a rich sinner, and though it may be hard to woo and win him, Jesus was as ready to die for him as for the poorest of men.

See Jesus seeking for the wicked poor. He entered a town one day, and found that there was one poor blind man who was counted so low and unworthy that he was the most despised man in the community, and was not permitted to enter the synagogue, and had He asked who was the most wretched man in the place He would have been told that it was this very blind man — too low to associate with his kind. That poor fellow was the very one in all the town whose condition appealed most to the heart of the Savior. He sought him and found him. He healed him and restored him to good standing among his fellows. A man seeking friends in a strange city would wish to associate himself with the most popular, but Jesus would search out the most needy and save the most wicked man in all the place.

See Jesus seeking the wicked outcast. One day, while standing in the Temple court, a group of men came dragging into His presence a despised woman of the town. They charged her with an ugly sin, and said she had been caught in the very act. They reminded Him that it was the requirement of the law that she should be put to death. They would have Him decide her lot and declare judgment. They told the whole ugly tale of her revolting sin. It was so unclean that He, the pure in heart, would not look them in the face while they recounted it; and so, in sheer modesty, He turned aside and stooped down as though He would write on the floor and kept His face averted until they had told their story; and when they were done, without looking up, He said, "He that is without sin among you, let him be the first to cast a stone at her," and then by and by looking up He discovered that her accusers had fled, and He, infinite Purity, was left alone with her—infinite impurity—upon the Temple floor. He spoke words to her that cut her to the quick. The sight of Him awakened deepest repentance and sorrow for her sin. He saw there the repentant heart, and speaking words of pardon sent her away with a new joy in her soul and a new song on her lips. Those men who brought her into His presence would not have dared associate with her on the street; but the loving Savior saw in her a possible disciple, and His great heart went out in love for her who had been regarded as an outcast in the town.

May 4
His Imperatives
by Newman Smyth (1843-1925) USA
Excerpted from "The Imperatives of Jesus," *The Reality of Faith*,
published by Charles Scribner's Sons, New York, New York in 1884

"But I say unto you..."
Matthew 5:44 (KJV)

Jesus speaks in imperatives. He commands human nature. The Sermon on the Mount is a sermon in the imperative mood. It is gracious, but it is imperative. Its blessings are commandments. Jesus reconstructs by His supreme personal authority the law and traditions of the people. It is enough for His command that He speaks it. "You have heard that it has been said: but I say unto you." "Verily, verily I say unto you." He does not argue with men; He commands them. He speaks words of invitation, but His invitations have behind them the imperatives of truth. His word, "Come unto Me," is both an invitation of heavenly grace and a command of duty. His words, "Blessed are the poor in spirit," "Blessed are the pure in heart," and so on, are words of supreme authority as well as promises of grace. Jesus never speaks for Himself or for His Kingdom one apologetic word. He makes demands of righteousness and truth upon us.

Glance again over the Gospels, and observe with what clear and ceaseless consistency Jesus' speech keeps up to the great imperatives of His Kingdom. Like the successive strokes of a bell ringing out over the hills and down the valleys, these imperatives of Jesus sound forth across the ages: Repent; believe; come; follow Me; take up your cross; seek first the Kingdom of God; keep My commandments. On all occasions, and before all men, Jesus kept His attitude of command, while He lost no human grace or gentleness by His constant and unmistakable attitude of authority over men. He went into the Temple, and stood among the rulers of the people as their Lord. He opened the Scriptures in the synagogue, and interpreted the law and the prophets as the Master even of those sacred rolls. He spoke with authority over Moses. He walked the beach of Gennesaret, and when the people came crowding around Him, He taught as One having authority. He talked with a willful woman at Jacobs' well, and she who had had seven husbands, and yet could carry her head high through that village in Samaria, finds her pride broken, and is at last humbled before the Stranger, who quietly told her all things which ever she had done.

In the still evening Rabbi Nicodemus comes to Him—now surely he who through the day and among the people has kept up a brave show of knowledge of the truth, and yielded his authority to none who questioned him, will acknowledge in private conversation with a master of Israel His own questionings and limitations, and the two sitting together upon the housetop under the stars will be but as children of the infinite mystery from which we are born. But hardly had the courteous salutation of Nicodemus been addressed to Jesus, when instead of the humble and half deprecating answer which would have been for any man of us the natural answer, clear and full upon the night air sounds Jesus' "Verily, verily I say unto you!"—to be repeated again as Nicodemus in astonishment asks the question of bewilderment, "How can these things be?" and to be followed and enforced by the supreme commandment, "You must be born again!"

And what man or woman of us is there who knows enough to contradict Jesus Christ? Who of us has learned anything to justify us in setting up our thought of life against Jesus' thought of it? our desire for happiness against the blessings of Jesus' gospel? our plan for immortality against Jesus' revelations of the way of eternal life? Who of us has authority to contradict the Master of the disciples, the Christ of the Gospels, the Lord of history, the Son of the Father, the Creator of the World, the Judge of all?

May 5
His Infinity - 1
by Albert Benjamin (A. B.) Simpson (1843-1919) Canada
Excerpted from "The First and the Last," *The Names of Jesus*, published by The Christian Alliance Publishing Company, New York, New York in 1892

> "I am Alpha and Omega, the beginning and the end, the first and the last."
> Revelation 22:13 (KJV)

This expresses the eternal pre-existence of Christ. We find Him constantly declaring this in His own addresses in the Gospel of John. "He was before me," is the witness of John the Baptist to Him. "I came from the Father and am come into the world," is His own testimony. "Before Abraham was, I am." Even in the Old Testament we have some wonderful pictures of the eternal Christ. "His name shall be the Everlasting Father (or the Father of Eternity)," is Isaiah's picture. "His going out has been of old, even from everlasting," is Micah's picture. "The Lord possessed Me in the beginning of His way, before His works of old I was established from everlasting, from the beginning, or ever the earth was, when there were no depths, I was brought forth. When there were no fountains abounding with water, before the mountains were settled, before the hills, was I brought forth. When He prepared the heavens I was there. When He set a compass upon the face of the deep, then I was by Him as one brought up with Him, and I was daily His delight; rejoicing always before Him; rejoicing in the habitable parts of His earth, and My delights were with the children of humanity." This is Solomon's inspired picture of the eternal Logos, and His ancient love to the world, and the people that He was coming in the fullness of the ages to redeem.

This expresses His pre-eminence. This also is most clearly taught by the Holy Spirit in the Scriptures, and claimed by Christ Himself. "That in all things He might have the pre-eminence," is the Father's purpose regarding His dear Son, for His is the pre-eminence of deity. He is higher than all others, higher than all angels; very God of very God; the brightness of the Father's glory, the express image of His person, the King of kings and Lord of lords. There is no doubt that this is what He claimed Himself, and for this claim His life was threatened again and again by the Jews, and taken at last in His final judgment and crucifixion. "He ought to die, because He has made Himself the Son of God," was their charge. The hands into which we commit our souls are divine and infinite hands. The ransom which has been paid for our sin is of the infinite value of deity. The grace that is sufficient for our full salvation is the grace of the infinite God. The kinship to which He has raised us is nothing less than to be partakers of the divine nature, and sons and heirs of God, and joint heirs with Christ. Let us not fear to bring forth every crown and honor Him Lord of all.

This expresses His relation to the work of creation and Providence. This thought is expressed by the Apostle Paul in his epistle to the Colossians in these strong and significant words: "For by Him were all things created that are in Heaven, and that are in earth, visible and invisible, whether they be thrones or dominions, or principalities or powers; all things were created by Him and for Him; and He is above all things, and by Him all things consist." This expresses Christ's relation to the natural creation, and to the affairs of Providence. It was through His hand that the material universe was framed; it is by His constant superintendence that the whole machinery of Providence is carried on. By Him all things, literally, "hang together." He is the cohesive force that holds the whole universe in order. All power is given to Him in Heaven and in earth. Like the Roman centurion, all beings and forces are at the service of His will, and He can say to this one, "Go," and he goes, or to this one, "Come," and he comes, and to all things, "Do this," and they do it.

May 6
His Infinity - 2
by Albert Benjamin (A. B.) Simpson (1843-1919) Canada
Excerpted from "The First and the Last," *The Names of Jesus*, published by The Christian Alliance Publishing Company, New York, New York in 1892

> *"I am Alpha and Omega, the beginning and the end, the first and the last."*
> Revelation 22:13 (KJV)

This verse also expresses His relation to the Bible. Christ is first in these sacred pages. The one objective of the Holy Scriptures is to reveal the person and portrait of Jesus. This is the key to its interpretation. This is the glory of its pages—Jesus in the story of creation, already planning the new creation; Jesus supreme above the ruins of the Fall; Jesus in the ark, the rainbow and the dove; Jesus in the sacrifice on Mount Moriah; the ladder of Jacob, and the story of Joseph, Jesus in the Passover lamb; the desert manna, the smitten rock, the pillar-cloud, the smoking sacrifice, the fragrant incense, the suffering scapegoat, the enrobed priest, the golden candlestick, the sacred ark, the sprinkled mercy seat, the hovering cherubim, the magnificent Shekinah, the glorious tabernacle and all its ministries and furniture; Jesus in the land of promise, in the Temple of Solomon, in the story of Joshua, the Psalms of David, the throne of Solomon, the visions of Isaiah, and the panorama of ancient prophecy as it unfolds toward the advent, the manger, the cross and the throne; Jesus in the Apostles; Jesus in the Apocalypse. The testimony of Jesus is the Spirit of prophecy. The face of Jesus can be traced like water lines in fine paper back of every page, for He is the Alpha and the Omega—the first and the last of this Holy Book.

This expresses the relation of Jesus Christ to redemption. He is the first in the plan of salvation. Long ago He was heard exclaiming, "Lo, I come; I delight to do Your will, God; My ear You have pierced." It has all been accomplished through Him, and His glory is all to return to Him, and He forevermore to stand as the center and head of God's grandest work—the restoration of a ruined race, the salvation of sinful people. Christ is not only first in redemption: He is all. This winepress He has trodden alone. None can share with Him this glory. His was all the cost. His alone the honor shall ever be. In Heaven no name as the Lamb is so marvelous. No song so loud as that which celebrates His redeeming love, and therefore all that receive this great redemption must give Jesus the supreme glory, or they cannot share it.

This expresses His relation to our individual salvation, for every soul must acknowledge Jesus as the first. "You have not chosen Me, but I have chosen you," He tells us. The first desire to come to Him came from Him. The very hunger that longed for Him was His grace beginning to enter our hearts. He has loved us with an everlasting love, and, therefore, with lovingkindness has He drawn us. Not only has He pardon for us when we repent, but is exalted to give repentance to Israel and the remission of their sins. Not only will He fulfill our earnest prayers; but He makes intercession within us with groanings which cannot be uttered. Not only will He meet us in blessing if we will come to Him; but He will even take our will and work in us both to will and to do His good pleasure.

His arms reach down to us at the lowest depth. His grace is beforehand in all its manifestations. Christ will take us at the very start of Christian life, and from the very beginning will count us His disciples, and then will set us free. Oh, let us fully learn this precious truth, and always take Him for the very thing we need the most and the first, and even the very thing for which we ourselves are responsible, and yet insufficient; and He will not only do His glorious part, but He will enable us to do ours.

May 7
His Influence
by William H. G. Thomas (1861-1924) England/Wales
Excerpted from "The Influence of Christ," *Christianity is Christ*,
published by Zondervan Publishing House,
Grand Rapids, Michigan in 1900

The remarkable thing about Jesus Christ is that men have invariably had to take sides for or against Him. Indifference has always been impossible. Men have had to declare themselves either as His friends or as His foes. In considering the question with which we are now concerned, it is therefore valuable to inquire what those have thought of Christ who for any reason have not submitted their lives to Him.

We have a remarkable chain of testimony to the impression made by Jesus Christ Himself during His earthly life. Among His contemporaries were those who, when sent to apprehend Him, came back without their prisoner, saying, "Never man spoke like this Man." Men of keen intellect like Pilate and Herod could not find any flaw in His conduct, while at His trial no two witnesses agreed together. Napolean the Great said that Alexander, Caesar, Charlemagne and himself founded empires dependent upon force, while Jesus founded one on love, with the result that millions would die for Him.

We cannot overlook the evidence of Christ's influence, as men are brought face to face with the deepest problems of life. What are we to say of the problem of human sin? Call it what we like, the fact by any other name would be as bad. Where can we find the power to deliver man from evil, to overcome the evil principle within, and to give the conscience rest and peace amidst the burdens of life? Cotter Morison [English historian, 1832-1888] in his *Service of Man*, which on its publication twenty-two years ago was spoken of as the most powerful attack on Christianity during that generation, frankly admits that there is no remedy for a bad heart, that society has a right to exterminate the hardened criminal, and to prevent him from leaving offspring as bad as himself. There is no good news in this for the outcast, the depraved, the abandoned, the hopeless. To tell such people that they are to be eradicated is to confess the ghastly failure to deal with sin. Nor can education, or philosophy, or even social reform cope with this gigantic power of evil. Yet thousands and millions today, as in all ages, are testifying to the power and glory of Christianity in dealing with their sin and wickedness. These are facts which stand the test of examination and carry their own conclusion to all who are willing to learn.

What, too, shall we say about human weakness, the inability to live righteous lives, the constant struggle and defeat in the face of what seem to be omnipotent foes? Science, with all its discoveries and glories during the past century, has no word of hope for the individual. It may be true, as Charles Darwin [English naturalist, 1809-1882] says, that all organized beings are slowly advancing towards perfection, but meanwhile what joy or comfort is this to the individual who longs to live a holy life, and who finds himself powerless to resist the forces within him and around him? And there is no answer apart from Jesus Christ.

We are therefore justified in calling attention to the influence of Christ through the ages as one of the greatest, most direct, and most self-evident proofs that Christianity is Christ, and that Christ has to be accounted for. It is impossible to consider this question solely as one of history; it touches life at every point today.

May 8
His Inoffensiveness
by J. Stuart Holden (1870-1934) England
Excerpted from "The Blessedness of the Unoffended," *Life's Flood-Tide*, published by Robert Scott Roxburghe House, London, England in 1913

"These things have I spoken unto you, that you should not be offended."
John 16:1 (KJV)

One of the greatest perils of the Christian life lurks in the common pathway of discipleship. It is the peril of being offended in Christ. The fellowship to which the gospel summons us inevitably inspires a constant new and humiliating discovery of self; an unvarying disturbance of established order in our lives, as His will corrects and opposes our own; and a ceaseless effort to attain to the ideal; that is, to make our lives as followers, increasingly correspond to His as Forerunner. The danger is just here — that we are apt to break down under the test and training of it all, to go back and walk no more with Him, in short to be offended in Him. It is always possible, despite every sincere profession of the soul, that what God meant for blessing should become blight to us by our misunderstandings. It is always perilously possible that the light of today may become deep and impenetrable darkness tomorrow, by reason of our failure to obey and keep step with Him, by reason of our lagging behind or turning aside from the compelling guidance of Christ's companionship. Men have, in this way, unconsciously and imperceptibly put themselves far out of the range of Christ's saving influences; and have become, like the derelicts of the ocean, occasions of danger and disaster to countless other lives.

But Christ, with that absolute frankness which is a large part of His attractiveness to men, cannot be held to blame for such pitiful defections. For He never disguises the otherwise unthought-of possibility. In His Gospels He combines welcome with warning as none other has ever done. His Word, while it opens the very heart of God to our consciousness, opens also our own hearts to us. By Him we come to know the Father, and by Him also we come to know ourselves. He reveals the entire faithfulness of God to us; but He also reveals the instability of our own wills, and the untrustworthiness of our own emotions. He treats us not as ideal but as real men; and forewarns us of the destruction that wastes at noonday, as well as of the pestilence that walks in darkness. Hence it is that to the most earnest and self-convinced of us all He says, "Blessed is he whosoever shall not be offended in Me." The implication is obvious and ominous. But the reality and richness of His grace is the sufficient and silencing answer to every one of our fears. The blessedness of the unoffended, despite all the danger without and the weakness within, is the possible acquisition of each one. And it is blessedness indeed.

We may translate and expand this saying of Christ as being, "Blessed is he who does not find in Me any cause for stumbling; who can keep his feet in My ways; who is not tripped up by any obstacles in the path into which I have directed him." Spoken as they were on the eve of His departure, when the fierce tests of discipleship were about to be experienced by His followers, they imply that they will need to fix their souls on the things He has told them concerning His purpose and power, if they are to avoid the peril of stumbling and going away from Him. For they are bound to come into experiences of test and strain as they carry out their consecration vows; and "in those days," says Christ, "be true to your own best experience of Me. Rest on that which no man can take from you—the personal knowledge you have of My grace. Hold to those things I have spoken and shown to you. Be loyal to Me. Trust Me entirely, despite every unexplained mystery and seemingly unnecessary tribulation. Then you shall not be tripped but strengthened by these very things which are all of My ordering."

May 9
His Insight - 1
by William L. Watkinson (1838-1925) England
Excerpted from "The Genesis of Evil," *The Transfigured Sackcloth and Other Sermons*, published by Sampson Low, Marston & Company, London, England in 1893

And then Jesus added, "It is what comes from inside that defiles you. For from within, out of a person's heart, come evil thoughts, sexual immorality, theft, murder, adultery, greed, wickedness, deceit, lustful desires, envy, slander, pride, and foolishness. All these vile things come from within; they are what defile you."
Mark 7:20-23 (NLTSE)

Our Lord here declares the human heart to be an originator; that the vices which darken the world take their rise within us; in the mystery of the soul He teaches us to seek for the mystery of iniquity. Some of our thinkers find man to be a very superficial creature indeed; they treat him as being the simplest bit of mechanism; to them he is an organ of whose entire contents they can give an exact and complete specification; no, to change the figure, he is nothing more than a hollow reed moaning or melodic just as it is breathed upon by the restless wind. They find nothing unaccountable in him, nothing mysterious in his vices or virtues; the laws of matter and motion explain his whole life, character, conduct, doom; there is no problem suggested by man that is more unsolvable than the problems of chemistry and astronomy. But He who knew us best saw in us an abyss of mystery, a creative, inscrutable, intense, supernatural element, and in this element He finds the genesis of that evil by which the world is cursed. While many vainly scrutinize the objective world for the causes of evil, Christ looks within and finds the secret of our woe in the weakness and willingness of our heart.

Sin does not originate in any lack of intellectual light, or power, or discipline, so the world will not be renovated by intellect. It is as clear as anything can be that intellect and morals are dissimilar; superiority of genius does not imply moral excellence, as superiority of goodness does not imply intellectual force. We have seen all too often the finest artists living foulest lives; oracles of science mastered by the lowest vices; the most brilliant lights of literature obscured by the vapors and choked by the ashes of sensual life. Culture may know the best that has been said and written; but to do the best when you know it, is the real problem of life, and this problem culture very generally fails to solve. "What is called civilization drives away the tiger, but breeds the fox." The Italian statesman, Signor Crispi [1819-1901], in a great speech called liberty and science "the religion of the future"; but if the creed of the future contains no other doctrines than these, some very dark chapters will have to be added to the history of the world.

Education is all in the right direction, but the knowledge of letters, science, philosophy, government, taste, will never correct that deep fault of our nature out of which springs the transgression of the moral law. The wretchedness of the world is created by men who "do err in their heart," and the cure for this is not in mathematics, in science, or in art. Intellectual culture does not touch the inertia, the blindness, the ingratitude, the selfishness, the cruelty, the willfulness, which bring our acutest sense of guilt, our bitterest experiences of woe. And careful observers are beginning to see that the redemption of the intelligence is not the redemption of the heart; that the race will not be saved by intellect; and that it is easy to expect too much from the spread of knowledge. The sooner we all come to this conclusion the better. It will be a good thing every way when society quite comprehends that reason alone does not incite people to right doing; that men may be entirely sane and exceptionally intellectual and yet commit the most atrocious crimes; that we must believe in depravity as well as in disease. The schoolmaster does splendid service, but he hardly touches the fundamental evil.

May 10
His Insight - 2
by William L. Watkinson (1838-1925) England
Excerpted from "The Genesis of Evil," *The Transfigured Sackcloth and Other Sermons,* published by Sampson Low, Marston & Company, London, England in 1893

And then Jesus added, "It is what comes from inside that defiles you. For from within, out of a person's heart, come evil thoughts, sexual immorality, theft, murder, adultery, greed, wickedness, deceit, lustful desires, envy, slander, pride, and foolishness. All these vile things come from within; they are what defile you."
Mark 7:20-23 (NLTSE)

The text condemns the theory which finds the origin of evil in the power of circumstances. In opposition to those who hold that circumstances determine character, our Lord says that out of the heart come the evil things of human conduct; in the secret bias of the soul, not in unfavorable surroundings, do evil words and deeds find generation. Now the science of our day corresponds with our Lord's teaching on the inwardness of character. It has been thought that the theory of evolution strengthens the belief in the power of circumstances by teaching that the special form and color of things are determined immediately by the neighborhood in which they spring. But evolution does not teach any such thing. So far as plants are concerned, it is recognized that their characteristics are from within—they vary primarily, not because of something special in their locality, but from a mysterious, innate tendency to variation for which no scientist can account. "External conditions can never cause an inheritable change of form, whether advantageous or the contrary; nor can it determine the development of an organ nor its abortion. Structural peculiarities, advantageous and disadvantageous, present themselves in individual varieties, quite independently of any direct influence of external conditions" [Anton Kerner, Austrian botanist, 1831-1898]. From within, out of the secret heart of the plant, comes its special size, shape, color, markings, perfume.

And sin will not be cured by circumstances. God forbid that we should speak lightly of those who seek to improve the race through the improvement of its conditions. We revere them, we hail them as fellow-workers in the same magnificent cause. But if we are to bless men effectively, we must get to the fountainhead of their sorrows—the thought and imagination of their heart. As Jeremy Taylor [English Anglican cleric, 1613-1667] says, "You cannot cure the colic by brushing a man's clothes." No bettering of the lot of the individual will necessarily make his spirit sweet, contented, pure. Neither will the favorable environment make the virtuous and happy community. Eden, Sodom, Canaan, proved this in the old world, and there are plenty of proofs of it in the modern world.

We see here the necessity for that regeneration upon which Christ insists. The heart is the fountain of evil; it must be changed and become the fountain of good. "Marvel not that I said unto you, You must be born again." It is not a new brain that we need; the most logical intellect will not save us. It is not new limbs that we need; new eyes, or hands, or lips, or tongue, or feet, will not help us. It is not new conditions that we need; the most serene, unexacting, ideal states of actual life will not make us virtuous or prove us to be so. We need all the faculties and powers of our inward being renewed. We need our conscience to bear us witness in the Holy Ghost; our imagination to eye the most supreme ideals of light and beauty, and urge its flight thereto as the eagle seeks the sun; our will by virtue of a divine strengthening to become imperative and invincible; our affections to be filled, dominated by the sovereign love of God. Nothing but this new heart and right spirit will meet the case. The regeneration of the man himself is the supreme burden of revelation.

May 11
His Intercession
by George H. Morrison (1866-1928) Scotland
Excerpted from "The Interceding Savior," *The Gateways of the Stars,*
published by Hodder and Stoughton, London, England in 1931

Wherefore He is able also to save them to the uttermost…
seeing He ever lives to make intercession for them.
Hebrews 7:25 (KJV)

There are times in life when it is very helpful to know that somebody is praying for us. It strengthens us when we are prone to faint. When some difficult duty lies ahead; when we have to undergo an operation; when death has taken away a loved one, and we are overwhelmed with loneliness, the certainty that friends are praying for us is a mighty support to our trembling hearts, and often ministers quietness and confidence. I have often heard missionaries say that what sustained them was their assurance of the prayers at home. During the war [World War I] many of our boys used to speak of the difference this made. It reinforced their hearts and kept them strong to know that folk at home were praying for them. Indeed, I have found that many who never pray are eager to have the prayers of others, when facing a crisis in their lives.

Now our text tells us that somebody is praying for us, and that somebody is our risen Savior. That is the only meaning which our text can bear, and with all its mystery we thankfully accept it. We light on the same truth again in the song of triumph in the eighth chapter of Romans. John, too, in his old age, dwelt on the consolation of that thought (1 John 2:1). And if we only let it sink into our hearts, however great the intellectual difficulties, we still find it the good news of God. Others may forget us in their prayers; there is One in Heaven who never does forget. Others may fail us when their lamp burns low; He ever lives. We are enveloped by the prayers of One who loves us and has the ear of God, and therefore is able to save unto the uttermost. Nor was this ministry begun in Heaven, it was carried over from the days on earth. Our Lord on earth was an interceding Savior. One remembers His words to Simon Peter, recorded in the Gospel of Luke: "Simon, Satan has desired to have you, but I have prayed for you that your faith will not fail." And if our Lord so prayed when He was here, why should it be thought incredible that He continues that ministry in Heaven? Does not Satan desire to have us just as he desired to have Simon? And often when our foot has almost slipped, have we not escaped out of the fowler's snare? And why should we be charged with being mystical because we adoringly ascribe our rescue to the intercession of the risen Lord? Did He not say, "I will ask the Father, and He shall give you another Comforter"? Have we never experienced with an inward certainty that in the hour of need that Comforter has come? All fresh provisions of the Holy Spirit, whether for service or for suffering, are indications of a praying Savior.

Again, we remember another intercession, "Father, forgive them; they know not what they do." And if He prayed that prayer when on the cross, we may be perfectly certain that forgiveness followed. Did He not say beside the grave of Lazarus, "I knew that You always heard Me"? How little any of us know what we are doing! How often we say, "If I had only known!" Then springs remorse, and agony of conscience, and thoughts which reproach us in the silent night. In such seasons may we not lift our hearts to Him who ever lives to intercede, and hear Him praying for our human ignorance as once He prayed upon the cross? So much of our sin is not deliberate. Evil is produced by lack of thought. We are such ignorant and foolish beings that we can rarely follow our actions to their issues. But He is praying for us just as He prayed on Calvary, and He is able to save unto the uttermost, because "He ever lives to make intercession for us."

May 12
His Intimate
by Eugene Russell Hendrix (1847-1927) USA
Excerpted from "The Hidden Word—The Ripening of St. John," *Christ's Table Talk*, published by The Publishing House of the M. E. Church, South, Nashville, Tennessee in 1908

The Fourth Gospel is preeminently the "Gospel of Conversations" of Jesus. Who would better remember and record them than the bosom friend of Jesus? The table companion at every meal, we naturally look to John to preserve for us the dinner parables and the matchless table talk in the Upper Room. Because Christ's words were hidden in John's heart, the Holy Spirit the more readily called them to memory. We have in John's Gospel substantially the very words that Jesus gave His disciples, and doubtless the words which the Father had given Him. The chosen spokesman of our Lord becomes not only the vehicle for bringing to us the gracious words of Christ, but also the best embodiment of these teachings in life and character. To John, Christ was indeed the Word—the Word that was in the beginning ever "toward God," as if to receive and convey the very mind of God that when we had the mind of Christ we might see the Father also. How sacredly would John preserve every word that proceeds out of the mouth of God! He would live by them, and not by bread alone. Thus they bore the peaceable fruits of righteousness.

Doubtless John often recalled the words of the Psalmist and made them his own: "Your words have I hid in my heart that I might not sin again You." John is not only the best fruit of our Lord's ministry, but he is the best exponent of our Lord's method in making a saint. "Now you are clean through the words that I have spoken unto you," said Christ in His last table talk when speech and prayer so perfectly blended in the Upper Room. To lodge in prepared hearts the living words, and to water them with His blood that they might bring forth abundant fruit, was the purpose for our Lord's coming. His last words were for His own: "For I have given them the words which You gave Me; and they have received them, and have known surely that I came out from You, and they have believed that You sent Me…I have given them Your word…Sanctify them through Your truth: Your word is truth." As, like Mary, John kept and pondered in his heart all these words, his character became Christlike. His ripe old age showed the beauty of holiness — the perfecting of a saint.

The beloved disciple gives us the most perfect example of the grace of waiting and its perfect work. In his patience he won his soul. It was a heroic achievement, not simply a mere passive result. That last third of the life of John the aged was the ripening period, when its best fruit was matured. It was indeed "borrowed time" that he lived on, beyond the usual threescore and ten; but it seemed borrowed from eternity. John seemed to live in eternity for the last third of his life. Doubtless there is no true life that is not lived in eternity, whence we get our deepest motives and our highest inspirations. There can be no worthy aspirations which do not come from such inspirations. Few people wake up to the real meaning of life until the invisible begins to seem more real than the visible. John had reached that period when the fisherman is forgotten in the seer. If ever he had worshiped his net, as men of affairs are so prone to do, his eagle eye now beholds the sea of glass, and the opened heavens show the great white throne of God. But far more awaited John than he saw on Patmos. A score or more of years, with their ripening influence, must come before he could write that immortal prologue of his Gospel or reproduce from the Holy of Holies our Lord's intercessory prayer. In the rugged Greek of the book of Revelation, written probably before the destruction of Jerusalem, John shows his apprentice work as a writer. Many years needed to elapse before the finished style of the fourth Gospel told of the mind that had pondered deeply the secret things of God; and as the Holy Spirit brought to John's remembrance all things that Jesus had spoken, his became the pen of a ready writer.

May 13
His Intolerance - 1
by J. Stuart Holden (1870-1934) England
Excerpted from "The Intolerant Christ," *Life's Flood-Tide*, published by
Robert Scott Roxburghe House, London, England in 1913

"He that is not with Me is against Me."
Matthew 12:30 (KJV)

Now at first sight the use of such a word as intolerance to describe Christ is almost repugnant to us. It sounds harsh; for we are accustomed to think of Him as of One so full of love as to be without severities of any kind. Of broader mind and more charitable judgment than any who preceded or who have succeeded Him, can it be that we find anything akin to intolerance in Him? Is He not too large and generous to have nothing of the smallness of mind by which we usually identify the intolerant man today? Is not the divine nature too ample to admit of what at any time seems irritable and impatient? For we do not usually commend intolerance as being the quality of the truly great. On the contrary, we rather pity the man who is so small as to be intolerant of all but his own views and his own order, and who intolerantly excludes and condemns those who are not in agreement with him. And in this we do well. For nothing is so unbecoming and unlovely as an intolerant man.

But herein lies the essential difference between the intolerance of Christ and of all others, most of all of His professed disciples. Their intolerance is the expression of imperfect and fragmentary knowledge. His is the intolerance of One who knows! He knows the why and wherefore of the mission on which He has been sent by the Father. He knows the subtlety and strength of the sin which He has come to combat for, and in, men. He knows the wide range of possibility in every life to which He makes appeal, the full value of the capacity and aptitude which He seeks to deliver from the grip of destructive forces. He knows the grieved love of the sadly-wronged God, and the yearning of the Father-heart over the alienated affection of the deceived child. And, knowing all this, He would be less than divine were He not intolerant of all that arrays itself against God's purpose of recovery and deliverance, of all that binds and blinds men to their true life, of all that impairs and incapacitates them, of all that deceives and denies them, of all that outrages the love which is everlasting in its patience and faith.

Then, His intolerance is not only the expression of His knowledge but of His love. It is impossible to think of Him as the true lover of men, apart from just this intolerant sternness, which at all times declares absolute truth in its bitterness. There is an intolerance in moral and spiritual issues, which is the only possible voice by which love can declare itself, and by which truth can win recognition for itself. And this is the intolerance of the Son of God.

It is seen, for instance, in the high claims which He makes for Himself. "I am the Bread of Life"; "I am the Light of the World"; "I am the Way, the Truth, and the Life." That He can make such claims without any loss of modesty or show of mere egotism, that He can so declare Himself without any toleration of possible rival, is expressive of an undisturbed consciousness of divinity, in short, that He has indeed come from God to men, and that He is God's full and final word to them.

How intolerant, too, is He in the commands which He lays upon men. "Seek first the Kingdom of God"; and again, "If any man come unto Me and does not hate his father and mother, and wife and children, and brethren and sisters, yes, and his own life also, he cannot be My disciple"; and again, "Follow Me." And only an intolerant demand for wholehearted allegiance and discipleship could be an effective gospel unto such a redemption. He cannot be Lord *at* all if He is not Lord *of* all.

May 14
His Intolerance - 2
by J. Stuart Holden (1870-1934) England
Excerpted from "The Intolerant Christ," *Life's Flood-Tide*, published by Robert Scott Roxburghe House, London, England in 1913

"He that is not with Me is against Me."
Matthew 12:30 (KJV)

The same intolerance marks His imposition of self-discipline upon His followers. "If your eye offends you pluck it out and cast it from you. If your hand offends you, cut it off and cast it from you." Sin is the enemy; and, in respect of it, any toleration is at once disloyal and disastrous. And conscience and memory unite in confirmation of His intolerance, hailing it as being the only effective way of dealing with sin's defiling enslavements. Were Christ to be in any degree less intolerant in the matter of sin, or to impose a less harsh and rigorous discipline upon those who would follow Him, conscience would shrink from accepting Him. For there is that within every man in regard to his own sin which, at any rate in his best moments (and never let us forget that it is then we are most truly ourselves), shrinks and recoils from anything like deferring or excusing of the willful transgression. Nothing but the drastic, the radical, the intolerant, can ever satisfy the clamorous need of the human soul in its sin-created agony. It turns from any cheap and easy way of peace with an instinctive refusal which is self-protective. It is drawn to Christ by the intolerant conditions upon which alone His power of deliverance may be known.

But it is, perhaps, most conspicuously in His discriminating division of men that this spirit and quality is seen in Christ. He banishes all uncertainty and disposes of all vagueness and that for all time in declaring that "he that is not with Me is against Me." In moral issues mere neutrality is quite impossible; and it is of the very nature of love to make this absolutely clear. Nor can this issue be evaded. Men must take sides when brought within the zone of Christ's compelling personality and mission. There is always "a division among the people because of Him." For while there is so much in Christ to quicken love and stimulate faith, there is always much to stagger the unwilling and unready. The intolerance which allowed no deterrence from the pathway of redeeming sacrifice; which turned a deaf ear to affectionate appeal, and with steadfast face set out on the pilgrimage of the cross, nor rested until all was accomplished, now seeks the highest place in the hearts of men. For this is the intolerance of a hungering love.

Obviously it is destructive of self-interest, of sinful affection, of unholy thought and action, of worldly compliance, and of all that is frequently found in violation of the throne of God in the lives of men. The issue is thus always between self-will and the will of God. And it is self-determined. We either actively align ourselves with Christ in His attitude toward these things, or passively declare ourselves against Him. We crown Him or crucify Him. And it is our spiritual sympathies which pronounce upon us. He does not judge us by our mental assent to the articles of a creed. As a matter of fact, He formulated no creed; for no creed could fully define Him, nor sufficiently express His intent and power. Nor does He judge us by our allegiance to a system of belief or worship. As a matter of fact, He imposed no system; for no system could contain or convey a grace boundless as the ocean and limitless as the universe. No! He simply says that the one who is not with Him in all the active sympathies of life, not in living agreement with His program, nor in loyal cooperation with His power, is against Him.

Let us see to it that we meet His claim with a responsive intolerance which forbids the withholding of anything that He savingly demands of us. For this is the genius of "the life that is life indeed." And they that are "with Him are called and chosen and faithful."

May 15
His Intolerance - 3
by George H. Morrison (1866-1928) Scotland
Excerpted from "The Intolerance of Jesus," *Wings of the Morning*, published by A. C. Armstrong and Son, New York, New York in 1907

"Anyone who isn't with Me opposes Me..."
Matthew 12:30 (NLTSE)

Our Lord had just performed a notable miracle healing a man who was possessed by a devil. It had made a profound impression on the people, and had forced the conviction that this was indeed Messiah. Unable to dispute the miracle itself, the Pharisees tried to challenge the power behind it, and in their cowardly and treacherous way they suggested there was something demonic about Christ. With a readiness of resource which never failed Him, Christ showed in a flash the weakness of that argument. If He was the friend of the demons, was He likely to make a brother-demon homeless? Then moved to righteous anger by these slanders, He said, "Anyone who isn't with Me opposes Me."

I want to speak on the intolerance of Jesus Christ. However startling the subject may appear, and however the sound of it may shock us, I am convinced we shall never understand our Lord if we fail to understand His intolerance. We have heard much of the geniality of Jesus, and of the depth and range of His compassion; nor can we ever exaggerate, in warmest language, the gracious and generous facet of His character. But it is good that the listening ear should be attuned to catch the sterner music of that life, lest, missing it, we miss the fine severity which goes to the perfecting of moral beauty. Wherever the spirit of Jesus is at work, there is found a sweet and masterful intolerance. The one thing that the gospel cannot do is to look with easy good nature on the world. And if this passionate urgency of claim has ever marked the activities of Christendom, we must try to trace it to the fountainhead and find it in the character of Christ.

We trace the intolerance of Christ, for instance, in His attitude towards hypocrisy. One thing that was unendurable to Jesus was the shallow profession of religion. You can always detect an element of pity when Jesus is face to face with other sins. There is the yearning of infinite love over the lost; the hand outstretched to welcome back the prodigal. But for the hypocrite there is no gleam of pity, only the blasting and shriveling of wrath. "Woe unto you, scribes and Pharisees, hypocrites!" It is the intolerance of Jesus Christ.

We trace it again in those stupendous claims that Jesus Christ put forward for Himself. The Lord our God is a jealous God, and the Lord our Savior is a jealous Savior. "I am the way, I am the truth, I am the life"; "No one comes unto the Father but by Me"; "No one knows the Father except the Son, and to whomever the Son will reveal Him." What do you make of these amazing claims, and of that splendid intolerance of any rival? Yet all these words are in the Gospels' record as surely as "a bruised reed shall He not break." Do you say there are many doorways to the Father? Christ Jesus stands and says, "I am the door." Do you say there are many shepherds of the sheep? Christ stands in His majesty, and says, "I am the shepherd." Full of pity, full of mercy, full of a great compassion, Christ is intolerant of any rival; He stands alone to be worshipped and adored, or He disappears into the mists of fable.

Again I trace this same intolerance in the allegiance which Christ demands from us. He is willing to take the lowest place upon the cross; but He will not take it in your heart and mine. But the moment He enters the kingdom of the heart, where He is King by conquest and by right, there everything is changed, and with a great intolerance He refuses every place except the first. "He that loves father or mother more than Me is not worthy of Me."

May 16
His Intrusiveness
by George H. Morrison (1866-1928) Scotland

Excerpted from "The Intrusiveness of Christ," *The Unlighted Luster*, published by Hodder and Stoughton, London, England in 1909

...when the doors were shut...for fear of the Jews, came Jesus...
John 20:19 (KJV)

In studying the life of Christ on earth I have often been struck with that note of the inevitable. People tried to escape Him—begged Him to depart—yet though all the doors were shut, Jesus confronted them. I think of the Gadarene demoniac in the tombs. He was an object of terror so that everyone fled from him. He had shut out his nearest and dearest by his wildness, but for all his wildness he could not shut out the Lord. "What have we to do with You, Jesus, Son of God—are You come here to torment us before our time?" He could escape from his chains; he could not escape from Jesus. Behold! he is now sitting clothed and in his right mind. Or I think of Christ in relation to Jewish history, and I feel once again that He was unavoidable. For the whole struggle of scribes and Pharisees and priests was to close the door on Christ and keep Him out. They refused to acknowledge Him and they would make no place for Him; He was a gluttonous man and a wine-bibber; not this Man but Barabbas! Everything that malevolence could do was done; everything that spite could suggest was swiftly practiced to discredit the Name and sully the reputation of this Prophet who mourned with tears over Jerusalem. Did it succeed? Christ kept out from the destinies of Judaism? Ah, friends, every page of Jewish story reveals the futility of that endeavor.

The most potent influence in Judaism is Christ Jesus. He is the Daystar of its only hope. They closed the door on Him—beat Him off—said He is done with now; but for all that they could not shut

Him out. If that was true in history I want you to believe that it is true now. Whatever walls you raise, Christ passes through them all and gets to you. There are deeds that we did long since, perhaps twenty years ago, but to this hour unexpectedly they rise and meet us. There were moments of exquisite happiness in our past, and even today their memory is like music. You cannot shut out the thought of intense hours; no change of years will prevent them coming through. Christ is unavoidable. I want that thought to sink into your hearts. Close every door against Him if you will; the mystery is that you do not shut Him out.

Sometimes He comes through the closed door just because all life is penetrated with Him. We talk of the Christian atmosphere we breathe, but the atmosphere is more than Christian, it is Christ. We may have closed the door on Him, but He is here. We cannot date one letter in the morning but we mean that so many years ago Christ was born. He meets us at every turn of the road, in every newspaper, and in every problem. Our life is so interpenetrated with Christ Jesus that to avoid Him is an impossibility.

Sometimes He meets us in a noble character, in a person who is a living argument for religion. And though we have resolved to have nothing to do with Christ, yet we feel in a moment that Christ is by our side. Creeds may mean nothing to us; we may have left off going to church; the dust may have gathered thick upon our Bibles; but accidentally we meet some man or some woman, having the hallmark of the genuine Christ, and through the shut door we know that Christ is here.

And sometimes it is in our deeper hours that He so comes. It is in the darker and more tragic moments of our life. We closed the door on Him when we were strong and vigorous, for we did not want the intrusion of the cross; but when life's deeps are uncovered then it is God we need, and through the shut doors Christ is in the midst.

May 17
His Invincibility
by Clarence E. Macartney (1879-1957) USA
Excerpted from "Have New Foes Risen Against Christ?" *Twelve Great Questions About Christ*, published by Fleming H. Revell Company, New York, New York in 1923

Is there anything of which one can say, "Look! This is something new"? It was here already, long ago; it was here before our time.
Ecclesiastes 1:10 (NIV)

Almost the first sentence of the Bible is, "God said," and the first sentence of temptation in the Bible is, "Has God said?" The great question of religion is, whether or not God has spoken to man, and whether or not we have a true record of that revelation. Has He, whom dimly we take to be our Creator and our God, come out from the darkness and the silence, and spoken a word to man? The destiny of a race hangs upon the answer to that question. Christianity presents itself to humanity as God's word, His speech, His revelation, for the good of man. "And God said," is the chord struck so magnificently at the beginning of the book. It follows us with its deep reverberations wherever we go in this many-chambered palace of the Bible and of Christian faith. "And God said," "Hear you the Word of the Lord!" "Thus says the Lord!"

Yet, at the very beginning came the Tempter with his sly insinuation, "Yes, and has God said?" This first sentence of unbelief will be the last also, for to create doubt as to whether or not God has spoken, is the only way in which the powers of darkness can persuade the soul to rebel against God and refuse the great salvation which He has provided. All forms of unbelief, ancient, medieval and modern, are in substance but a repetition of that first question put to the woman by the Tempter. God has never said anything to a fallen race which was not immediately questioned, denied, ridiculed. For every, "Thus says the Lord!" there has been an answering, "Has God said?" The attack on the Bible, on God's Word, on revealed religion, is as old as man's mind. Should anyone say to us, then, concerning some reported attack upon Christianity, "See, this is new!" remember it existed long ago in the ages which were before us. The same enemies have launched their fiery darts against the Church and the Bible. The mind that invented them was just as keen, and the arm which hurled them was just as strong, as are the mind and the arm which devise them and hurl them today. Yet the Church and the Bible remain.

Christianity presents itself to men as a remedy for sin. But man, ancient, medieval, or modem, has never liked to confess that he is a sinner. Hence he has either openly rejected Christianity, or what is more common, and today most prevalent, he has tried to restate it and reinterpret its great doctrines so that they shall apply to this imaginary being who is not a lost sinner. But the attempt breaks down. Christianity is a religion intended for sinners and cannot be made to fit any other kind of man. The present chaotic condition of Christianity, so far as its beliefs are concerned, is due entirely to the fact that the great presupposition of Christianity — that man is a lost sinner who can do nothing for himself, and must perish unless Christ comes to save him — is either bitterly denied or coolly ignored. We may talk as we will about the "new knowledge," the "progress of science," "progressive revelation," the "new world" we live in, the "static" rather than the "dynamic" idea of faith, and so on through all the catalogue of the favorite terms of Modernist theology; but that is not the cause or the origin of neo-Christianity, "the gospel which is not another," which is being preached in so many of our churches today. The real cause and source of it is man's unwillingness to take God's remedy for sin. No man can become a Christian without the act of faith, and that act of faith, that taking Christ as Lord and Savior, presupposes taking one's self as a sinner. That men should refuse to do this is nothing new under the sun.

May 18
His Joy – 1
by William M. Clow (1853-1930) Scotland
Excerpted from "The Joy of the Way to Calvary," *The Day of the Cross*,
published by Hodder and Stoughton, London, England in 1909

But Jesus turning to them said, "Daughters of Jerusalem,
weep not for Me..."
Luke 23:28 (KJV)

All the way from Pilate's judgment-seat to Calvary has been called the *Via Dolorosa*—the way of pain. If by that is meant that it was a way whose every step might well evoke our tears, whose simple record should renew and deepen our sorrow, the name is appropriate enough. But if the name is used to express the mind of Jesus, if it is His sorrow we have in view, its insight is at fault, and its use bestows no honor on Jesus. It is due to the Romish taint which has infected our thinking, and fastened our eyes on the physical sufferings of the cross, forgetful of what the reticence of the Gospels and the express triumph of the Epistles might have taught us—the radiant victory of the spirit over the flesh.

Jesus has been called the Man of Sorrows—outside the New Testament. The nearest approach in the Gospels to that misleading name is the mention of the ignorant and mistaken understanding that He was the prophet Jeremiah, a misunderstanding Jesus at once brushes aside. The truth is that, in most of its aspects, Jesus lived a singularly joyous life. The most careless reader cannot escape feeling the calm and serenity of His words, and the perfect peace which pervades His life. Contentment may express the high achievement of Paul, but it is too shallow a word to apply to the life of Jesus. Calm was not life's crown with Him. He had abounding joys. The silence that dwells among the lonely hills, the shadows on the Lake of Galilee, the array of the lilies, the glory of the grass of the field spoke to Him with a voice which no poet's ear ever heard. His delights were with the sons of men, and He found tender solace in their homes, and uplifting gladness in their love. When we think of His Incarnation, a shadow falls upon our spirits as its humiliation forces itself upon us, but we forget the eager will behind it, which made its narrow limits a constant joy. His youth in Nazareth, with His dawning consciousness of His mission, was a time of the leaping pulse and eager desire. His poverty—of which we, in our ignorance of an Eastern life, and our gluttony for shameful comfort, have made too much—gave Him an unburdened life. "A man's life," He said, "consists not in the abundance of the things which he possesses." "Take no thought for the morrow." Ah! when we understand the sources of joy, when we penetrate the secret of Jesus, we realize that, despite His loneliness and separateness in His higher experiences, despite the burden of men's sins and sorrows, and despite the last awful hour on the cross, no human heart ever thrilled with a joy to match that of Jesus. And when we regard Him closely as He passes up to Calvary, we find that from the depths of His joy a stream is flowing which cannot be quenched. Then we understand why He could say to His disciples, as He stood on the threshold of the agony of Gethsemane, and felt the very shadow of the cross: "These things have I spoken unto you that My joy might remain in you, and that your joy might be full."

Look at Jesus now, as He walks the way to Calvary! The night—that searching and disciplining night, for all who were awake through its eventful hours—had passed away. Its festive joy and discerning love had found relief in the High Priest's prayer after the supper. Its sleepless envy and spineless fear have issued in the pitiless deeds of the courtyard and judgment seat. The morning has ushered in the great day. Flesh and heart have fainted and failed. Simon of Cyrene bears His cross, and now He is going forward to the last deed of all. A high elation is on His spirit, and a rush and surge of joyous feeling, overmastering pain and quenching sorrow, swells in His heart.

May 19
His Joy – 2
by William M. Clow (1853-1930) Scotland
Excerpted from "The Joy of the Way to Calvary," *The Day of the Cross*, published by Hodder and Stoughton, London, England in 1909

But Jesus turning to them said, "Daughters of Jerusalem, weep not for Me..."
Luke 23:28 (KJV)

The wail of the women of Jerusalem breaks on His ear. He stops and turns, and because He will not have them misunderstand Him, and give a false accompaniment to His crowning act; He chides them for their tears. The joys of sense have been taken from Him. Of all the joys that man can take away, He has been bereaved. But He has the joys of the Spirit. He has His deep delight in spiritual things. And it was that inner, spiritual, eternal joy, welling up out of His victorious spirit, which sustained Him, and made the way to Calvary an uplifting triumph.

Let us think about this joy of Jesus on the way to Calvary. As He walks in the way to Calvary, as He looks back on all the way God has led Him, as He sees in clearest light the will of God, and presses on to do it, as He goes forward, the trembling of His worn-out frame has left Him in the high and holy delight of His perfect confidence in God, and so He cries, "Weep not for Me."

In one aspect, the day of the cross is the darkest, saddest, most tragic in the world's history. Yet it was the day of Christ's highest joy. As He goes up the way of weeping, spent, forsaken, marked for death, these women of Jerusalem wailed and lamented Him. He turns and looks upon them, and the triumph-song breaks from His lips, "Daughters of Jerusalem, weep not for Me, but weep for yourselves, and for your children." For He was going to the deed which crowned His life, He was accomplishing the purpose of His heart, He was on the threshold of His highest service and sacrifice, and His joy was almost full. Ah, brethren, if you have ever felt the deep joy of making some poor wasted heart glad, if you have known the leaping of the spirit when some abandoned life has been saved from shame, if you have known even the thrill of blessedness when you have led some little child to Christ, you can realize what must have been the spiritual delight of the Son of God in that day of service and of sacrifice when He died to set His people free.

And now, as He sees the beams which shall make His cross, as He is fulfilling the eternal sacrifice, as He, unloosing the bonds of sin, as He, opening the Kingdom of Heaven, as He is within a few hours of the moment when He shall cry, "It is finished," and go home to wait for His reward, His joy is greater than human heart can conceive. What word could have been more suitably upon His lips to these compassionate daughters of Jerusalem, what word is to be spoken yet to men among us who dwell overmuch on the sorrows of the way, but "Weep not for Me."

The joy in His service and sacrifice were consummated on the cross. But the joy in the spiritual well-being of men still throbs in the Human Heart that beats on the throne of God. He still "sees of the travail of His soul, and is satisfied." Not only when He saw Peter's impulsive soul chastened into steadfast strength; not only when He saw John's fiery heart glowing with love; not only when He saw Thomas's doubting spirit strengthened in faith; but now — today — when He sees our faces turned towards Him, when He sees us laying aside all malice, and all guilt, and all hypocrisies, and envies and evil speaking; when He sees us overcoming by faith, this joy fills His spirit. This is "the joy set before Him," for which He endured the cross and despised the shame, the joy which shall be fulfilled, "when all the ransomed Church of God is saved to sin no more."

May 20
His Judgment - 1
by George H. Morrison (1866-1928) Scotland
Excerpted from "The Judgment of the Son," *The Afterglow of God*,
published by Hodder and Stoughton, London, England in 1912

"The Father...has given all judgment to the Son..."
John 5:22 (ESV)

The great impression made by the life of Christ is not an impression of judgment but of love. Here, we say, is a Person of such compassion as never was witnessed on the earth before. There is a depth of tenderness about Him that is infinitely attractive and endearing. There is a wealth of the most helpful sympathy—a passionate desire to be a friend. There is a tenderness that is unparalleled; a sensibility to all distress; a love so deep and strong and true that life was not sufficient to disclose it.

We come to see that wherever Jesus was, there was the element of judgment. As He moved along these ways of Galilee, men and women knew that they were loved. With a like instinct, too deep for understanding, they knew continually that they were judged. The moment they stepped into that lowly presence—the moment they looked into His face and heard Him speak, they felt they were standing at a judgment bar. It was not that they felt that they were known. We may feel that we are known and not be judged. We may be perfectly conscious that someone knows our motives, and yet it may never cause the slightest self-reproach. But there was always self-reproach where Jesus was. People were ashamed of themselves, they knew not why. His life was an unceasing act of love, and yet it was an unceasing act of judgment.

Sometimes it was His words that carried judgment, and carried it in quite a casual way. That is one office of the casual word, to reach the conscience and stir it unawares. None of us like to be directly judged. We are apt to resent the word of condemnation. To charge a person with such and such a fault is very often the way to harden their heart. But we all know how the casual word, said in our presence but never aimed at us, has a strange way of getting at the conscience. Have you not occasionally felt uneasy when the conversation took a certain turn? It was not meant for you, and yet it reached you; it found you out and made you feel your guilt. And what I say is that the talk of Christ had that strange power, in unequalled measure, of making people feel mysteriously guilty. Sometimes He hurled an open condemnation. Sometimes He cried, "Woe unto you, you Pharisees." But what I want you to feel is that it was not such that was the bitterest condemnation of His lips. It was those words which He was always speaking, and which were never meant to wither and condemn, and yet which had that strange and incredible power of waking the agony of self-reproach.

Sometimes it was His deeds that carried judgment, and here again, in general, indirectly. Directly, He judged a barren fig tree once; but it was not in this way that His acts judged men and women. He did them not to judge them, but to save them. They flowed from a heart that was the home of love. And yet when they fell upon the human conscience, they had a strange power of awakening self-reproach. "Depart from me, O Lord, for I am a sinful man." You remember how Simon Peter once cried that? And what had happened to make him cry that cry? Had Christ condemned him with a tongue of fire? It was not that which caused the bitter cry. It was the net that was so full of fishes. It was an act so wonderful and kind that Peter saw, and seeing loathed himself. Have we not all experienced that judgment—the silent judgment of some noble act? Nothing was said, but something fine was done, and seeing it so done, we were ashamed. And I say again that in the acts of Jesus, all of them acts of love and acts of grace, there lay the power, in unequalled measure, of touching men and women with a strange self-reproach.

May 21
His Judgment - 2
by George H. Morrison (1866-1928) Scotland
Excerpted from "The Judgment of the Son," *The Afterglow of God*,
published by Hodder and Stoughton, London, England in 1912

"The Father...has given all judgment to the Son..."
John 5:22 (ESV)

Sometimes it was His looks that carried judgment, and looks are often powerful to do that. There are looks that are the cause of keener pain than any scolding of an angry lip. And if in human eyes where sin has lodged there is this power of awaking self-reproach, how awful must it have been in eyes like Christ's? I do not wonder that the rich young ruler was sorrowful, when I read that Christ had looked on him and loved him. I do not wonder that the crowd was stricken when Jesus looked on them with anger. I do not wonder that when Jesus turned and looked on Simon Peter in the hall, the heart of Peter was broken with the look, and he went out into the night and wept. Will anyone say that was a look of anger? My brother and sister, it was a look of love. And the past was in it, and all its tender memories, and the dear dead days that were beyond recall. And it saved Peter when the night was past to think that the Lord had turned and looked at him; but first down to the very depths it judged him. No wild rebuke would ever have done that. It would have hardened him, and made him degenerate. One look of Christ did more than all the Law of Moses. One look of Christ outmatched a thousand threatenings. One look of Christ showed in what height and depth the Father had given all judgment to the Son.

It was not only by what He did that Jesus judged; it was more by what He was than what He did. Is there any one of us right now who has not known how character can judge? Is there not somebody you know and love, who silently condemns you when you think of them? It is not that they are wanting to condemn you; nothing may be farther from their thoughts—and yet when you meet them, and when you see what they are, you are ashamed of all that you have been. That, I take it, is what the gospel means, when it tells us that the saints shall judge the world. There is not a saint, and not an earnest soul, but unconsciously is judging every day. And people may mock them, and scorn them, and call them idle dreamers or visionaries, and yet who knows what self-reproach is stirring before that character of love and beauty? Think how complete the character of Christ was, how beautiful, how perfect in its finest and its strongest. Then tell me if you have ever realized how people must have felt, and felt as in a flash, when on the highway or in the summer field they found themselves in the presence of the Lord? They were ashamed, and knew not what it meant. They were convicted, yet not a word was spoken. Away deep down new thoughts began to burn of what their life might be and ought to be. It was the unconscious influence of character; the only perfect life the world had known. It was the witness, although they knew it not, that the Father had given all judgment to the Son.

Then in the third place, it was an unceasing judgment. It was in action every hour He lived. The judgment of character is always that, just because character is always character. Our legal judges are not always judges. They have their seasons when they sit in judgment. And then they lay aside their robes of office, and they go back to private life again. But in Christ the robe of office was Himself, never to be laid aside in life or death, and that means His judgment is unceasing. You feel it when He worked and when He spoke. You feel it when He went alone to pray. Men were convicted when they knew He prayed, and they came and cried to Him "Teach us to pray." Right from the baptism on to the cross of Calvary; right from that hour on to this hour, Christ has been judging men and judging women, and judging everything people's hands have produced.

May 22
His Keeping - 1
by Andrew Murray (1828-1917) Scotland/South Africa
Excerpted from "Jesus Able to Keep," *The Spiritual Life*, published by Tupper & Robertson, Chicago, Illinois in 1896

In the second Epistle to Timothy, the first chapter and the twelfth verse, you have these words: "I know whom I have believed and am persuaded that He is able to keep that which I have committed unto Him against that day."

I got a request from some twelve or fifteen brethren in the ministry, or in the work of God, asking me to give a testimony as to my own personal experience in the Christian life. And before I speak of these words I want, in a few short sentences, to tell you how God has led me. What God has done to me is not mine but His own, and if it can help you, I cannot withhold it. And yet, I am somewhat reluctant to speak of my experience, for this reason: When a man has got a clear, distinct experience to tell and a very definite story about something God has done for him, a clear passing out of one state of the Christian life into another, it is often very helpful and very stirring. But that is not my story. I was away in South Africa, almost alone, and I had to fight and stumble my way along, and owing to that I had no such clear path as I could have wished for; but let me tell you.

If I speak of my life, my Christian life, the first fifteen years, perhaps, I call a time of darkness and of struggling after the light. I could divide my Christian life into three periods: The time of darkness, the time of the vision of the light, and then the time of the richer experience. I was, as a young minister, most earnest. I was counted a most faithful gospel preacher, and I was diligent in the enormous parish that was entrusted to me. I loved my work and yet all the time my spiritual life was one of deep unhappiness. I was bound in the chains of misunderstanding and prejudice. One thing that I thought was that a Christian must go on sinning every day. I really thought that this was a must. As a result of that, I had no definite expectation that God would keep me from it. I am sorry to say that that was my belief, and then along with that I had no understanding that obedience was a possible thing. I look back with shame when, in later years, I began to see the place that obedience ought to take in a Christian life. I remember how little I understood that—that Christianity is to give up yourself to entire obedience to God. I never saw it.

And then, along with that, I had no real faith in the keeping, sanctifying power of God's Holy Spirit or of Jesus Christ. Yet I was most earnest, studying the matter of sanctification, praying about it, but I got very little light. But it was a time on which God looked with mercy, for it was a time of great desire and often of crying to God, and God hears cries.

When God has created a need, He will fulfill it. Oh, if there are any hungry and thirsty souls, walking in darkness and struggling along, and saying they cannot understand it, or trying to understand it, and complaining that they can't reach it, I say to them, lift up your hearts to God in trust. The God that created your heart for Himself, and the God who made you His child in Christ, He will provide for your holiness if you trust Him more. Look away from all teaching. Use it as a help when you can, but look away from it to the living God. He made you and He can make you holy.

May 23
His Keeping - 2
by Andrew Murray (1828-1917) Scotland/South Africa
Excerpted from "Jesus Able to Keep," *The Spiritual Life*, published by Tupper & Robertson, Chicago, Illinois in 1896

I suppose for fifteen years after my conversion, I went on, and then came the time when, in England, there was a great stir about the higher life, and I got some of these books and they helped me wonderfully, and I then began to say, "Yes, there is a better life." It was at that time, now thirty years ago, in a time of revival in my Dutch parish in Worcester, South Africa, that I wrote "Abide in Christ" in Dutch. It was not, perhaps, exactly the same as now, but the substance. It was at that time that my heart was feeling after the truth and beginning to find it, beginning to get hold of something—a little of the blessed experience of better knowledge of God and of more trust in Him. And yet I have to confess with shame that, at that time, I often stumbled. One thing was, I had never been taught the absolute necessity, the supreme importance of literal, immediate, actual obedience to God. Someone said to me, about that book, "I think you have put it more from the privilege side than from the duty side." Perhaps that is true. I had not, at that time, sufficiently seen the call to absolute obedience.

So it went on, year after year. I enjoyed more of God, I enjoyed more rest, I enjoyed more peace, I got more victory, and I learned to trust God more. The path God led me in was not that of one decisive crisis, but step by step. Mind, I have great faith that God is willing to take a man in by a sudden step, by a crisis in his life, and I count it a very blessed thing, and I think the reason that God did not take me in that way was simply that I was not properly instructed. I had no Christian friends of experience around me to help, and when you haven't any help in that way, you often fail on some little point of obedience or faith, and then you fall back again. But then God led me on, in His great mercy, I at times failing, yet at times in great peace, until later on—it would be difficult to say exactly how long, for there was no actual transition—I can see that when I contrast the last fifteen years of my life with the first fifteen, I praise God for a very great difference. And what I praise God for is this: The rest of faith. I can see that He has taught me to rest in Him and to trust Him and to believe, even if my faith does not always rise to its fullest height, but yet to continue in the abiding belief that my God is working in me; that my God loves me with a wonderful love, and that as I yield entirely to Him He will do a perfect work in me.

Oh friends, that is what we need, those who don't have it. To come into that rest, that rest with God, which leaves everything with Him. And what God has done more for me is this: He has helped me, I trust to greater and more continued obedience. I do not say it is perfect, but by the grace of God I have learned to do His will, and to do it as a thing unto Himself, personally, and I have found the peace and blessing of it.

One thing more. It has pleased God to use my labors for the helping of His children, out in the land where I live and elsewhere, and I cannot sufficiently praise His goodness that it has pleased Him to use me as a vessel, an earthen, empty, broken vessel, into which He has poured out His life and of His love, and of the living water to bring to others. There is my simple, short testimony. There was a time, a third of my Christian life, that was in great darkness; there was perhaps another third seeking God and the light and rejoicing in it and yet not getting full access; another third in which God has brought me out deeper into the enjoyment of His life and His love—praised be His holy name. I feel, above all, how helpless I am to speak about what I thought to speak, about the Lord Jesus Christ. He is ready, in His almighty love and power, to take hold of every child of God, however far back or low down he is, if he will give himself into His almighty keeping. May God Himself exalt His blessed Son in each of us.

May 24
His Keeping - 3
by Andrew Murray (1828-1917) Scotland/South Africa
Excerpted from "Jesus Able to Keep," *The Spiritual Life*, published by Tupper & Robertson, Chicago, Illinois in 1896

You know the words of the text, "I know Him, whom I have believed, and I am persuaded that He is able to keep that which I have committed unto Him against that day."

The commitment. What does that mean? People have sometimes asked, What was it that Paul committed to Christ? Some have said it was his life, in the midst of so much persecution and danger; others have said it was his ministry, the work that he had to do, as an apostle; others have said it was his own soul, with his spiritual life and his hope of the crown of righteousness. I think it is impossible to separate these things. I think Paul meant them all, for he had committed himself wholly to Christ Jesus. He said, "I cannot keep myself. I have got a very precious thing. I have got a heart and a life and a wonderful soul created by God, but I cannot keep it. Sin and the world and the flesh and the devil are all tempting me and wanting to rob me of my powers; what shall I do? I will give it up to Christ to keep." And he did. He gave himself wholly. His head, his heart, his mind, his affections, his will, his powers, his body, his righteousness, his property, his religion, everything, he gave up to Christ, and said, "Lord, do with it as seems good in Your sight and keep it for me." That, dear friends, is simply and exactly what a man has got to do if he wants to enter into the higher life.

The great mischief with Christians is that they have given over their souls to Jesus to keep and say, "Lord, keep my soul and let me never perish." That is what many people pray. But they have said, "Lord, let me keep my will, let me keep my own mind, and read and think what I like; let me keep my position and let me keep my own money." They ask to keep a great many things and they never, never, can have peace or rest. The Lord Jesus comes and says He wants all, *all*, ALL. And that is the solemn question with which I come to every Christian.

Brother, have you given up everything you have into the keeping of Jesus? Or do you not often talk about just what you like? About this and that man you say exactly what you choose, sharp or foolish things, just as you like. You haven't given up your tongue to Jesus. Your thoughts! Do you not often spend your thoughts upon yourself or upon the world, just as you like? You have never yet said to the Redeemer, "My mind, with every power, belongs to the Holy Christ, who bought me with His blood." I want you to come, right now, if you have never said so, and say, "Christ shall have all."

I want to go deeper. I want to say, are there sins of which you never have said, "I give that up to Christ?" There is the love of the world. Are you going to say, "I am going to part with the world and to give this heart, this life of mine to love Christ, to love Christ only, to love Christ with the love that the Holy Spirit has given me." Dear friends, you all want the higher life, the life of faith, and the life of Christ, but remember, we must pay the price. We must get rid of everything and Christ Jesus must have us all in all. May God, by His Holy Spirit, work conviction in the hearts of His children.

May 25
His Keeping – 4
by Frances Ridley Havergal (1836-1879) England
Excerpted from "Christ for Us," *Kept for the Master's Use*, published by James Nisbet & Co., London, England in 1879

"So will I also be for you."
Hosea 3:3 (KJV)

The very pledge implies our past unfaithfulness, and the proven need of even our own part being undertaken by the ever patient Lord. He Himself has to guarantee our faithfulness, because there is no other hope of our continuing faithful. Well may such love win our full and glad surrender, and such a promise win our happy and confident trust!

But He says more. He says, "So will I also be for you!" And this seems an even greater marvel of love, as we observe how He meets every detail of our consecration with this wonderful word.

His Life "for you!" "The Good Shepherd gives His life for the sheep." Oh, wonderful gift! not promised, but given; not to friends, but to enemies. Given without condition, without reserve, without return. Himself unknown and unloved, His gift unsought and unasked, He gave His life for you; a more than royal bounty — the greatest gift that Deity could devise.

His Eternity "for you." All we can ask Him to take are days and moments — the little span given us as it is given, and of this only the present in deed and the future in will. As for the past, in so far as we did not give it to Him, it is too late; we can never give it now! But His past was given to us, though ours was not given to Him. Oh, what a tremendous debt does this show us!

His Hands "for you." Literal hands, literally pierced, when the whole weight of His quivering frame hung from their torn muscles and bared nerves; literally uplifted in parting blessing. Consecrated, priestly hands; "filled" hands (Exodus 28:41; 29:9) — filled once with His great offering, and now with gifts and blessings "for you."

His Feet "for you." They were weary very often, they were wounded and bleeding once. They made clear footprints as He went about doing good, and as He went up to Jerusalem to suffer; and these "blessed steps of His most holy life," both as substitution and example, were "for you."

His Voice "for you." The "Voice of my beloved that knocks, saying, Open to me, my sister, my love"; the Voice that His sheep "hear" and "know," and that calls out the fervent response, "Master, say on!" This is not all. It was the literal voice of the Lord Jesus which uttered that one echoless cry of desolation on the cross "for you," and it will be His own literal voice which will say, "Come, you blessed!" to you.

His Wealth "for you." "Though He was rich, yet for our sakes He became poor, that you through His poverty might be made rich." Yes, "through His poverty" the unsearchable riches of Christ are "for you."

His Will "for you." Think first of the infinite might of that will; the first great law and the first great force of the universe, from which alone every other law and every other force has sprung, and to which all are subordinate.

Himself "for you." "Christ also has loved us, and given Himself for us." Jesus Christ, "Who His own self bore our sins in His own body on the tree"; "this same Jesus…Whom having not seen, you love"; the Son of God, and the Man of Sorrows; my Savior, my Friend, my Master, my King, my Priest, my Lord and my God — He says, "also for you!"

May 26
His Kingdom - 1
by William Nixon (1803-1900) Scotland
Excerpted from "The Kingdom of Christ on Earth," *All and In All*, published by Johnstone, Hunter & Co., Edinburgh, Scotland in 1882

Jesus answered, "My Kingdom is not of this world..."
John 18:36 (KJV)

Christ as a King is not of this world. He was greatly inferior to worldly rulers in outward condition. "He made Himself of no reputation, and took upon Him the form of a servant, and was made in the likeness of men." They are born in palaces and nursed on couches of splendor; He was born in a stable and laid in a manger. They are trained amidst all outward advantages; He lived at Nazareth in subjection to laboring parents, and grew up as the carpenter's Son. They grasp at temporal dominion; He refused it when put within His reach and pressed on His acceptance. They have around them the rich, the mighty, and the noble; around Him were harmless women and simple fishermen. They rise to their sovereignty by the force of temporal power; He rose to His sovereignty by the force of truth. They display themselves in all outward magnificence; His highest public display took place when, amidst the acclamations of the multitude, He entered Jerusalem on an ass's colt. Their authority is upheld too often by the sacrifice and sufferings of others; He secured His authority by His own sacrifice and sufferings. They triumph over their enemies by destroying them; He triumphed over His by being taken by their wicked hands and crucified and slain.

All the emblems and accompaniments of His royalty as God-Man, Mediatorial King, proclaim its infinite greatness. Earthly kings occupy thrones of visible splendor; but Jesus fills the throne of the universe. Their brows are decked each with a royal diadem; but to set forth His sovereignty over all nations and other worlds, it is said that He has on His head many crowns. The sound of their reputation may for a time fill great regions of the earth; but He has a name which is above every name that is named, not only in this world, but also in that which is to come. They dwell in literal palaces; but He has a palace in every heart that loves Him: He also inhabits eternity; and in the Heaven of heavens, as His special residence, He dwells in the midst of a glory to which no man can approach and live. They are surrounded by officers and servants of all ranks and stations; but He is surrounded by myriads of glorious creatures that minister before His throne. They have legions of soldiers whom they send forth to maintain their dominion and their honor; but He is followed and served by the hosts of Heaven, who go everywhere to execute His purposes, whether of judgment or of mercy. They may boast of their dominions; but He is head over all things. They may at times feel as if nothing could withstand them; but He is the only resistless ruler of the universe; Heaven, earth, and hell are subject to His will.

But what does this character of the King prove with reference to the Kingdom? It proves everything. It proves that so far as His Kingdom can be stamped by Him with His own likeness, it will not be a kingdom of this world. And He does stamp it with His own character, He forms it after His own image. He calls it into existence, and so gives to it what character He pleases. He is the Creator, Redeemer, and Sanctifier of His Kingdom, as well as its King. He makes and fashions it according to His own will. He is not like earthly kings who cannot change the nature of the materials that make up their kingdoms. He exerts Almighty power over the materials of which His Kingdom is composed. Its character, therefore, corresponds to His own; and as He is not of this world, so neither is His Kingdom. The subjects of Christ's Kingdom are not of this world. That is to say, the means by which He turns them into subjects of His Kingdom, and the character to which He forms them, are spiritual, heavenly, and divine.

May 27
His Kingdom - 2
by William Nixon (1803-1900) Scotland
Excerpted from "The Kingdom of Christ on Earth," *All and In All*, published by Johnstone, Hunter & Co., Edinburgh, Scotland in 1882

Jesus answered, "My Kingdom is not of this world…"
John 18:36 (KJV)

The spiritual nature of Christ's Kingdom is proved by the laws that rule in it. They are heavenly in their origin. The laws of earthly kingdoms, framed by earthly rulers, partake of the mingled wisdom and folly, reasonableness and passion, caution and impulse of the human heart, and of the pride and selfishness and cruelty inherent in our fallen nature. The laws of Christ's Kingdom issuing from the eternal throne, embody the mind of the all-perfect, glorious God, are a transcript of His infinite perfections, the offspring of His combined holiness, justice, goodness, and truth, so that the law of Christ's Kingdom is holy, and the commandment holy, just, and good. The Word of God is the statute book of Christ's Kingdom; and the authority of that Word, and of Him from whom it comes, is the only authority that can, without sin, without, in fact, a blasphemous assumption of the divine prerogative, be pleaded for the enforcement of any laws whatever, within the Church or Kingdom of Christ. Even good laws, that is, laws good in themselves, derived from any other source, such as civil government, have on that ground no more rightful force within Christ's Kingdom or Church, than the laws of France, however good, have within the kingdom of Britain. The laws put in operation within the Church, must be not only good, but derived from the divine word, the only fountainhead of all law for the Kingdom of Christ on earth, and enforced on the authority of that word alone.

The laws of Christ's Kingdom are heavenly in their sanctions. The laws of earthly kingdoms are enforced by the temporal rewards that accrue to the loyal, and by the temporal punishments that overtake the disobedient and rebellious. But the laws of Christ's Kingdom are enforced by admission to spiritual privileges or exclusion from them, and by the prospect of the future and everlasting rewards and punishments that will be bestowed on saints and inflicted on sinners respectively.

The laws of Christ's Kingdom are heavenly in their end. The purpose of human laws in civil society, is to keep in outward order the inhabitants of a land. For that purpose, the authority and dominion of earthly rulers extend only to the outward persons and temporal property, the bodies and substance of those who are subject to their power. When they come to the boundary line, separating the region of conscience from the region of the bodies and substance of the people, the dominion of earthly rulers ceases. Human laws and lawgivers cannot justly, or without enormous wrong, extend their authority and power so as to attempt coercively to control the consciences and hearts of men. But the inward spiritual nature of man is just the region where the laws of Christ's Kingdom chiefly take effect. Their great design is to enlighten His people's understandings, to subdue their wills, to regulate their consciences, to govern their hearts, to control their affections and desires. Christ's Empire is an Empire of truth and love. He sheds abroad in their hearts that love which is the fulfilling of the law. They thus delight in His law after the inward man. They love it, and make it their meditation all the day. And thus by the Spirit it is so written in their hearts, and so embodied in their lives, that they are turned into living epistles of Christ, to be known and read of all men.

In the view of Jesus' words to the Roman governor about His Kingdom, and of its destined and approaching supremacy on earth, the ruling powers had better have a care of how they deal with this Kingdom of Christ, or any of its sections within their territory. It does not exist for them; but they exist for it.

May 28
His Knocking
by David James Burrell (1844-1926) USA
Excerpted from "See Him at Your Door," *We Would See Jesus*,
published by American Tract Society, New York, New York in 1914

The Savior stands knocking at the door of every heart, saying, "If any man hears My voice and opens the door, I will come in to him and will dine with him, and he with Me." Look out of your window and you shall see Him. What will you do about it?

A man's heart is his castle. Reason and Will are two mighty bolts by which it is fastened even against God. He addresses Himself to the reason, saying, "Come, now, and let us reason together; though your sins be as scarlet, they shall be as white as snow; though they be red like crimson, they shall be as wool." But suppose our intellectual powers are convinced, what then? Though the upper bolt be drawn, the lower bolt holds fast. We may yield a mental assent to all the arguments and entreaties of divine grace and yet be unreconciled with God: For, in the last reduction, the stubborn will must yield or God cannot come in. There lies the trouble. "You will not come to Me that you may have life."

It is difficult to imagine how God could have created a man in His own likeness and after His image without endowing him with a sovereign will. He might have made a graven image or a mannequin; but this would not have been a child of God. It is obvious that the possession of a sovereign will carries with it the power of disobedience. In this we are differentiated from all the lower orders of life. The stars of the universe obey God. The fowls of the air and the beasts of the forest and the fishes of the sea all yield to His command; but man has the power to say, "I will not." It thus appears that the token of our divine birthright is the danger signal of our destiny. The same endowment that brings us into familial relation with the Father involves the possibility of an awful revolt and infinite departure from Him. If, therefore, God would have access to my soul He must stand there and knock and live with my decision. It is written of Him that He will not "turn aside the right of a man." If He draws me, He must draw me with "the cords of a man."

But why should the man in the closed house—a sinner, eating his heart out with shame and misgiving—refuse to admit the gracious Son of God? Oh, surely there must be some misunderstanding here! He comes to dine with us! The feasts of Vitellius [Roman emperor, 20-69AD] have gone into history. It was not an uncommon thing for him to spend the revenues of an entire province on a single banquet. His table was furnished with lampreys from distant seas, with nightingales' tongues and peacocks' brains and all manner of rare delicacies. Those were famous feasts; but they were nothing compared to those which the Son of Man proposes to furnish for the delight of all who will open unto Him. Here is water from the King's well, wine from the King's vineyard, apples and pomegranates from the King's orchard. Here is the joy of pardon, "Son, your sins are forgiven." Here is "the peace of God which passes all understanding." Here is "the hope that makes not ashamed." Here are all the consolations of the heavenly grace; and here is the gracious presence of the King of kings shining like a blessing upon all.

Did we but know the goodness in the heart of Him who stands waiting at our door we surely would not exclude Him. It is written, "God sent not the Son into the world to judge the world; but that the world should be saved through Him." Salvation is the gift He brings us. Why then this attitude toward Him? Hark! The voice is pleading still: "Behold, I stand and knock; if you open unto Me I will come in and dine with you."

May 29
His Knowing
by James Russell (J. R.) Miller (1840-1912) USA
Excerpted from "Comfort in Christ's Knowledge of Us," *The Hidden Life*,
published by Thomas Y. Crowell & Company,
New York, New York in 1898

To many people the thought of Christ's perfect knowledge of them is an unwelcome one. It awes them and troubles them. But if we are living as we should live, if we are true to our purpose and sincere in our striving, the consciousness that Christ knows all about us should give us great comfort.

Too often this thought of the divine omniscience is presented as an element of terror. Children are told that God sees them; and the fact is presented to them as one which should inspire dread, and they are made to fear God's eye. The words "You, God, see me" are quoted and commented upon as if it had been in a stern view that the Lord appeared to Hagar. Really, however, it was of a friendly revealing that these words were first used. Under God's all-seeing eye was a shelter of love for the poor woman. So it is always that God looks down upon His children, and His look is ever kind. He is our Friend, not our enemy; and His feeling toward us is very gracious and loving. The thought of His perfect knowledge of us should never be an oppressive one; and it will not be so if we understand even a little of His yearning interest in us, and if we have even a faint understanding of His infinite patience.

True, our life is full of failures and blemishes. We mean to be loyal to Christ, but the world is hard, and we are very weak. At best, we get only little fragments of the beauty of Christ into our character. We are Christ-like only in dim, blurred resemblances in our disposition and conduct. We intend to be gentle and loving; but we tarnish our days oftentimes with unhappy attitudes, irritable bickering, inappropriate complaints, and selfish striving. We intend to be strong in faith, allowing nothing to make us fear or doubt; but our trust fails us many times, and we grow fearful in life's stress. We mean to be consistent Christians, to live blamelessly in this evil world; but our strength is small, and temptations are hard; and where is the day which is not spoiled by failures?

When we come into the presence of Christ with our broken vows and our stained records, what can we say? Can we look up into His blessed face and declare that we love Him, with the memory of all our faults, inconsistencies, and failures fresh in mind? Is not our poor Christian life a denial of our fair profession? We might say that we are sorry, and will not repeat these sins and follies; but have we not been saying this over and over, perhaps for years, and then almost immediately repeating the things we deplored and promised never to repeat?

What shall we do? If Christ were only a man like ourselves, judging love by its deeds, we could not hope for His patient bearing with us. Men are not so tolerant of our failures. They grow weary of our broken vows. They do not know our inner life; they cannot see the sincerity which is in our heart beneath all that would seem to prove us insincere. But here it is that we find the comfort in Christ—in His perfect knowledge of us. He not only knows the sin and wrong that are in us, but He also knows whatsoever in us is true and sincere. He sees the little true love—little, yet true—that there is amid the weakness, the broken vows, and the sad failures.

This love that is in the heart of Christ is a wonderful love. It is a love that never tires of us. It is Christ's perfect knowledge of us that gives such infinite patience to His love and grace. He knows the sincerity that is in us; He sees, too, the possibilities of good that are in us—not what we are now, but what we are to be when the work in us is finished.

May 30
His Law
by David James Burrell (1844-1926) USA
Excerpted from "The Great Law of Christ," *God and the People*, published by Wilbur Ketcham, New York, New York in 1899

Bear one another's burdens, and so fulfill the law of Christ. For if anyone thinks he is something, when he is nothing, he deceives himself. But let each one test his own work, and then his reason to boast will be in himself alone and not in his neighbor.
For each will have to bear his own load.
Galatians 6:2-5 (ESV)

The Great Law of Christ is so-called for three reasons: First, because He gave it. Second, because He exemplified it in His own life among men. He bore His own burden; for, indeed, there was a burden which He alone could bear; in which no friendship could relieve Him. At the gateway of Gethsemane He said to His disciples, "Wait here while I go and pray over there." And there, under the deep shadow of the olive trees, He drank His bitter cup; as it is written, "I have trodden the winepress alone and of the people there was none with Me." He made no complaint, no murmuring. His prayer was, "If it is possible, let this cup pass from Me"; but when it became apparent that the bitterness of death was the necessary condition for the world's redemption, He calmly agreed, saying, "O My Father, not My will but Yours be done." And thereupon He set His face steadfastly toward the cross. Such was the courage of the Perfect Man.

But furthermore He exemplified the Great Law in bearing the burden of others. It is written "He bare our griefs and carried our sorrows. We did esteem Him stricken, smitten of God and afflicted; but He was wounded for our transgressions and bruised for our iniquities. The chastisement of our peace was upon Him." His heart went out toward all sufferers. His ears were open to every cry for relief. He fed the hungry, opened the eyes of the blind, wiped away the leper's spots, ministered to sorrow, wept by the open grave; and at last He climbed up Calvary staggering under the burden of the whole world's sin. Ah, that was the most wonderful deed of sympathy, of self-sacrifice, of practical generosity, that the world ever saw. His heart broke in compassion for the world's pain, and His hands were stretched out in divinest love to all the children of men.

And third, the Great Law of Christ is so-called because He laid it down as the fundamental principle of His Kingdom. The universal observance of this Law will bring in the Millennium. It corresponds to the physical Law of Gravity, by which all the worlds of the solar system are kept in proper relation to each other and to the central sun. If those for whom Jesus died were under the domination of this Law, as the stars of the universe are under the control of gravity, there would not be one lost or wayward soul in the universe. This was in the mind of Jesus when He said, "I pray for these; that they all may be one; even as You, Father, are in Me and I in You, that they also may be one in Us: that the world may believe that You did send Me."

In the Great Law, thus briefly stated, we find the sum and substance of the duties of the Christian life. Our success in right living is measured by our imitation of Christ as the Burden-bearer. Mere sentiment is of little worth. Our religion is a matter of practical importance; it is to do good as we have opportunity unto all men. We come into sympathy with Him in the thick of the world's conflict. We die with Him when our hearts break in sympathetic touch with the world's agonizing heart. This is "the cure of souls"; this is the law of love; this is the fellowship of Christ. He entered into our estate; He passed through the doorway of human homes, toiled in the workshop, joined the company of wayfaring men, knelt by the bedsides of the sick and dying to give comfort.

May 31
His Leadership
by Phillips Brooks (1835-1893) USA
Excerpted from "The Leadership of Christ," *The Battle of Life and Other Sermons*, published by E. P. Dutton & Company, New York, New York in 1910

"In My Father's house are many mansions...I go to prepare a place for you...and I will come again and receive you unto Myself."
John 14:2-3 (KJV)

This is Christ's way. Wherever He would have His disciples go, He goes first Himself, and through the door which He has opened He draws them by His love. That is the whole philosophy of Christian culture. And that is the meaning of the Incarnation. God entered into human life; made Himself one with it as He only could have done with a nature that was originally one with His own. He became human as He could not have become beast or stone. Then in that human nature He went out into humanity. He opened yet unopened gates of human possibility. He showed what people might be, how great, how godlike! As we think of the Incarnation deeply, these three stages come in one thought. First, God in Christ seems very near to us as we think of His love. Then He seems very far above us as we think of His holiness, and then again He seems to bring us very near to Himself as we feel His power. He is one with us.

In this way we trace Christ's treatment of those first disciples. And what then? Here we live at this late day. Is any such method at work, any such culture possible now? My dear friend, one thing is certainly true about Christ. That all that He has ever been He must forever be. All that He was to those first disciples, He must be ready to be to anyone, even the least of His disciples always. His power is nothing at any one point if it is not powerful at all points; nothing, if not eternal. How is it possible, then, that Christ should do for you and me what He did for Peter and John, and Matthew and Nathanael? It is not hard to see, and to many people living just such lives as we live it has become the most real of experiences. Jesus, the Jesus of the Gospels, fastens His life to our life. By His life and death, bearing witness of His love, He entwines Himself into our being. To love Him becomes a real thing. He is close by our side. He is right in our lot every day.

Then as we go on living this way with Him some crisis of our life occurs, some need for action. We are put to some test, and as we stand doubting, or as we go and do the act in our low way, Christ, right by our side, does it in His higher way. Not that His hands visibly touch our tools and do the work we have to do. But it becomes evident to us what He would do under our circumstances, what one thing it would be possible for Him to do as we are situated. It is very different from what we are actually doing. We are fawning to people's opinion, compromising principle, telling a lie. And it is made manifest to us that Jesus in just those same circumstances would defy people's judgments and stand by principle and tell the truth. We are not up to that. We see Him leave us. He goes out from us. But if we really love Him, if our life has grown one with His, He does not leave us really. His going on into principle, honor, truth, and God is a pledge and promise that in those holy homes there is a place for us, too, and soon we are restless unless we follow Him, and the gates of that nobler life which He has opened shine before us, and His love draws us on to be with Him.

When Christ has led His disciples on and on from stage to stage of spiritual growth, at last He opens the door and gives them entrance into Heaven. Whatever other joy and glory may be waiting for us in Heaven, the glory and the joy which will be most to us, and which we ought most of all to anticipate, is that there will be new regions of spiritual life thrown open, new and deeper experiences of the soul made possible, deeper knowledge of God, deeper knowledge of ourselves, deeper delight in purity.

June 1
His Liberation – 1
by Handley C. G. Moule (1841-1920) England
Excerpted from "Christ the Liberator," *Christ Is All*, published by
Hodder and Stoughton, London, England in 1920

"If the Son shall make you free, you shall be free indeed."
John 8:36 (KJV)

Here stands One who claims this great potency and prerogative, to make me free, and free indeed. And my inmost self responds to the offer with the sense of need of freedom, moral freedom, spiritual freedom, freedom from a torturing conscience, freedom from a terrible captivity of will, freedom from the guilt of sin before my eternal Judge, freedom from the power of sin within my conscious self. You need, as a sinner, to be free; and perhaps right now you have advanced from a mere admission of need into a profound sense of want, a "hunger and thirst after righteousness," an indescribable longing, and aspiration, and request to be that which the Eternal would have you be. And here, here in this written page, in this authentic record of a life which assuredly man did not invent, and which is, therefore, fact, here speaks this voice of promise, "You shall be free indeed"; here stands this living Promiser, "I am the Son; I can make you free." And just in proportion to our craving for a freedom of the soul, will be the intense attention with which we shall look the Promiser in the face, and from His very words, and manner, and person extract the assurance of His capacity to fulfil. "Do you believe that I am able?" "Lord, I believe; and he worshipped Him."

Have you ever taken the matter in hand, and tried to educate the inner slavery into liberty, and to force down the inner rebellion into order, in a strength of your own? Very possibly you have. And perhaps, in a sense, you have succeeded. A vile habit has become less frequent; possibly it has quite ceased. But is it not miserably partial work; a scraping of the surface, a whitewashing of the sepulcher? There is no peace at the center of your being. You are but "holding the wolf by the ears"; or at best, if the wolf is driven out, the serpent has glided in, and vice has left the nest warm for pride.

"If He makes us free," then, compared with the most intense efforts of our will apart from Him, "we shall be free indeed." The Son can indeed bring a blessed freedom into the inner world; let us, let me, recognize that fact with growing joy. Tempted Christian, have you really put the Lord in command of your heart? Are you really, through grace, willing that He should be the absolute Ruler there? Have you quite simply put Him first, first before ambition, first before worldly interests, first before man's praise and blame? Are you quite willing to "commit the keeping of your soul to Him in well-doing?" And, being so willing, are you simply looking to Him to work—using His means of grace, and not least the secret means, the privately pondered Bible, the exercise of secret prayer—but using them as guides after all to Him, the Lord the Son, who died for you and rose again? Then I humbly but boldly say to you, take your strongest temptation, take your weakest point, write across it in your soul the great words, "He is able"; and humbly commit it, in calm expectant faith, to Him as to a living Redeemer. Hear Him as He says, "My grace is sufficient for you"; and look in His face as He says it. Is it not a true word from the Lord of truth?

You shall find it wonderfully true. I do not say that inner conflict will never come; I do not say that you will need no more to watch and pray; God forbid. But I say that you shall joyfully experience great victories instead of little; deep changes instead of shallow; continuity of inner peace instead of one that is erratic. I say that the experience of the Lord's success with a case as difficult as yours, as difficult as mine, shall be within you a spring of indescribable rest, and joy, and gentle power.

June 2
His Liberation - 2
by Arthur J. Gossip (1873-1954) Scotland
Excerpted from "What Christ Does for a Soul," *20 Sermons by Famous Scotch Preachers*, published by George H. Doran Company, New York, New York in 1924

To Him who loves us and has freed us from our sins by His blood, and has made us to be a Kingdom and priests to serve His God and Father...
Revelation 1:6 (NIV)

What exactly has Christ done for you? What is there in your life that needs Christ to explain it, and that, apart from Him, simply could not have been there at all? If there is nothing, then your religion is a sheer futility. But then that is your fault, not Jesus Christ's. For when we open the New Testament it is to come upon whole companies of excited people, their faces all aglow, their hearts dazed and bewildered by the immensity of their own good fortune. Apparently they cannot think of anything but this amazing happening that has befallen them, quite certainly they cannot keep from laying almost violent hands on every chance passerby, and pouring out yet once again the whole bewildering tale. And always as we listen they keep throwing up their hands as if in sheer despair, telling us it is hopeless, that it breaks through language, that it won't describe, that until a man has known Christ for himself he can have no idea of the enormous difference He makes. He gave me a new spiritual standing, so he says; I was a serf, born into slavery, and I am free, and it was Christ who did it. That is a part of what He has brought me. He gave me a new spiritual standing. If only someone could blot out the past, could grant me a new start, could save me from my failure! If! If! But that's precisely, says Apostle John, what Christ did for me! And indeed we can see Him at it, as we follow through the Gospels' pages, and watch Him coming here and there on crushed and crouching figures, who have accepted their defeat, surrendered to themselves, have long stopped even trying, can read their condemnation in every hard eye, and themselves resigned to it as just. And yet Christ spoke to them as if they too had souls; and gave them of His very best, quite evidently sure they also could respond to it; let them see frankly that whatever the past is, He for one still believed in them with all His heart. And, with that, the incredible happened, and a soul awoke where you and I would have said that no soul could be. We must take it at Christ's hand. For nothing exasperated Him more than the strange unambitious ease with which we are satisfied. Verily, verily, He keeps saying disappointedly to us who have settled down so soon, you will see greater things than these. Why do you camp just across the border of the Kingdom, or barely in it, when you could progress and take it, all the length and breadth and fullness of it as your own? As Luke says in his glorious opening of the Acts, "the former treatise have I written unto you of what Christ did and taught as a beginning." Even Calvary, he felt, did not exhaust Jesus Christ. And whatever you and I may have received from Him, however wonderful it is, it is at most only a preface, a first chapter, a beginning; there is infinitely more. This bare, unimpressive life of ours, with the lean shoulder of your natural character showing all too often through the thin layer of better things superimposed, like wind-blown soil, is not the most He can do for us. He gave me a new opulence, says John, and we also must accept it at His hand.

And last of all, first of all, and most of all, He gave me a new character. For that I suppose is the meaning of that phrase about us being priests to God, and His Father. But a priest is at least meant to be one who can't live for himself, like other people, but for others; who is so hurt by the sufferings and sorrows of his fellowmen that he can't get it out of mind, but has to go to God on their behalf, and stagger back with help and encouragment for them. And we are all priests, none of us can live for himself—have all caught the infection of our Lord's unselfishness—cannot but see that life is given to us to spend upon our fellowmen.

June 3
His Life

by Horatius Bonar (1808-1889) Scotland
Excerpted from "The Power of Christ's Resurrection," *Light and Truth*,
published by James Nisbet & Co., London, England in 1870

Always bearing about in the body the dying of the Lord Jesus, that the life also of Jesus might be made manifest in our body. For we which live are always delivered unto death for Jesus' sake, that the life also of Jesus might be made manifest in our mortal flesh.
2 Corinthians 4:10-11 (KJV)

The Life here spoken of is not the substitutional or sacrificial; at least not in the substitutional or sacrificial aspects. It is Life as a root, or fountain, or vital power. It is not a life given *for* us, but a Life given *to* us. It is the Life of the risen Christ; resurrection Life; His risen Life deposited as in a vessel for us, and showing out all its fullness in counteraction to the death which is in us and around us. It is in reference to this Life that Paul reasons, "If when we were enemies we were reconciled to God by the death of His Son, much more being reconciled, we shall be saved by His Life"; that is, if a dying Christ did so much for us, what will not a living Christ do? Let us look then at this vessel and its contents; this well and its life-giving water. "Truly it has been said, Christ is Life, others only live." Mark this "Life of Christ."

It is large. The vessel is spacious; and its contents are proportionate to its capacity. The amount of Life contained in the vessel is infinite, and being infinite, it assures us that no amount of death, or danger, or weakness on our part, can prove too great for it to counteract and overcome. O vastness, O infinity of Life, what is there that You cannot do for us? What is the extent of death, in a human soul or body, when compared with this Life divine? Good news indeed!

It is constant. This life is not erratic. It does not come in tides, ebbing and flowing; nor in seasons, sometimes winter, and again summer; nor in swings, as day and night. It is continuous, unbroken, ever flowing. It is the river which ceases not. It is the deep, deep well which never runs dry.

It is free. Priceless in every sense it is. Without price, and beyond price! "Free" is the word inscribed on this divine vessel. No condition, no merit, no price! The Life is a gift; and that gift is absolutely and unconditionally free.

It is suitable. It takes up every act of our being, and extends to every region, every circumstance, of our life. It pours itself into every faculty, and feeling, and organ. It meets us at every point. It brings out from its unsearchable riches the very things that we require in every necessity.

It is powerful. Omnipotence is in it. It is not the mere skill of the physician, or the effectiveness of His medicines (a thing of experiment or probability). But it is the irresistible power of a divine vitality, which no kind nor amount of creature-death can neutralize or conquer.

It is available. We might say, it is placed at our disposal, and within our reach. It is not in the heavens, that we should have to ascend there; it is not in the depths, that we should have to dig down further. It is near; it is the nearest thing in the universe; as near as He is in whom we live and move and have our being. It pours itself in through faith; through the Word; through prayer; through praise; through the sacraments. We are surrounded by this mighty Life. It is within us; it is around us; a well of water springing up into everlasting Life. It makes our life a continual resurrection. Like Abraham, we lay our life (as he did Isaac) on the altar; like Abraham, we receive it again from the dead. We live in and through the living One. Because He lives, we live also. Our life is hidden with Christ in God. Christ Himself is our Life.

June 4
His Light - 1
by Joseph A. Seiss (1823-1904) USA

Excerpted from "The Light of the World," *Beacon Lights: A Series of Short Sermons,* published by General Council of the Evangelical Lutheran Church, Philadelphia, Pennsylvania in 1900

Then Jesus spoke again to the people, He said, "I am the light of the world. Whoever follows Me will never walk in darkness, but will have the light of life."
John 8:12 (NIV)

The purest and least tarnished thing in the world is light. Snow is pure, ice is pure, water is pure, air is pure; but all of them may be marred, polluted, and made the instrument of pollution. It is not so with light. Man's hand cannot soil it. No corruption can infect it, or stick to it. Nothing can defile its rays, or attach pollution to its beams. And such is Christ. All creatures have shown themselves liable to sin and moral taint; but Christ passed through a world of sin, and the hell of its punishment, as a sunbeam through a hospital, and came out as pure and blessed as He sprang from God Himself. He took on Him sin's form, that He might endure sin's due; but its stain He never knew. In Bethlehem's manger He was the Holy Child; and to Heaven He returned the spotless Lamb of God. He lived a human life, tried by all its cares and sorrows, oppressed with all its necessities and temptations, grew up among its corrupt children, associated with its erring population, encountered its subtle passions, suffered its coarseness, its rebuffs, and its villainies, and died a martyr to His efforts to reform its defections; but in all this "He did no sin, neither was guile found in His mouth." He was pure, for He is Light.

Light is also as bright as it is pure. Things are bright in proportion as they are full of light. The day is bright when no clouds shut out the sun. The prospect is bright when illumined by the greatest number of rays. The hope is bright which is freest from gloomy forebodings and fullest of the light of promise. And such is Christ. He is brightness, "The brightness of the Father's glory." The brightness of every Divine perfection.

Light likewise is free. It comes without cost, and it comes ungrudgingly. No poverty is so great as to exclude its blessings. It gilds the halls of the great and the huts of the humble, and all alike without money and without price. Nor is there an open crevice in all the wide world into which it is unwilling to enter, or where it fails to throw in its heaven-lit smiles. It is free. And so is Christ. He is the Savior of the poor as well as of the rich, and on the same terms of free grace to each and all willing to accept Him. He is the true Light, ready to lighten every person that comes into the world.

It is also the nature of light to be all-revealing. Darkness obscures the vision. Where darkness prevails perception is limited. A pit may open at our feet; a murderer may be waiting in our path; a dagger may be aimed at our heart; each touch may be a stain and each step defilement; but darkness prevents our knowing it. Only when daylight comes can we see and know the truth.

And Christ is the great Revealer. By Him we come to know God and our true selves. By Him we learn who and where we are, what our needs are, and how to relieve them. One of the hardest things in the world is to make people believe that they are guilty and lost beings. The reason is, they are in the dark. They need the light to show them themselves. And that light is Christ. Only allow a man to compare himself with Jesus, and try himself in the light of Christ's life and teachings, and it will not be long until he sees that self of his to be a mere mass of guilt, that world of his love a monster, whose very embrace is filth and whose cup of joy is death.

June 5
His Light – 2
by Henry Robert Reynolds (1825-1896) England

Excerpted from "The Light of the Knowledge of the Glory of God," *Light and Peace*, published by E. P. Dutton & Co., New York, New York in 1892

The light of the knowledge of the glory of God in the face of Jesus Christ.
2 Corinthians 4:6 (NIV)

"The unfolding of Your words gives light" (Psalm 119:130). The transformation into thought, of the blended glory and sympathy, and the interwoven majesty and tenderness of the Christ, has created a new dawn in the mid-day of nature.

The light brighter than the sun which broke over the consciousness of Paul on his way to Damascus illuminated every truth which he had already made his own. It reversed for him the highest wisdom of the past, and cancelled his inheritance in the privileges and pride of centuries. The knowledge of the glory of God in the face of Jesus Christ became so brilliant an illumination, threw such floods of light on deep problems, on obscure and unsuspected places of thought and of human experience that he found himself in a new world, with new ideas of all things in Heaven and earth, in time and eternity.

It illuminates all the facts and laws of nature. The cross of Christ provides a new observatory for the universe. The heavens have a new meaning to us, for, if Christ is what He says He is, He is more and greater than they; and the death of the Son of God means more to us than if we saw the whole constellation of Orion, with all its suns and nebulas, blotted from the skies.

The knowledge of the glory of God in the face of Christ illuminates and enlarges and deepens our idea of God.

Further, while such a revelation of what man may become and ought to be makes evident to us the difference between what is possible and what is actual, we obtain the most terrible disclosure of the nature of sin, and the only light which makes it tolerable. Our first religious ideas have often proved to be a sense of conflict with God. The conviction haunts us that we have broken with the Almighty; that we have forfeited all hold upon Divine protection; that we have willfully entangled ourselves in the consequences of broken law; that we have incurred the issues, which no obedience, no repentance, no sacrifice of ours can pay or remove. The sense of evil, of increased severance from God, and the sense of coming doom are forced upon us by conscience and by the sense of dryness.

The light of this knowledge falls on the otherwise unsolvable mystery of sorrow. I will not try to establish this mystery, or portray the dark shadow, or weigh the burden of life. We all know it by bitter loss and pain. When we come into the light of this knowledge of the God-Man, a new meaning is given to our sorrow and to all sorrow. The widespread incidence of human grief may silence our wail but it will not touch the secret of our agony. But once we permit this light to shine upon our darkness, we find ourselves called into the fellowship of the Son of God, and we are reconciled.

When this light shines upon us, we have a message to the world of heathenism, and to the nations that are groping in darkness; we have in the brotherhood of our Lord a commission which will go straight to the evils that are festering in the heart of our modern civilization. We have what we know to be the abundant justification of the existence and mission of the Church. We are certain that we have in it a remedy for all sin, all guilt, all conflict with Providence, and war between man and man. We have the open secret and the abiding possession of a peace that passes all understanding.

June 6
His Likeness
by Newman Smyth (1843-1925) USA
Excerpted from "The Christ-Likeness of God," *The Reality of Faith*, published by Charles Scribner's Sons, New York, New York in 1884

This is why we work hard and continue to struggle, for our hope is in the living God, who is the Savior of all people and particularly of all believers.
1 Tmothy 4:10 (NLTSE)

There is latent in this Scripture a double energy of truth which the providence of God is now calling forth for the more thorough Christianization of Christianity. A historic power of Hebrew faith is in this Biblical expression, "The living God"; and there is further Christian energy of truth in these words, "Who is the Savior of all men, specially of them that believe." God is living, now, here, on earth, everywhere; and God is our Savior. Christ is usually called Savior; but this name of Christ Paul here transfers directly to God. In several texts God is called our Savior. God, then, is to us what Christ is. God Himself, then, is essentially Christ-like. He must have in Himself some Christ-likeness, for He is, as Christ, our Savior. Let the energy of these two truths once enter into a person's heart—the truth that in everything we have to do with the living God, and the truth that our God is the Christlike One, and they are enough to revolutionize a person's life.

These truths, that God is the living Presence, and that God is Christian in all the depths and glories of His being, are truths now seizing upon our religious thought, and pervading our best religious literature with new power of the Spirit. I say it reverently, that the Almighty Lord and Ruler of this universe is a Christian Being. In all our reasoning and speech about divinity and human destiny, we need to recognize simply and fully this essential fact of revelation that our God—the living God—is of all beings the most profoundly and really Christian. At all times, and in all relations, we are to conceive of God both as the living Presence, and as the Christ-like One.

At different periods in the history of the Church, the Spirit whom Christ promised should lead His disciples into all truth seems to have fixed the mind of the Church upon some particular truth which was needed at that special time for man's growth in the knowledge of God. Thus, in the first centuries, the mind of the early Church was riveted upon the nature of the wondrous person of Christ; and the Nicene creed was the result of three centuries of thought about Christ. In the Reformation the truths of free grace and the sole sovereignty of God became the strengthening bread of life for believers. God leads His people at different times to different phases and powers of the truth according to their present need. And is not His Spirit still leading us, if we will put away our own opinions, and seek to learn those things of Christ which for our own peril of faith we need to have shown to us?

God Himself is to be seen through Christ, and Christ is to be studied through all that is best and worthiest in the disciples' lives. Therefore through human hearts also which reflect in any wise Christ's spirit, we may seek to realize what God is. God is in Christ. God, I have been saying, is Christian, essentially and eternally Christian. Therefore if you would know God, you must live according to Christ. Every sin is so much ignorance of God. Through goodness only can He who is the Good be known. To know God our Savior we must become Christ-like. If any man does not have the Spirit of Christ, he is none of His.

June 7
His Living - 1
by Andrew Murray (1828-1917) Scotland/South Africa
Excerpted from "Christ Liveth In Me," *The Spiritual Life*, published by Tupper & Robertson, Chicago, Illinois in 1896

We want to have a clear idea of what we, in our Christian life, aim at. The question is, what is the work that Christ does to bring us near to God? In what way does He enable us to live as God wants us to live? We too often think of Christ as an outward person here on earth, who hears and helps us. A man may come and give me $10,000, and so be my helper, but there is no further union between him and me. The man may be a great benefactor, but there is no organic union between him and me. I may never see him again. Many people look upon Christ as such a separate, outward Savior. They never can fully enjoy His salvation. I must believe that even as Christ is in Heaven, so He is here in me, His branch. He comes into my inmost life, He occupies that life, He lives there, and by living there He enables me to live as a child of God. Some think that when Christ dwells within us He comes somewhere in the region of the heart, and He lives there. We are two separate persons, Christ one and I one, and somehow He works in me at times. No! That is not the way. Christ comes into me and becomes my very life. He comes into the very root of my heart and being. He comes into my willing and thinking and feeling and living, and lives in me in the power which the Omnipresent God alone can exercise. When I understand this, my soul bows down in adoration and confidence toward God. I live in the flesh, the life of flesh and blood, but Christ dwelling in me is the true Life of my life.

The words which I want to say are very simple and well-known. "Christ lives in me. I am crucified with Christ, nevertheless I live, yet not I, but Christ lives in me" (Galatians 2:20). Now, the point to which I want to direct attention is that if Christ is to live in me

He does not live in me by a blind force, nor without my knowing it. He calls me to come and see what His life is, and so, if I desire His life, I must give up mine. I must also give up all wrong ideas about what the life of Christ really is. I cannot have the life of Christ, in power, in me, unless I seek to know truly what the life is that He lived. Oh! come and let the living Christ live in you. And to that end, seek to know the life He has set before you in His example. Not that we are able to imitate Christ. But because Christ lived His life for us, and imparts it to us, therefore we can do it.

What folly it would be for a child of three years to say, All that my father can do I can do. And how can I say, I can live as the mighty Christ did? What folly! To attempt to walk as Christ did. And yet, the Bible tells me I must do it. The Bible also tells me I can do it, because "Christ lives in me." If I allow the living Christ to take possession of my will and desires, I can walk even as He walked. Let us come to the life of Christ, and try and find out what is that life that He lived on earth with His Father. That is exactly the Christ who lives in us. There are not two Christs, only one, the Christ that lived on earth is the Christ that lives in my heart. The great mark of Christ is that He lived in the deepest humility and dependence upon the Father. He said, "I can do nothing of Myself." Don't you see, from the beginning to the end, God was everything in that life. That will be the beauty, blessedness and strength of my life, when I learn, like Christ, to know that in everything God is all, and when the motto of His life becomes mine: "For God, to God, through God, are all things."

My life comes from God. I come from God. I have nothing of myself, and everything I get I must get from God. Who is going to maintain it? God, alone, can maintain what He has begun. He must work it out to completion. He must perfect it to the very end. So my life is given by God. The life of Christ and the life of my soul are both given from God in Heaven, received from Him, and must be kept day by day, in deep consciousness, it belongs to God. God, alone, can keep it right, maintain it.

June 8
His Living - 2
by Andrew Murray (1828-1917) Scotland/South Africa
Excerpted from "Christ Liveth In Me," *The Spiritual Life*, published by Tupper & Robertson, Chicago, Illinois in 1896

It is the highest folly for me to think I can keep my life myself. Have you ever studied that? I have received, from the living God, the living Christ in me, and I am not to try and live out that life, but I am to take it to God and acknowledge, "My God, You have planted it in me; You, alone, can keep it." Do this if you want to realize what that dependence is, how Christ lived His whole life in dependence upon God's will and God's strength and God's might. He said, regarding that question of strength, "The Son can do nothing of Himself." Was that really true? Yes. He said, "The words I speak, I speak not of Myself, but as the Father shows the works, I do them." He said in regard to His will, "I came not to do My own will." I cannot trust my will. I do not know what I ought to do. I wait fully, that the Everlasting God might work out what is right. If Christ, the Holy One, needed to say that, don't you think you and I need it ten thousand times more? And that is what we want Christ to come into us for, to breathe in us that very disposition.

The very highest virtue of any Christian life is only to let God have His way. Only to give God the opportunity of doing His work in us, and coming day by day, hour by hour, to the place of absolute dependence upon God, and to learn one lesson: "Oh, God, I have nothing. I do not know anything, I am nothing, nothing, and I can only do what God makes me." And now, how is Christ to bring me near to God? He cannot bring me near to God in any other way than the way He came Himself. What was that way? The way of the deepest self-denial, the way of the most entire surrender to God. He was forever expecting God to work in Him, to look to God for strength. He prayed to God for guidance. He cried to God in His trouble. God was everything, everything to Him, and Christ was content to be nothing. Are you willing to have this Christ to come into your life?

The great reason why our Christian life does not advance more is that we try to do too much ourselves. We are far too self-active and self-confident. We, perhaps, never learned the simple elementary lesson that the only place for me before God is just to be nothing and God will work in me. Look at the angels in Heaven, the seraphim and cherubim. Why are they such bright flames before the throne of God? Because they are nothing, nothing in them to hinder God, and He can let the glory of His presence burn right through them. And why was Christ so perfect, and why did Christ gain such victory, and why did Christ please God so? It is this one reason: He allowed God to work in Him from morning until night, and every step was just in dependence upon God. He said, "Father, guide Me," "Father, I wait upon You," "Father, work in Me," and when Christ comes to live in us, do believe me and God's Word, the first and chief thing He wants to work in you is an absolute dependence upon your God. Pray to God to teach us that Christ in us needs a life of absolute, entire dependence upon God.

Now the great question that stirs the Church is: Why are Christians so feeble? And the great question with many is: What can we do to get the full Christian life, to live as God promises we can live? What can we do to become just such children of God as the Father is able to make us, branches of the Living Vine, to the glory of God? My beloved Christians, let me bring you to the point. What have you to do? First of all, we must look upon this Christ, and ask ourselves, Am I willing to give up everything, so that this Christ can live in me? You saw and you know how Christ lived in Paul. Why, it was as if Christ had become incarnated in Paul. The same zeal for God, same love for souls, and same readiness to sacrifice everything. Everything great in Paul was the complete Christ-life in him. There have been Christians since that day in whom you could see the very form of Christ in them.

June 9
His Loneliness
by John Caird (1820-1898) Scotland
Excerpted from "The Solitariness of Christ's Sufferings," *Sermons*, published by William Blackwood and Sons, Edinburgh, Scotland in 1858

"I have trodden the winepress alone."
Isaiah 63:3 (KJV)

Jesus was indeed a lonely being in the world. With all the exquisite tenderness of His human sympathies, touched with the feeling of our every sinless infirmity with a heart that could feel for a peasant's sorrow, and an eye that could beam with tenderness on an infant's face, He was yet one who, wherever He went, and by whomsoever surrounded, was, in the secrecy of His inner being, profoundly alone.

The point to which I would confine your attention is this, that there were connected with the nature of this mysterious Sufferer certain features or conditions which rendered His sorrows such as no other of our race could endure, certain facts which gave to them, as to His whole history, a character of elevation and wonder, beyond the range of mere human experience. So that forasmuch as amid all the sons and daughters of sorrow that crowd the page of human history, Jesus yet stands forth "the Man of Sorrows," the Solitary Sufferer of humanity; passing through a strife which none but He might encounter, bearing in His lonely spirit the awful pressure of a sorrow which none of mortals except Himself ever bore, He might indeed with emphasis proclaim, "I have trodden the winepress alone."

One of the most obvious of these is that all His sorrowing and sufferings were, long before their actual occurrence, clearly and fully foreseen. They were anticipated sorrows. Every calamity and affliction that awaited Him was disclosed to Him in all its certainty and severity from the very commencement of His history, and the terrible anticipation of approaching evil accompanied Him through His whole career on earth. This, obviously, is one feature of the mournful history of Jesus in which He stands alone; one condition of His earthly experience which must have lent a bitterness to His sorrows from which those of all other mortal sufferers are exempt.

A circumstance which distinguishes the sorrows of Jesus from those of all ordinary men, and which gives to this greatest of sufferers a characteristic of solitariness in their endurance, is this, that they were the sorrows of an infinitely pure and perfect mind. No ordinary human being could ever suffer as Jesus did, for His soul was greater than all other souls; and the mind that is of largest scope, or that is cast in the finest mold, is ever the most susceptible to suffering.

The feelings of Jesus in contemplating the sin and wretchedness of humanity, the mournful prevalence of evil in the world, were not those merely of a most holy and tender-hearted human being. Let me add as one other consideration tending to show how very unique a sorrow was His, how very solitary Jesus must have been in His sorrow, that it was the sorrow of a Creator amid His ruined works. The feelings of Jesus, in beholding, and living among, the moral ruin and degradation of mankind, were not those merely of an exquisitely pure and sensitive human spirit: They flowed from a far deeper and more profound source. It was not merely the gentlehearted and pitying Man of Nazareth that trod our fallen world; it was nothing less than the world's great Creator, who, concealed in that humble guise, surveyed and moved for thirty years among the ruins of His fairest, noblest work, lying widespread around Him! For are we not borne out by Scripture authority in the affirmation that grief for the moral ruin of humanity is an emotion to which the Divine mind is not a stranger?

June 10
His Love – 1
by Adolphe William Monod (1834-1916) France
Excerpted from "The Endearing Attribute," *Pulpit Eloquence of the Nineteenth Century*, published by Dodd & Mead, New York, New York in 1874

God is love.
1 John 4:8 (KJV)

What suspense! That which philosophers have so ardently and vainly sought—that of which the wisest among them have abandoned the pursuit—a definition of God! Here it is, and given by the hand of God Himself. "God is"—what is He about to tell us? What is God "who dwells in the light whereunto no man can approach, whom no man has seen, nor can see"—whom we "feel after, if possibly we may find Him, though He is not far from any one of us"—who constrains us to cry out with Job, "O that I knew where I might find Him! If I go forward, He is not there; backward, but I cannot perceive Him; on the left hand, where He works, but I cannot behold Him; He hides Himself on the right hand that I cannot see Him." What is He, that all-powerful God, whose word has created, and whose word could annihilate everything which exists—"in whom we live, and move, and have our being"—who holds us each moment under His hand, and who can dispose as He will of our existence, our situation, our abode, our circle of friends, our body, and even our soul? What, in short, is this holy God, "Who is of purer eyes than to behold iniquity," and whom our conscience accuses us of having offended; of whose displeasure nature has conveyed to us some vague impression, but of whose pardon neither conscience nor nature has given us any intimation—this just Judge, into whose hands we are about to fall—it may be tomorrow, it may be today—ignorant of the sentence which awaits us, and knowing only that we deserve the worst. What is He? Our rest, our salvation, our eternal destiny—

all is at stake—and methinks I see all the creatures of God bending over the sacred record in silent and solemn expectation of what is about to be revealed concerning this question of questions.

At length the momentous word "love" appears! Who could desire a better? What could be conceived comparable to it, by the boldest and loftiest imagination? This hidden God, this powerful God, this holy God—He is love! What more do we need? God loves us. Do I say He loves us? All in God is love. Love is His very essence. He who speaks of God speaks of love. God is love! O answer, surpassing all our hopes! O blessed revelation, putting an end to all our fears! O glorious pledge of our happiness, present, future, eternal!

This love I would lead you to see concentrated in a fact—in one single fact—which is sufficient for John, and which will equally suffice for us, if we rightly comprehend it. "In this," continues John, in developing his idea, "in this is manifested the love of God toward us, because that God sent His only-begotten Son into the world, that we might have life through Him. Herein is love, not that we loved God, but that He loved us, and sent His Son to be the propitiation [payment and reconciliation] for our sins."

This love of God, ever before your eyes, will impart itself to you, and renew your whole being. It is by feeling one's self-love that one learns to love; and selfishness reigns, only because we are ignorant of the love of God. "He that loves not, knows not God." You will love because you have been loved. You will love God, because God first loved you. You will love your neighbor, because God has loved both him and you. Do you not see the new life for which such a change will fit you? Happy are you, if the love of God so penetrates you, that, in whatever view you are regarded, no better description of your character can be given than that which love inspired John to write of God! He is love! His words are love! His works are love! His zeal is love! His labor is love! His joys are love! His tears are love! His reproofs are love! His judgments are love!

June 11
His Love - 2
by John Cunningham (1819-1893) Scotland
Excerpted from "The Religion of Love," *Scotch Sermons*, published by Macmillan and Co., London, England in 1880

The love of Christ constrains us.
2 Corinthians 5:14 (KJV)

"The love of Christ constrains us"—to what? To live not to ourselves, but to Him who died for us. In other words, constrained by the love of Christ, and taught by the self-sacrifice of Christ, we ought to live unselfish lives. A consecrated love should be our motive, a Christian life should be our end.

I think there can be no doubt that love—love not for self but for others—is a powerful propeller and regulator of human conduct. Some have indeed attempted to reduce all love into selfishness. I cannot at present examine these theories; suffice it to say, I do not believe them, and proceed upon the supposition, surely not a very unjustifiable one, that there is such a thing as disinterested love in the world. I care not whether it is instinctive or not; it is there, and wherever it is, it is beautiful and good. I have hitherto spoken of the hope of reward and the fear of punishment as two powerful incentives to virtuous behavior. But is there no other? Can you think of no other? For instance, are none kept in the straight path of purity and integrity because they know that any deviation from it would grieve and distress those whom they love? Are there not many who would rather do anything and suffer anything than cause a pang to a parent's heart? Are there not some who have been kept back from crime just by this consideration?

What would we not do for those whom we love! What burdens would we not bear! What hardships would we not undergo; what sacrifices would we not cheerfully make! History not unfrequently traces the heroic to such affections as these; and believe me, there is a humble heroism in many homes, which finds no record in the historian's page. There is sometimes a patient industry, continued until "the head grows dizzy and the eyes grow dim," for the support of an aged parent; there is sometimes a faithful watching for long months and years by the bedside of a sickly sister; and, if a visitor there, you may see how carefully the drooping head is pillowed, and how anxiously the slow ebb of life is observed, and how gently every kind office is performed, and how no word of complaint is spoken, though there should be weary days and wakeful nights and an aching head. Sometimes, again, how bravely is the battle of life fought in the face of poverty and misfortune, without flinching and without fear, with stout hands and a sturdy heart, for there are little ones at home to be cared for; and what will the head and heart and hands of a parent not combine to do for these! These are good deeds, recorded in Heaven though unnoticed on earth, and they spring from the constraining power of love.

Such is the influence of love in some of its many ramifications. It holds society together. It keeps the vicious in check, and spurs on the virtuous to be more virtuous still. It is more stringent in restraining from crime than law enforcement and penitentiaries. In truth, all the officers and judges and jailers in the world could not put down crime were it not for this, and the appeals of the pulpit are effective only when they touch a chord already existing in the human heart. Take away this principle, and vice like a rank and noxious vegetation would soon overspread society. But by its gentle and scarcely perceptible constraints love makes the bad good, and the good better; and it is universally felt that they must be very bad indeed who can overleap all its fences and violate feelings so peculiarly sacred. It is thus that the love of Christ constrains us. In other words, love for Christ, as the highest ideal of human perfection, the point where the human and Divine merge into one, is the basis of our Christian morality.

June 12
His Love - 3
by James W. Alexander (1804-1859) USA
Excerpted from "Dying for Friends," *Discourses on Common Topics of Christian Faith and Practice*, published by Charles Scribner, New York, New York in 1858

"There is no greater love than to lay down one's life for one's friends. You are My friends if you do what I command."
John 15:13-14 (NLTSE)

Friendship is a sacred word, belonging as truly to Christianity as to morals. It is such a relation of man to man, that from mutual esteem, admiration and attachment, rather than from regard to interest, each contemplates the person of the other with satisfaction and generosity, each desires the welfare of the other, and delights in his company; and consequently each is ready to fulfill the wishes of the other and to make sacrifices for his pleasure. It is a flowing of soul to soul. It is—so says the Roman adage—to will and to refuse the same things. Wretched is he who cannot go to experience for his definition; for "poor is the friendless master of a world!" We need not go to the touching records of David and Jonathan in the Old Testament. The Gospels assume that in the circle around our Lord, there was one disciple whom Jesus loved. Friendship never rose to so sanctified an exaltation. We do well, therefore, against certain perverse philosophers, to include friendship among the Christian virtues, and to practice it in the daily interaction of life. Even in common society, its triumphs are sometimes beautiful and dignifying, but it is nowhere so pure and unearthly, as where it exists between souls which have been touched by the Spirit of God. Then it is a fountain which wells forth from the cross of the heavenly Friend.

But we are this day to ascend a yet loftier height, and to contemplate a friendship which exists between Christ and the believer. The word seems to acquire a new and heavenly acceptance when we apply it to Him who is above all blessing and all praise.

This relation of friendship is sustained by the Lord Jesus to His people. His whole life was a series of blessed friendships. There are no pictures of attachment like those of Bethany and the Upper Room. The Twelve, the Seventy, the holy women who accompanied Him, the thousands of less distinguished disciples, all stood to Him in the relation of friends. It was not merely John, who reclined on His bosom, or James and Peter who shared His more sacred moments, or Lazarus whom He loved, or Mary and Martha who ministered to Him; but all who listened to His words and sought His companionship. He was so unlike us who preach His gospel in degenerate times, that He associated visibly and at the banquets of the Pharisaic great, with persons who had lost their character, and was designated as the friend of publicans and sinners.

Jesus Christ is still the most accessible Being in the universe. The death of the Lord Jesus Christ for His people is pronounced by divine authority to be the grand argument of His love; and they feel it to be so. It was not the simple article of death, the bare separation of soul and body which He contemplated. He saw the mysterious shadow of Gethsemane, the agony and bloody sweat. He saw the midnight assault, the arrest, the hurrying by torchlight from tribunal to tribunal, the whip, the scourging, the robes of scorn, the insults of the populace, the exposure, the humiliation, the blasphemy, the crown of thorns. He saw the accursed tree, the nails, the spear, the desertion, the blood and anguish, the complicated dying. He saw this to be a substitution, a suffering for others, for friends, for those who should forsake and deny Him, for millions who were as yet His enemies. And seeing all this, He said, with an emphasis which we can now better understand, "Greater love has no man than this, that a man lay down his life for his friends."

June 13
His Magnetism - 1
by John Henry Jowett (1863-1923) England
Excerpted from "The Magnetism of the Uplifted Lord," *The Transfigured Church*, published by Fleming H. Revell Company, New York, New York in 1910

"And when I am lifted up from the earth, I will draw everyone to Myself."
John 12:32 (NLTSE)

The context gives us the needed light to see our way. "Now there were certain Greeks among those that went up to worship at the feast: these therefore came to Philip...and asked him, saying, 'Sir, we would see Jesus.'" The personality of Jesus was already becoming attractive, the magnet was beginning to draw, the sons and daughters were coming from afar! "Philip went and told Andrew: Andrew went, with Philip, and they told Jesus." And what will Jesus say when this first little group of inquirers from the outer world are at His door? "And Jesus said, 'The hour is come, that the Son of Man should be glorified!'"

Here is the beginning of the glory He seeks, the drawing of all people unto Him. Here is the little band of advance scouts which precede a host which no one can number. But this little company is only like a small handful of precocious blades of corn upon an otherwise barren field. They are almost before their time.

So the magnet is to be the Lord Jesus in the wonderful energies of His transcendent sacrifice. "And when I am lifted up." "As Moses lifted up the serpent in the wilderness, even so must the Son of Man be lifted up." No one can really feel the pressing mystery of the cross who does not enter it possessed by the conviction of the sinlessness of Jesus, and realizing something of the vast range of consciousness in which His spirit moved; His sense of the absolute oneness of Himself and God; His unwavering sense of the voluntariness of His surrender to the powers of people and the pains of earth, "No one takes it from Me"; His expressed consciousness, that, by the raising of the eyes, He could call to His aid legions of attendant forces which would make Him invincible; His calm assurance that "all things had been given into His hands"; His submission to the cross in that assurance; all these remove His death from the ranks of common martyrdom, and place Him in an astounding and glorious isolation. His martyr Stephen was forced into death: Jesus walked into it.

Our Lord declares that it is in the energy of that transcendent sacrifice that His personal magnetism is to be found. The energy of His love as displayed in His life, compared with the energy of His love as displayed in His death, is as dispersed sunshine compared with focused sunshine, sunshine concentrated in a burning heat. And it is this focused sacrificial energy of His death, "The last pregnant syllable of God's great utterance of love," which our Lord declares is to be the ministry of attraction, by which everyone is to be drawn to Him.

Nothing so overcomes the deathly and the deadly in people as "the preaching of Jesus Christ and Him crucified." It breaks up their frozen indifference. It makes them graciously uneasy. It disturbs them with promising unquietness. It awakens moral pains by restoring the moral circulation, and it accomplishes resurrection through the pangs of hell and the sorrows of death. But the sacrificial Lord does more than inspire initial unrest. He converts the uneasy stirrings into definite spiritual movement. He not only breaks up inertia, He determines direction. He awakens individuals, and He also draws them. He draws people towards Himself, and they move to a close and personal communion. There is nothing else which works in that way, and to such swift and personal devotion. Then in the energies of this sacrificed Christ we are not only to find the dynamic of redemption, but the secret of human camaraderie.

June 14
His Magnetism - 2
by Joseph E. Smith (1830-1910) USA

Excerpted from "The Attraction of the Cross," *The West Virginia Pulpit of the Methodist Episcopal Church - Sermons from Living Ministers*, published by Frew, Campbell & Hart, Wheeling, West Virginia in 1883

"And when I am lifted up from the earth, I will draw everyone to Myself."
John 12:32 (NLTSE)

The cross attracts, because, as nothing else does, or can, it reveals God. It conceals, while it unveils His glory. We see God only by the rays which converge on Calvary. I go out at noonday, and lifting my eyes to Heaven, dare, for five minutes, to gaze upon the unclouded sun; and I am stricken with blindness for my boldness. But by and by there is seen in the Western sky a hand like a cloud shooting straight from horizon to zenith and spreading its black wings northward and southward like an avenging spirit, wrapping the earth in a mantel of wrath. And now, from the eastern sky there comes another, black as the banner of night, rushing like a war horse to the charge. They meet in mid-air, with the roar of thunder, and the gleam and flash of forked lightning, that sets the heavens ablaze. Borne on the tempest's breath are rain and hail, that come like a deluge on land and sea; and presently, when the storm is hushed, when the sun, glowing like a ball of fire, hangs suspended over the western hill, while the hoarse thunder is dying away in the distance, and the cloud, like the banner of a retreating army, is slowly ascending the distant hills, there, on its departing folds the sun has imaged himself in the glory of the rainbow. I gaze upon it with eye undimmed. I drink in its wondrous beauty, I am entranced by its splendor. The noonday glories are diluted and accommodated to my organ of vision. Brethren, thus is it with God. No man has seen Him at any time. We could not behold Him and live. And so, God has shrouded His glories in the person of His incarnate Son. He set Him down amid the toils and trials and tears of humanity and bid us see the Godhead shining through.

See in the words He spoke, in the miracles He did, and in the life He lived, the thought and purpose and glory of God. And then, on the cross of Calvary He gathered up all of beauty and of glory that the human eye could bear or the heart endure, and through its pain, and death, and darkness He has proclaimed that "God so loved the world that He gave His only-begotten Son that whosoever believes in Him should not perish but have everlasting life." Yes, this is the glory of the cross; it reveals God, and, revealing Him, it saves man. Here is a sun that never sets, a tie that never breaks, a power that never fades. For eighteen centuries it has been scattering the mists of prejudice, lifting the veil of ignorance, crushing the power of hate, and wringing adherents from the ranks of its enemies. The Man! Oh, how it lifts the entire man. How it enlightens the mind, convinces the judgment, purifies the affections, sanctifies the will, consecrates the energies of soul and body, for time, and for eternity, to God. How blessed the promise; prince or beggar, sage or savage. Out from that cross today is going a mysterious power that is grappling with all hearts. It claims all souls as His legitimate empire. They are His by right of purchase. He moves upon them now for conquest. Already its victories are marvelous. It has lifted Christians out of their denominational littleness and narrowness, and strife into the largeness and broadness of Christian sympathy. It has lifted nations out of barbarism, savagism and slavery into the culture and liberty of Christian civilization. It is lifting them out of fraud and oppression and wrong into the rights and privileges of the highest humanity. The cross is revealing the beauty of holiness, the magnificence of truth, the divinity of love, the grandeur of man, and the glory of God. It is attracting the gaze of the world. It is binding to itself the hearts of the nations; until the last sinner, lifted from his sins and allied to his God, the universe shall swing about the cross as its center forever and ever.

June 15
His Manifestations
by George D. Watson (1845-1924) USA
Excerpted from "The Three Manifestations of Jesus," *The Secret of Spiritual Power*, published by The McDonald & Gill Co., Boston, Massachusetts in 1894

In the third chapter of the first Epistle of John we have presented to us three manifestations of Jesus, each one of which is directly connected with our salvation and glorification. In verse three, "When He shall appear we shall be like Him." In verse five, "He was manifested to take away our sins." In verse eight, "The Son of God was manifested that He might destroy the works of the devil." Each step in the elevation of man is directly connected with some revelation or manifestation of the Lord Jesus as the direct cause.

"He was manifested to take away our sins." The sins are emphatically ours. The law is broken by our wills, our choice, our consent; the evil dispositions are indulged in by our hearts; our faculties and powers have been the instruments of transgression. Our actual sins form a cloud. But the word "sins" does not refer to the act itself, but to the moral quality of the act, so that when the bad moral quality of our actions are removed, it is emphatically true that our sins are taken away.

"He was manifested to destroy the work of the devil." Actual sin is traced to the sinner, original sin is traced to Satan. The greatest work of Satan was to corrupt the human heart, and the carnal mind is emphatically a result of his work. Every Christian who has gone through with perfect inward crucifixion knows that we can be conscious of having every Christian grace, and, at the same time, conscious of an inherent perversity, which is the opposite of every grace. We feel it and hate it. We know it is in us but not of us, that it is a foreign element to our true normal human nature.

Now the question is how this inward corruption can be destroyed. So many try growth, development, repression, and any and every deception except the remedy mentioned here, a special manifestation of Jesus as the direct cause of heart cleansing. But what can it mean to destroy the carnal mind? It will be easily understood if we remember that sin is not an entity, that it has no substance or existence apart from a moral creature, that it is of the nature of a pain, or a fever, or a dream, none of which can exist apart from some living being. Thoughtless persons sometimes ask, "Where does inbred sin go when cleansed away?" The sufficient answer is where does a fever go, or a headache go, when the body is restored to normal health? Just as fever can exist only in the disorder of the blood, so the carnal mind exists only by some fundamental disorder of the moral heart, which is to the soul what blood is to the body. And when the earnest Christian, struggling for perfect heart rest, understands Jesus as the only and all sufficient and present Cleanser, the Holy Ghost will so manifest Him as a Sanctifier, that the leprosy of inward sin instantly vanishes as darkness when a light enters a room.

"When He shall appear we shall be like Him." This is the final manifestation of Jesus in His capacity of Redeemer. According to the Scripture, redemption is not complete until the body is raised from the dead and soul and body glorified in the heavenly presence of the Lord. Though our sins are taken away, and though the carnal mind is destroyed, there are yet a multitude of infirmities, limitations, afflictions, which beset and load down more or less the saintliest persons. The pure in heart are conscious of these hindrances, and yet, at the same time, conscious that they are not sin in the Scripture sense of that word. There is a transcendent work, utterly beyond our thoughts, which is to pass like angelic lightning over our whole being at the glorious appearing of our Savior. We may conjecture a thousand blissful changes such a sight will produce in us, but it is all summed up in the words of the Holy Ghost: "We shall be like Him, for we shall see Him as He is."

June 16
His Martyrs – 1
by James W. Alexander (1804-1859) USA
Excerpted from "Consolation Derived from a Review of Christian Martyrdom," *Consolation: Discourses on Select Topics, Addressed to the Suffering People of God*, published by Charles Scribner, New York, New York in 1852

The sufferings of Christ's faithful martyrs not only furnish a proof to the truth of Christianity, but demonstrate its power to support the soul under the greatest sufferings.

When our Lord, in predicting the arrest and trial of His disciples, says to them, "And it shall turn to you for a testimony," the meaning is, your persecutions, when foes shall lay their hands on you, this shall turn to you for a testimony: It shall afford you an opportunity to testify for Christ in the most striking circumstances, and with the greatest effect. The word rendered "testimony" is kindred to our word "martyr" which is only the Greek for "witness"—one who bears testimony. You shall, by means of your faith and endurance, be witnesses for My gospel.

Martyr is a witness; but, in the language of the Church, one who bears witness to Christianity by his death; while the term confessor was applied to those who, before persecuting magistrates, firmly risked punishment for confessing Christ. The confessor became a martyr by shedding his blood. In this sense we constantly speak of "martyrs and confessors." The ancient historians reckon exactly ten persecution periods; but it is scarcely possible to confine the number to this. They arose from the iron determination of the heathen powers to suppress the true religion; for I pass over the earlier persecutions under the Jews, from Stephen onward.

The history of the martyrs is a testimony to the power of Christianity to support the soul under great suffering. Persons of all ages, of all conditions in life, and of both sexes, exhibited under prolonged and cruel torments a strength, a patience, a meekness, a spirit of love and forgiveness, a cheerfulness, yes, often a triumphant joy, of which there are no examples to be found in the history of the world. They rejoiced when they were arrested; cheerfully said goodbye to their nearest and dearest relations; gladly embraced the stake; welcomed the wild beasts let loose to devour them; smiled on the horrible apparatus by which their sinews were to be stretched, and their bones dislocated and broken; uttered no complaints; gave no indication of pain when their bodies were enveloped in flames; and when condemned to die, begged of their friends to interject no obstacle to their joy (for such they esteemed martyrdom), not even by prayers for their deliverance. What sustained these sufferers? It was their belief in Christianity. They never pretended that it was anything else. If anything may be regarded as established, even by the concessions of adversaries, it is that the Christian system imparted to the humblest and weakest a fortitude and a constancy which were unknown to the schools of philosophy. This was, indeed, the chief humiliation of the persecutors. Exhausting their whole resources in vain against aged men, feeble women, and inexperienced children, they were at length driven to wilder means, as discovering that Christianity could not be quenched in blood. These aspects of martyrdom, my brethren, should by no means be neglected. That thousands should have died so supported is not an uninteresting fact in the world's history.

The testimony of martyrs in their pangs is a testimony against our lukewarmness and unbelief. It is impossible to reflect on their history and not own this. Theirs was Christianity in earnest. How different from ours! If you can so poorly bear the daily crosses of life, and are so easily intimidated by the sneers or the inconveniences that befall you; if amidst these days of easy and honorable Christianity, you find it so hard to be Christians, how will it be when you come into the storms of mighty conflict?

June 17
His Martyrs - 2
by John Henry Jowett (1863-1923) England
Excerpted from "The Disciple's Sacrifice," *The Passion for Souls*
published by Fleming H. Revell Company, New York, New York in 1905

I fill up in my flesh what is still lacking in regard to Christ's afflictions.
Colossians 1:24 (KJV)

"I fill up that which is still lacking." Not that the ministry of reconciliation is incomplete. Not that Gethsemane and Calvary have failed. Not that the debt of guilt is only partially paid, and there is now a threatening remnant which demands the sacrifice of human blood. The ministry of atonement is perfected. There is no outstanding debt. "Jesus paid it all." In the one commanding sacrifice for human sin Calvary leaves nothing for you and me to do. In the bundle of the Savior's sufferings every needed pang was borne. And yet "I fill up that which is still lacking." The sufferings need a herald. A story needs a teller. A gospel requires an evangelist. A finished case demands efficient presentation. The atoning Savior must express Himself through the ministering Paul. The work of Calvary must proclaim itself in the sacrificial saints.

"I fill up that which is still lacking." That is not the presumptuous boast of perilous pride; it is the quiet, awed aspiration of privileged fellowship with the Lord. Here is an apostle, a man who thinks lowly enough of himself, counting himself an abortion, regarding himself as "the least of the apostles, not worthy to be called an apostle," and yet he dares to whisper his own name alongside his Master's, and humbly to associate his own pangs with the sufferings of redemptive love. "I fill up that which is behind of the sufferings of Christ." Is the association permissible? Are the sufferings of Christ and His apostles complementary, and are they profoundly cooperative in the ministry of salvation? Dare we proclaim them together?

Here is an association. "In all their afflictions He was afflicted." "Who is weak and I am not weak; who is offended and I burn not?" Is the association alien and uncongenial, or is it altogether legitimate and fitting? "In all their afflictions He was afflicted"—the deep, poignant, passionate sympathy of the Savior; "Who is weak and I am not weak"—the deep, poignant, passionate sympathy of the ambassador. The kinship in the succession is vital. The daily dying of the apostle corroborates and drives home the one death of his Lord.

Here, then, is a principle. The gospel of a broken heart demands the ministry of bleeding hearts. If that succession is broken we lose our fellowship with the King. As soon as we cease to bleed we cease to bless. When our sympathy loses its pang we can no longer be the servants of the Passion. We no longer "fill up the sufferings of Christ," and not to "fill up" is to paralyze, and to "make the cross of Christ of no effect."

My brethren, are we in this succession? Does the cry of the world's need pierce the heart, and ring even through the fabric of our dreams? I am amazed how easily I become callous. I am ashamed how small and insensitive is the surface which I present to the needs and sorrows of the world. I so easily become enwrapped in the soft wool of self-indulgency, and the cries from far and near cannot reach my easeful soul. Except when I spend a day with my Lord, the trend of my life is quite another way. I cannot think about them because I am so inclined to sleep! A numbing settles down upon my spirit, and the pangs of the world awake no corresponding sympathy. I can take my newspaper, which is ofttimes a veritable cupful of horrors, and I can peruse it at the breakfast table, and it does not add a single tang to my feast. I wonder if one who is so unmoved can ever be a servant of the suffering Lord!

June 18
His Mastership
by Handley C. G. Moule (1841-1920) England
Excerpted from "Christ the Master," *Christ Is All*, published by Hodder and Stoughton, London, England in 1920

Whether we live, we live unto the Lord; and whether we die, we die unto the Lord: whether we live therefore, or die, we are the Lord's. For to this end Christ both died, and rose, and revived, that He might be Lord both of the dead and living.
Romans 14:8-9 (KJV)

It is this law, this constant spiritual fact, that Jesus Christ is the autocratic Owner of His followers, and then the result of it in His call to them to consent wholeheartedly to His Possessorship, to yield themselves completely to the Will of God in Christ. It is not just one of those truths which mean practically next to nothing while they are entertained, as it were, in the air and at a distance, but which for many even those convinced and devout Christians need only to be brought home, to be translated into here and now, in order to become discoveries as of a new world, revolutions that bring in a new age in the history of the soul. It is one thing to regard our Lord with sincere homage in a large and general sense, holding fast through His mercy all the great treasures of all-embracing belief about His glorious Person, resting the burdens of conscience on His Sacrifice and Intercession, and recognizing the duty of at least an implicit and constructive loyalty to Him in the main outlines of life.

It is another thing when the man discovers, with an insight perfectly calm and genuine, while yet it is given him from above, that what the Redeemer claims, and annexes, and appropriates, is nothing less than all the being, and all its action. It is a wonderful thing to discover that, not in figures and flights of speech, but in sober fact, "every thought is to be brought into captivity to the obedience of Christ," if Christ is to have His due; that the will is to be laid in simplicity at His feet; that all faculties of the mind, and all their growth and all their gains, are to be presented honestly to Him for His far-reaching purposes; that reputation, when and while it is granted, is only a trust for Him; that material possessions are only a trust for Him; that our time is His, all His, morning, noon, and night, without interval or vacation; that our tongues are indeed His, in their every word; that "whether we eat, or drink, or whatever we do," all of it is to be done "to the glory of God," in this sense of a reference of the whole of life to Him. "For whether we live, we live unto the Lord; and whether we die, we die unto the Lord…For to this end He died and lived again."

Deliberately and most humbly, as before Him of whom I dare to speak, I state thus, without lessening or moderation, the New Testament position about the claims of Jesus Christ upon the Christian. Have I overdrawn them? I cannot present them in all the breadth and depth, and at the same time the minuteness and precision, with which you will find them set forth in the New Testament as a whole. There, Christ is indeed all things in all His followers. There the Christian is a being whose true reason and true life is altogether and always in Jesus Christ. He is slave, and his Redeemer is absolute Owner. He is branch, and his Redeemer is Root. He is limb, and his Redeemer is Head. He is vessel, and the great Master of the house is always to have full and free use of him for any purposes of His own. He has no rights, and can set up no claims, as against his Lord: "If I will that he tarries until I come, what is that to you?"

Yes, my brethren, I cannot possibly overstate these claims of our most blessed Lord, with the writers of the Gospels and Apostles open before me. And they are claims which have no regard for times and seasons, for phases of thought and the spirit of the age. If they were valid once, they are valid now; for they are rooted in eternal truth and point straight to an eternal future.

June 19
His Meaning
by William H. G. Thomas (1861-1924) England/Wales
Excerpted from "The Meaning of Christ," *Christianity is Christ*,
published by Zondervan Publishing House,
Grand Rapids, Michigan in 1900

Facts can never be properly appreciated until an endeavor is made to penetrate behind them to their meaning. We have now reached the point when an attempt must be made to discover the meaning of all this emphasis on Christ. We have considered His character as perfect and sinless, His claim to Divine authority over mankind, His death as an atonement for sin, His resurrection as the demonstration of His Divine life, His Gospels as faithful records of His earthly manifestations, His Church as the perpetual testimony to His saving power, His grace as witnessed to by His devoted followers, His influence as acknowledged by some of His greatest foes. But what does it all mean? Why do we lay such stress on the Fact, the Person, and the Work of Christ?

The answer is, because Christ is before everything else a revelation of God. This, and nothing short of it, is the one and complete explanation of Christ. The idea of God is the dominating idea in all religions, and the idea of Christ as the Revealer of God is the dominating idea in Christianity. The supreme message of Christianity is, "There is one God and one Mediator between God and man, Himself Man, Jesus; one God, and one unique Mediator as the personal Revealer of God to man." No one can doubt that this is the meaning of the place given to Christ in the New Testament.

The Name of Christ is found everywhere therein, and always in connection with His personal revelation of God. It meets our gaze at all points, and proclaims with no uncertain sound that to us God has revealed Himself in Christ Jesus, that for us, for religion, for Christianity, for salvation, for life, Christ is God. The disciple's question addressed to Christ, "Show us the Father," is at once an admission of his own need and a confession of his belief that Christ could supply it; and the relation of Jesus Christ to God is set forth in the New Testament with no uncertain sound. "All things are delivered to Me by My Father" (Matthew 11:27). "He that has seen Me has seen the Father" (John 14:9). "He is the image of the invisible God, the radiance of His glory" (Hebrews 1:3). Jesus Christ, divine and human, is for all time and for all men the final, complete and sufficient manifestation of God.

> "The unchangeable sum of Christianity is the message: The Word was God, and the Word became flesh. This being so, it is clear that Christianity is not essentially a law for the regulation of our conduct; not a philosophy for the harmonious coordination of the facts of experience under our present forms of thought; not a system of worship by which men can approach their Maker in reverent devotion. It offers all these as the natural fruit of the Truth which it proclaims in the Incarnation and Resurrection of Christ. But Christ Himself, His person and His life, in time and beyond time, and not only any scheme of doctrine which He delivered, is the central object and support of faith" (Brooke Foss Westcott, British theologian, 1825-1901).

This, and this alone, constitutes essential Christianity. Whatever men may find and emphasize in Christ, His Sonship, His Messiahship, His Teaching, His Manhood, while these are all included in the essence of Christianity, they do not exhaust it. Christianity as Christ conceived of it transcends all these different aspects of embracing them in the one supreme and dominant truth of His personal revelation of God. The essential fact is that He brings God to man in order that He may bring men to God. Man's greatest, deepest need is God, and union and communion with Him.

June 20
His Meekness
by Alexander Whyte (1836-1921) Scotland
Excerpted from "Our Lord's Favorite Graces: Meekness and Lowliness of Heart," *The Walk, Conversation and Character of Jesus Christ Our Lord*, published by Oliphant, Anderson & Ferrier, Edinburgh, Scotland in 1905

"Take My yoke upon you and learn from Me, for I am meek and lowly in heart, and you will find rest for your souls."
Matthew 11:29 (KJV)

When our Lord says of Himself that He is meek and lowly in heart, it sounds to us, at first sight, somewhat like self-praise. And indeed not here only, but all up and down the four Gospels the same personal note and the same self-appraising tone prevails. That is until we are led to seek out, and with some anxiety, the proper explanation of that so unexpected and so startling manner of speech in our Lord. And then when we enter properly into that so universal habit of His and fully understand it, we see that it is just another evidence and just another result of the perfect purity, perfect humility, perfect simplicity, and absolute sinlessness of our Lord. He could say with the most perfect truth and innocence and modesty what no other person who ever lived could have said without presumptuous sin. He could say that He alone knew the Father, and that He alone could reveal the Father; and then He could say with the same breath that He was meek and lowly in heart, and all the time be as innocent of pride or self-praise as if He had only said how old He was, or how high He stood in His stature. And in the measure that we become like Him we also shall be able to speak about ourselves, and to describe ourselves, and even to appraise ourselves, and, all the time, to do so as truthfully and as attractively as He did. We shall then be free to tell to everyone what God has done in us and by us, thinking only of God's goodness to us, and of our consequent debt to Him and to all our fellows. And all that will be but another entrance of ours into that liberty wherewith Christ shall yet make us as free as He Himself was made free.

Now, what exactly is this thing here called meekness and lowliness of heart? And when and where do we see these most excellent graces exhibited in our Lord? Just open the Four Gospels and you will meet with the meekness, and the gentleness, and the lowly-mindedness of Jesus Christ in every chapter. Lowliness best describes His birth and the household in which He was brought up. And the same word best describes His everyday life all down to His death. He filled up all His appointed days on this earth with words and deeds of divine authority and divine power. At the same time His whole earthly life was sanctified and beautified with the most perfect meekness and lowliness of heart. On every page of the four Gospels you will read how He went about doing good with all patience and longsuffering and lovingkindness. How He turned His cheek to the person who struck Him. How He blessed when He had been shamefully treated. How He was a Man of Sorrows and acquainted with grief. He was wounded for our transgressions. He was bruised for our iniquities. He was oppressed, and He was afflicted, yet He opened not His mouth. He is brought as a lamb to the slaughter, and as a sheep before her shearers is dumb; for the transgressions of people He was stricken. And yet in all that His meekness and His lowly-mindedness were such that the yoke He bore was easy for Him, and the burden that was laid upon Him was made light to Him.

If being a creature of Almighty God does not teach you your own place under Almighty God, then consider yourself as a sinner against God, and such a sinner. You have not reflected enough on a thousand good reasons that God must have for the way He is yoking you and loading you. If you looked more at yourself, and at what your salvation must need at His hand and at your own hand to work it out, you would bow your neck to His will continually, and would hold your peace.

June 21
His Mind
by James Russell (J. R.) Miller (1840-1912) USA
Excerpted from "Having the Mind of Christ," *The Lesson of Love*, published by Thomas Y. Crowell & Co., New York, New York in 1903

The ideal Christian life is one in which the mind that was in Christ Jesus rules. But what is the mind that was in Christ? Is there any word that describes it? What was the very heart of Christ's mission? What one day was there in all His life when He showed forth most clearly the central glory of His character? Was there any one act in all the multitude of His wonderful works in which the radiant blessedness of His life was revealed in greater fullness than in any other? If you were asked to name the one day in the life of our Lord when He showed most of the splendor of His person, which day of all would you choose? Would it be the time of His transfiguration, when the brightness of His deity shone out through the robes of flesh that He wore? Would it be the day of His miracle of feeding the five thousand, or the day when He raised Lazarus? Or would you take some scene when He stood amid throngs of lame, sick, blind, and healed them all? Or would you say that the brightest moment of His earthly life was when He was riding into the city with great processions of joyous people crying, "Hosanna"?

None of these hours of human splendor was the hour of the fullest revealing of the heart of Christ. None of those radiant days was the day when most of His true glory was manifested. None of these achievements of power was the greatest thing Jesus ever did. The brightest day in all His earthly career was the day when He hung upon His cross. The revealing of His glory that was divinest was when men thought that He had sunk away in the deepest shame. The act that was the most magnificent of all His achievements was the giving of Himself in death for men. We could take all the miracles out of the gospel story and all the narrative of gentle and beautiful things, if only the cross was left. The cross is the fullest representation of the glory of Christ. If we ask, then, where, on what day, in what one act, the most complete revealing of Christ can be seen, the answer is—on Good Friday, when He died between two thieves.

"Let this mind be in you, which was also in Christ Jesus." The very hallmark of Christ-likeness is the stamp of the cross. We say we want to be like Christ. We say it in our prayers, we sing it in our hymns, we put it into our consecration services. But what do we mean by being like Christ? Are we not in danger of getting into our vision of it merely some surface gleams of divinity, an easy kind of life, a gentle piety, a dainty charity, a fashionable holiness, a pleasing service? When two disciples asked for the highest places, the Master spoke to them in serious words of His baptism and His cup, asking them if they were able to drink of the cup and be baptized with the baptism. When we say we want to be like Christ, He points us to His cross and says: "That is what it is to be like Me; are you able?"

The cross shows us a vision of what our life must be if we are following Christ. The cross stamps itself on every true Christian life. Some people wear crosses as ornaments. If we are Christians like Jesus, we will wear the cross in our heart.

The things that are really the brightest in your past life are not the honors you won for yourself, the brilliant successes you achieved, nor the prosperities which added to your importance among men, but the deeds of love which your hand worked in Christ's name for some of His little ones. The one brightest day in all your past life was the day you did your purest, most unselfish, most self-denying act for your Master, in serving one of His. It is only when we have some measure of Christ's self-renunciation that we have touched the truest and Christ-like things in life.

June 22
His Miracles - 1
by Clarence E. Macartney (1879-1957) USA
Excerpted from "Did Christ Work Miracles?," *Twelve Great Questions About Christ*, published by Fleming H. Revell Company,
New York, New York in 1923

"...Jesus of Nazareth, a Man approved of God among you by miracles..."
Acts 2:22 (KJV)

The two great pillars which support the temple of Christian truth and show it to be a revelation from God to man are the prophecies and the miracles. We hear much, today, about the modern spirit of unbelief. There is no doubt about the unbelief, but there is nothing modern about it. It is as old as the mind of man. But there is perhaps more dogmatic denial of Christianity than there has been for many a day, and the most popular ground of the denial is what is called the scientific ground. The creed of this denial of Christ amounts to this: "Receive nothing you cannot demonstrate, and believe nothing you cannot see." Such a creed is neither scientific nor religious. It is but the manifestation of the pride of man's mind, the sin that made the angels fall, and which still keeps men from accepting the dominion of Jesus Christ.

It is because of the spread of physical science that not a few within the Christian Church have been tempted to deal lightly with the supernatural and miraculous element in the Christian revelation. Because physical science knows nothing of miracles, a great many Christians are almost afraid to say that their souls are their own, and they act as if they secretly wished that their New Testament did not have all these accounts of the wonders which were done by Christ. Thus it has come about, that what God gave to men as one of the two great evidences of the truth of the divinity and authority of Christ, is mentioned almost with an apology by not a few writers and speakers in the Church. What the Savior Himself and His apostles pointed to as a proof and confirmation of Christian truth, men today regard as sort of a stumbling block, an embarrassing addendum to Christianity, excess baggage, as it were, which they would like to be rid of. This is one of the many ways in which the Church, in order to gain favor with men and win their support, has come perilously near to a compromise with the world itself. No greater tragedy could befall the Christian Church than to have men think that Christians were ready to throw away any portion of the divine revelation, for the sake of gaining the support of the mind of the age. The quiet disregard, or the implied denial of, certain great facts of the life of Christ as we have that life in the Bible, every mature mind must recognize to be, intellectually, absolute inconsistency. Christianity cannot be ethically divine and historically false. The man who is preaching the so-called ideals of the Christian faith and at the same time ignoring, or evading, or denying its facts, is indulging in a sort of theological agility, which, if followed and adopted by others, could have no other result but complete denial of Christianity — ideals, facts, hopes, and all. We want no soft, mossy bed of sentiment upon which to lie. We prefer the hard rock of fact, even though the facts cut and wound our pilgrim feet. Did Christ work these miracles attributed to Him in the Gospels? We know that the miracles are inextricably involved with the other facts of the life of Jesus, and that there is no Christ but the Christ who walked on the sea, and raised the dead, and made blind men to see. Men who talk about any other Christ are talking of a myth, a shadow, a vapor, for there can no more be a non-miraculous, non-supernatural Christianity than there can be a quadrangular circle. The question which we face, then, the issue with which we are dealing, is a very great one — did Christ work miracles? This means not merely did He feed five thousand men with five loaves and two fishes, or did He raise the widow of Nain's son from the dead, or did He heal the paralytic at the Pool of Bethesda, but something far greater, namely, was there any such person as Christ at all? Has the world a divine Redeemer in whom it can trust?

June 23
His Miracles - 2
by Clarence E. Macartney (1879-1957) USA
Excerpted from "Did Christ Work Miracles?," *Twelve Great Questions About Christ*, published by Fleming H. Revell Company, New York, New York in 1923

"...Jesus of Nazareth, a Man approved of God among you by miracles..."
Acts 2:22 (KJV)

It is objected that a miracle is a violation of law, or God as He reveals Himself in nature. God, it is said, would contradict Himself if He did anything in another way. But this implies that we know all about God and His ways. Instead of that being so, how small a portion we have seen! The general uniformity of nature to which deniers of the miracles appeal is a blessing to man. It would be a terrible world in which to live if we could not count on the laws of gravity, of heat and cold, of summer and winter, seedtime and harvest. But this uniformity is consistent with voluntary control, and therefore for good and sufficient reasons, as the Bible tells us it has been, could be interrupted. When we speak of the uniform type of nature all we mean is that an effect is something produced by a cause, and that all the effects we see are produced by natural causes. But we have no right to conclude that therefore a miracle is impossible, for belief in miracles does not imply that an effect took place with no adequate cause, but that an effect was produced by the immediate act or will of God, who ordinarily works through second causes, but sometimes, if the Bible is true, through an immediate act. Instead of being a denial of the law of cause and effect, a miracle is its highest illustration.

A god who made a world and then shut himself out from it so that he could never enter it again, never suspend, regulate, add to its laws of working, would not be God. He would be like a man who made a machine with whose laws of operation he could never interfere. What we call interference, suspending or changing of laws, may not really be such at all, but part of the great plan of God. To man it is a miracle, but not to God.

"This beginning of miracles did Jesus in Cana of Galilee," says John after the account of turning the water into wine, "and manifested forth His glory." It was the "beginning" of miracles. In other words, Jesus from the commencement to the end of His public ministry worked many miracles. Christianity claims to be a revelation from God confirmed and vindicated by mighty signs and wonders. The Gospels contain the records of thirty-three miracles and tell us that there were many others which they do not record. Try to take those stories out of the four Gospels, and how much of a Christ do you have left? The miracles are as a strand woven into the fabric of the garment of Christ's personality, and you cannot tear them out without destroying the fabric itself. The poor, minor, damaged Christ which some men try to hold up after they have gotten rid of the miraculous in the life of Jesus is not a Christ that the world has taken, or will take, seriously. The only Christ that we know is the Christ who walked on the sea, raised the dead, and called the dead out of their grave.

On two occasions Jesus referred to the miracle He had worked in feeding the multitude in the wilderness with the five loaves and the two small fishes. Just as the only Jesus we know is the Jesus who worked miracles, so the only Jesus we know is the Jesus who claimed that He worked miracles, testified in the most deliberate way that He did. But what sort of a man was this Jesus whom people, today, say they will take and worship, minus His miracles? They all agree that He was a perfect character. But how was He a perfect character if He did not work miracles, yet testified that He did? The holiest character that has appeared on the horizon of human thought, the kindest, truest, best, the One from whose brow truth flashed as the rays of light pour from the sun, bears witness that He worked miracles and did many mighty wonders.

June 24
His Missions - 1
by Jonathan Mayhew Wainright (1792-1854) USA
Excerpted from "A Plea for Missions," *Thirty-Four Sermons*, published by
D. Appleton and Company, New York, New York in 1856

Cast your bread upon the waters, for after many days you will find it again. Give portions to seven, yes to eight, for you do not know what disaster may come upon the land.
Ecclesiastes 11:1-2 (NIV)

The Royal Preacher [King Solomon] undoubtedly made reference to the obligation and the advantage of relieving the temporal wants of our fellow creatures; but we may, I think, discover in the same words an exhortation and an encouragement to alleviate their more urgent and more universal spiritual necessities. We are to cast the bread of life unsparingly and extensively upon the wide waters of this world's sinfulness and ignorance. We are not to regard it as lost or unprofitably spent because we do not instantly behold its good effects; we are to have confidence in the divine promise, that after many days we shall most assuredly find it, in its blessed influences upon the perishing nations.

Our attention then is to be directed towards the duty of sending forth the gospel of Christ, as widely as possible, even until it reaches the ends of the earth, and penetrates every desert place upon its wide circumference. "Cast your bread upon the waters." The mighty ocean covers much of the largest portion of this world on which we dwell; it can bear about with the greatest facility, and rapidity, and universality, the treasures that are entrusted to it; it encircles every island, washes the shores of every continent, and communicates with their deepest recesses by rivers and bays, its majestic arms. Here we find an illustration of the anticipations we are taught to indulge in regard to the extent of Christ's Kingdom, and an amplification of the words of prophecy, that "the earth shall be full of the knowledge of the Lord as the waters cover the sea." Here also we find the only boundaries which are to limit our thoughts and labors in the sublime cause of Missions. The gospel is not to be restricted to one nation, or kindred, or people—it is destined in its sure and irresistible progress to reach and pervade all. To what extent, as regards individuals, the kingdoms of this world are to become the kingdoms of our Lord and of His Christ, whether every living and accountable creature, in any one future age, will be brought to accept the offered terms of salvation, we know not; but of this we are assured, that God designs the gospel to be preached to all, and has appointed a period in the duration of the world when every intelligent being, from the greatest to the least, shall have the opportunity of knowing the truth as it is in Jesus. Where then are we Christians to limit our prayers, our projects, and our exertions? We do not confine our prayers—we daily beseech our Almighty Father that His Kingdom may come, and His will be done on earth even as it is in Heaven. In Heaven His will is universally performed, and His name adored by every blessed inhabitant there. Our prayers then reach forth in aspirations after a like universal exhibition of obedience and love here below.

When I consider what the Missionary cause is—that its design is to communicate to our brethren of the human family who are destitute of them, blessings and privileges which we esteem invaluable and essential; to impart knowledge which we possess to beings like ourselves, who are absolutely perishing for lack of it; and when I consider that by imparting we diminish not the smallest portion of our own privileges and advantages, I am in utter amazement that this cause is not more zealously promoted. And were it proper to introduce private feelings, I would add, that I am grieved and humiliated that it has not heretofore occupied a much larger space in my own meditations and labors.

June 25
His Missions - 2
by Jonathan Mayhew Wainright (1792-1854) USA
Excerpted from "A Plea for Missions," *Thirty-Four Sermons*, published by
D. Appleton and Company, New York, New York in 1856

Cast your bread upon the waters, for after many days you will find it again. Give portions to seven, yes to eight, for you do not know what disaster may come upon the land.
Ecclesiastes 11:1-2 (NIV)

Any system of professed Christianity which maintains light opinions of human depravity, and softened explanations of the threatenings of eternal damnation, cannot be expected to take a deep interest in the spiritual condition of the human race. When we notice what we esteem a slight disease, we are not particularly anxious about the means of cure—our remedies are mild and are slowly administered, and we are willing to trust to the healing power of nature. Not so when we observe the symptoms of one of those dreadful maladies which quickly send men to destruction; then we are alarmed and in earnest, and use vigorously and without ceasing, every method of stopping it, which science and experience can devise. Similar to this must be the feeling of those who are truly engaged in the missionary cause. Those who entertain different opinions of the extent of human depravity and its consequences, may talk about Missions, and attempt to excite among themselves some interest in their favor; but this is in self-defense, and because they are aroused by the reproach of lukewarmness. They can have no heartfelt devotion to this species of Christian compassion. It is not simply because Christianity will improve the temporal condition of those to whom it is communicated—saving the idolater from moral degradation, and from expensive offerings and sacrifices of human blood; restoring a woman to her just privileges, her mild control, and purifying influences, and thus bringing in its train all the benefits of civilized life—it is not on these accounts alone that we are to promote the spreading of our religion. Great, unquestionably, as are the moral and temporal advantages which accrue to those who are the subjects of missionary labors, this must not be our sole or our principal reason for promoting them. Would we aid Missions upon proper and efficient principles, we must aid them because they are means appointed by God for taking perishing sinners from a state of condemnation; for introducing the lost sons of Adam into the flock and fold of Christ; for extending the triumphs of the Redeemer over sin, Satan, and death; and for populating the mansions of the blessed with pure and rejoicing spirits, who might otherwise have been the hateful and blaspheming subjects of eternal condemnation and misery. These are the solemn and overwhelming considerations which present the cause of missions in all its extended importance, which connect it with the eternal realities of a future world, and which, therefore, are best calculated to enflame the attention of beings acting on their responsibility as immortal.

Those who have not these feelings and views can never be engaged in it, as they should be—heart, mind, soul, and strength. When mere temporal advantages are to be communicated to our fellow creatures, and moral renovation for the purpose of inducing them to live with greater purity and dignity "the life of today," when these are the only motives that compel us to the missionary cause, it will inevitably be pursued with the caution, the delay, the controlled feelings and views of a worldly policy. Let me know what opinions any set of men hold in regard to the distinguishing characteristic of the gospel of Christ, and I can almost predict how high the thermometer of their religious generosity will rise when applied to the atmosphere which envelopes the sin-darkened nations.

June 26
His Missions – 3
by Herman Harrell Horne (1874-1946) USA
Excerpted from "Jesus and Missions," *Modern Problems As Jesus Saw Them*, published by Association Press, New York, New York in 1918

What was to be the extent of the Kingdom of Heaven on earth? No limits whatsoever are finally put on its growth. This is the point of view from which to approach the study of Jesus and missions. Therefore, we will look first at His life, and then at His teachings, in relation to missions.

Even His infancy is associated in story and prophecy with foreign personages, countries, and people. Wise men from the East come to worship Him who was born king of the Jews. As an infant He is carried into Egypt. The righteous and devout Simeon saw in the infant Jesus the salvation of God "prepared before the face of all peoples; a light for revelation to the Gentiles, and the glory of Your people Israel" (Luke 2:31-32).

At the outset of His ministry, John the Baptist, as reported by John the evangelist, strikes the universal note in the mission of Jesus: "Behold, the Lamb of God, who takes away the sin of the world!" (John 1:29).

Early in His ministry the faith of the Roman centurion caused Jesus to marvel and to turn and say to the multitude following Him: "I have not found so great faith, no, not in Israel. And I say unto you, that many shall come from the east and the west, and shall sit down with Abraham, and Isaac, and Jacob, in the Kingdom of Heaven." There were to be no racial or geographical boundaries to the Kingdom.

Jesus actually faced the Gentile world in advance when the Greeks presented themselves to Philip as interpreter with the request:

"Sir, we would see Jesus" (John 12:21). What effect did this request have on Jesus? First, it caused Him to realize that the hour of His sacrifice, which was also the hour of His glorification, had come. He saw the first fruits from a foreign field that should be borne by the grain of wheat fallen into the ground and dying. By hating His life in this world He would keep it unto life eternal. Those who serve Him were to follow Him in so doing, that they might both be with Him and be honored by the Father. Then, this prospect of His physical death, though leading to such fruitfulness, His soul was troubled, He questioned whether He should pray for deliverance from it, only to check the rising question with the affirmation that for this very cause He had come to this hour, and then prayed that the Father would glorify His name. So mightily did the prospect of harvest in the Greek world affect His soul.

It is thoroughly in keeping with these universal missionary insights that the risen Christ should give the Great Commission, with its four universals, to the eleven disciples, claiming all authority, sending them to all nations, to teach them all His commands, and promising His presence all the days until the end. Finally, the risen and ascending Christ speaks to His chosen apostles: "You shall be My witnesses both in Jerusalem, and in all Judaea and Samaria, and unto the uttermost part of the earth" (Acts 1:8).

In the clarity and the power of all these words of mission in the good tidings brought by Jesus, the souls of all missionaries from Paul until now have been inspired and upheld. Followers of Jesus have no doubt about it—His gospel is for all. So it was intended and so the centuries have proven it to be.

June 27
His Mother - 1
by William M. Clow (1853-1930) Scotland
Excerpted from "Mary, the Mother of Jesus," *The Day of the Cross*, published by Hodder and Stoughton, London, England in 1909

Now there stood by the cross of Jesus His mother...
John 19:25 (KJV)

The Virgin Mary has been an almost forbidden theme to Protestant preachers. The other holy women of Scripture may be freely praised. The strong wisdom and resistless energy of Deborah, the quenchless faith of Hannah, the self-forgetting loyalty of Ruth, and the grace of the words and deeds of the women of the Gospels have had countless tributes paid to them. Mary, the mother of Jesus, is an almost unmentioned name. Let us consider the surpassing grace of this highly-favored — this "blessed among women."

Mary stood by the cross, patient and resigned, in the unspeakable anguish of her motherhood, is doing the typical deed of her life. No other could so fully have told the story or interpreted the mind of Jesus, yet no syllable, either of appeal or of protest or of sorrow, came from her. And as we think upon her character, it seems to express itself in three dominating traits.

Of these three outstanding features the first is her inwardness. It is difficult to express in a single word that quality which penetrates her whole thought and action, but there is no better word for it than inwardness. There is no truly great character, and no devout and holy spirit (especially among women) without this trait of inwardness — this quality of brooding silence, of reserve which no thought can penetrate, of a certain aloofness and separateness in the deeper experiences. The source of a true inwardness is the possession of a secret. Think of the secret Mary kept locked up in her heart. Recall the message of the angel: "The Holy Ghost shall come upon you, and the power of the Highest shall overshadow you; therefore that holy thing which shall be born of you shall be called the Son of God." A secret like that shadows a life, and gives a sober cast even to its joy. A secret like that controls every deed and word, gathers to itself all the aspirations of life, and interprets all knowledge of God and every event of His providence.

The second notable trait of Mary's character is her submissiveness. Art, with its keen eye for a passionate and typical situation, has often drawn Mary at the foot of the cross, and always in the attitude of perfect submission, not even lifting her eyes. Her sorrow can be matched by that of no other, yet she stands uncomplaining, fulfilling her last obedience, steadfast in her faith. That act of submission was but the summing up of her life, the closing and final expression of that grace which bore the rebuke at the marriage feast, accepted His perplexing words, "Do you not know that I must be about My Father's business," without further chiding, and first of all, when the secret of the Lord was with her, and He showed her His covenant, bowed low before the will of God with her meek answer, "Behold the handmaid of the Lord; be it unto me according to your word."

The third notable trait in Mary's character is her self-sacrifice. The sacrifice of the cross is the sacrifice of Jesus. But it was the sacrifice of the Father likewise "who spared not His own Son, but delivered Him up for us all." And it was also the sacrifice of Mary, who stood in meek acceptance to see her Son die. "A sword shall pierce your own heart also," Simeon had prophesied. Now standing by the cross she felt its sharp thrust, and she bowed her head as she made the mother's last sacrifice. "The Lord gave, and the Lord has taken away; blessed be the name of the Lord," was the psalm that she chanted in spirit.

June 28
His Mother - 2

by Walter Benwell Hinson (1860-1826) England/USA
Excerpted from "The Woman of Sorrows," *A Grain of Wheat and Other Sermons*, published by The Bible Institute Colportage Association, Chicago, Illinois in 1922

Now there stood by the cross of Jesus His mother...
John 19:25 (KJV)

I want to show you the massive compensation that repaid Mary, the woman of sorrows, for all her great grief. For Elizabeth gave her a title, though she was not aware of doing it. She called her the "Mother of my Lord." That was worth having a lot of sorrow for, was it not? A woman had the privilege of mothering Jesus! The mother of my Lord! Why it seems to me it would be worth going through hell to get a title like that. The mother of my Lord! But Mary also mothered the Lord. I shall believe until I die she patched Christ's clothes, because they were poor in that Nazarene family. And, after all, when you get far enough away from it there is a lot of satisfaction in a patch! And I should think there is a lot of satisfaction in patching, too. My old mother used to patch my clothes while she sang, "Guide me, O Thou great Jehovah." Many of the mothers of today neither patch the children's clothes nor sing hymns. But Mary mothered the Lord, and she patched His clothes—I shall always think that—and she heard Him say His prayers. And that is another thing where American mothers fail. And did you ever wonder from where Jesus got His wonderful knowledge of the Bible? I wonder how much of that Mary taught Him, and I wonder how much your boy knows of his Bible that he learned from your lips.

But I was talking about Mary's massive compensation, for she had it. When He was dying—and God only knows what sorrow He had on that cross, for no human being can ever imagine it—yet out of all His distress He looked at His mother and commended her to John, not to Peter, for Peter was one of those impetuous men who would have stumbled over Mary's feet someday, but John, who was the Apostle of Love. And Mary may have had a beautiful old age there with John! And today she has compensation up there in the stars, for none can take away from Mary the consciousness that hers was the bosom the Child slept on; and for His sweet sake she endured the torture of misrepresentation, and mistrust, and suspicion. And the thousand little kindnesses she showed to Jesus Christ she remembers up there, and they are like the wine of Heaven to her lips.

And it is the law that runs through your life and mine. Oh, there is never a tear you ever shed for Christ's sake but it shall have a rainbow of glory encircling it at the last. And the more tears you shed the more glorious you will be. And if your eyes are wet with tears of sympathy with Jesus, when you go into the next world God's own fingers will wipe those tears from your eyes. And every thorn that has pierced you for Christ's sake will grow roses for you up in glory. And the dollar you could ill afford when you gave it to Jesus Christ, will be, not a bit of gold up there, but it will become a smile and a praise from the face and lips of Jesus Christ.

So have another look at Mary, the woman of sorrows; and learn that her sorrow was caused by Jesus; and that afterward He turned it into a great and eternal rejoicing. Put then your feet down on the path of sorrow, for the path of sorrow — and that path alone — leads to the land where the sorrow is unknown.

June 29
His Mourners - 1
by Louis Albert Banks (1855-1933) USA
Excerpted from "The Three Marys Beside the Cross," *The Fisherman and His Friends*, published by Funk & Wagnalls Company,
New York, New York in 1896

There were standing by the cross of Jesus was His mother, and His mother's sister, Mary the wife of Clopas, and Mary Magdalene.
John 21:25 (KJV)

In the group that stood about the cross of Jesus on that awful day of crucifixion, all the faces were not bitter and full of hate. Among those there who were friendly were three women who were loyal and faithful to Christ to the end. The first one to be named is His mother, Mary. How natural it seems, and how true to our knowledge of human nature, that His mother should have been faithful when so many others forsook Him and fled. A mother's love is proverbial for its tenderness and constancy.

It is certainly a very interesting and suggestive fact that the sister of Mary should be with her, sharing the terrible danger and the tender devotion of this trying hour. She has no doubt been led to this supreme fidelity to Christ through her love for her sister — showing us the magical power of human influence in winning people to Christ.

There is another Mary at the foot of the cross — Mary Magdalene. When we think about it we are not astonished to find her there also. When she first became acquainted with Jesus she was a poor, wicked, demon-possessed woman. Christ was kind to her. He dispossessed her soul of the evil spirits, and in her great gratitude and love she became His devoted and loyal friend forevermore. Peter might deny the Master if he would, others might forsake Him and flee, but she owed all she was to Him and it never occurred to her that it was possible for her to desert Him in the hour of His trial. How many there are of us who have the same reason for loyalty that Mary Magdalene had! We, too, were poor, lost sinners. The devils of anger, and selfishness, and appetite, and passion, possessed our poor hearts, and were leading us, bound hand and foot, to be the slaves of evil. Then Christ came to us and inspired our hearts with the hope that there was for us something infinitely better; the hope that He was able to set us free from the bondage of sin and death. And when at last our faith was aroused, and we asked Him, He came into our hearts, drove out the evil spirits, and gave us the gladness of His peaceful presence.

He did all that for us. What have we done for Him? He is still being crucified among men. Are we showing forth everywhere our gratitude to Him? He asks us that we shall wear His name; that we shall tell men what great things the Lord has done for us; that we shall so testify to Him that others, hearing of His goodness to us, shall forsake their sins and accept Him. There is no greater sin than ingratitude. I put it home to your heart, I pray that the Holy Spirit may put it to your conscience, whether you are showing forth in your daily conduct and conversation the gratitude which is due from you to the Lord Jesus Christ.

And you who are not Christians, I urge upon you this blessed truth that the same Christ who cast out from the heart of Mary Magdalene seven devils, and gave her this great cause for thanksgiving, is able to save you from every sin which haunts you and masters you. Some of you are mastered by evil habits that have been growing for a long time. They seemed insignificant at first, and you lingered with them. You thought you could break them off when you pleased, but you are coming to understand that you are not your own master; that when you determine to do good, the devil who possesses you and to whom you have yielded the fortress of your heart makes you do evil. O my brothers and sisters who are conscious of overmastering sins and wicked habits, I pray that you may meet Jesus Christ! He is here now. He is in His Word.

June 30
His Mourners - 2
by Nehemiah Adams (1806-1878) USA
Excerpted from "The Women at the Sepulcher," *The Friends of Christ*, published by T. R. Marvin and S. K. Whipple & Co. in 1853

And there was Mary Magdalene, and the other Mary, sitting over against the sepulcher.
Matthew 27:61 (KJV)

It was "yet dark" on the first day of the week when these women came to the sepulcher. It was an interesting, a touching instance of that presumption to which love is prone, that these women should have gone to that place with the purpose for which they had prepared themselves. There was a guard around the tomb. Would that guard allow Christ's disciples to have access to His body? Surely not. Suppose that they would; how were these women to roll that stone away? They said to themselves, as though they had just thought of it, "Who shall roll away the stone from the door of the sepulcher?"

"And when they looked, they saw that the stone was rolled away, for it was very great." But someone had been there before them. "And behold, there was a great earthquake; for the angel of the Lord descended from Heaven and rolled back the stone from the door, and sat upon it. His countenance was like lightning, and his raiment white as snow; and for fear of him the keepers did shake, and became as dead men."

The angel that terrified the guard spoke kindly to the women, and assured them that Christ had risen; and he sent them to the disciples with the news. "They fled from the sepulcher with fear and great joy, and ran to bring His disciples word. And their words seemed to them like idle tales, and they believed them not."

John and Peter ran together to the sepulcher. John outran Peter, and reached the place before him, yet did not go in. He tells us himself that he did not go in. Peter soon arrives, and with the characteristic boldness with which he twice threw himself into the sea to meet Christ, he goes directly into the tomb. "Then went in also that other disciple who came first to the sepulcher, and he saw and believed." These wondering disciples left the empty sepulcher and went home. But Mary Magdalene stood without at the sepulcher weeping. What more can she want? "And as she wept, she stooped down, and looked into the sepulcher." But O, there is something there to see—two angels in white, sitting, the one at the head, and the other at the feet, where the body of Jesus had lain. They did not appear to Peter and John, but they were doubtlessly there.

"Woman, why do you weep?" said these heavenly friends. As soon as she had replied, "They have taken away my Lord, and I know not where they have laid Him," she turned suddenly, perhaps at the sound of a step, and saw Jesus standing, and did not know that it was Jesus. Jesus said to her, "Woman, why do you weep?" Jesus said unto her, "Mary!" She turned, and said unto him, "Rabboni! Master!" Jesus said unto her, "Don't cling to Me for I haven't yet ascended to My Father. But go find My brothers and tell them, 'I am ascending to My Father and Your Father, to My God and your God.'"

Having fulfilled this errand, Mary Magdalene, with the other Mary, falls into the company of believers and friends, undistinguished by any further mention of them, until, at last, they rise, one after another, to meet that Savior face to face, and to enjoy in Heaven the fulness of that love, of which the foretaste here was Heaven upon earth.